WITTGENSTEIN AND THE THEORY OF PERCEPTION

WITTGENSTEIN AND THE THEORY OF PERCEPTION

Justin Good

continuum
LONDON • NEW YORK

Continuum International Publishing Group
The Tower Building, 11 York Road, London SE1 7NX
80 Maiden Lane, Suite 704, New York, NY 10038

British Library Cataloguing-in-Publication Data
A catalogue record for this book is available from the British Library.

ISBN: 0-8264-8889-7 (hardback)

Library of Congress Cataloging-in-Publication Data

A catalog record for this book is available from the Library of Congress.

Typeset by Aarontype Limited, Easton, Bristol
Printed and bound in Great Britain by Biddles Ltd, Kings Lynn, Norfolk

Contents

Contents

Introduction

Towards a grammar of sight

The aspects of things that are most important for us are hidden because of their simplicity and familiarity. (One is unable to notice something – because it is always before one's eyes.) The real foundations of his enquiry do not strike a man at all. Unless that fact has at some time struck him. – And this means: we fail to be struck by what, once seen, is most striking and most powerful.[1]

What does it mean to see? Do you know? Don't we already know? If I didn't already know, then how could I even ask the question? And how would I know if your answer was valid? Well, that depends on what one interprets the question to be asking about. And what is the question asking about? That is, what could the question be used to ask about? As it turns out, quite a lot. The study of perception is endless. This is not a bad thing. The unending character of the inquiry does not stem from a lack of epistemological discipline but from the abundance of meaning contained within, or rather, refracted through, the concept of sight. Less like a thing or a relation and more like a web or a network of connections, the concept of sight is as complex as human life itself. This complexity makes the study of seeing a methodological challenge all around. It is challenging to the scientist studying the complex causal mechanisms underlying sight as a natural physical process. It is challenging to the sociologist studying the complex social ecosystems that the ability to see makes possible. It is a challenge to the artist who attempts to free her visual interests from the clutch and clinging of visual habit and inertia. Most importantly, it is a challenge to the ordinary, and mysterious, human individual and her community, whose practices of seeing make up a large part of her life's cognitive and ethical work and play.

How do we appreciate this complexity? How do we tame it theoretically without domesticating it conceptually? As necessary oversimplifications, theories and definitions of sight help us to grasp various patterns in its structure, highlighting certain features of its theoretical meaning and practical importance in human life. How can we grasp the genuine insights offered by theories of perception while at the same time remaining cognizant of the epistemological liabilities that every theoretical context involves? This question can be posed in terms of how to approach the study of perception from a genuinely interdisciplinary perspective, and even more broadly, from a perspective that bridges the theoretical–analytic mode of naturalistic explanation and the expressive–existential mode of the humanities. The later philosophy of Ludwig Wittgenstein offers a way to do this.[2]

Although the title of this book refers to Wittgenstein and to the theory of perception, it does not discuss Wittgenstein's theory of perception. In part, this is because he neither has such a theory, nor has any interest in having one. He is interested in questions having to do with the conceptual meaning of sight, with questions regarding the *grammar of sight*. These are the aspects of sight that, given a certain understanding of seeing, we cannot help but to know because they define that way of seeing. One begins to appreciate the complexity of the concept of seeing when one begins to appreciate the complexity of its grammar. To use one of Wittgenstein's metaphors, the concept of seeing is like a delicious artichoke with many leaves. When we construct a theory or a definition to capture its essential nature, we divest the artichoke of its leaves, trying to find the real artichoke hidden within. But the artichoke *is* its leaves. Wittgenstein offers us a technique for exploring the whole artichoke, for getting to the heart without losing the whole. This can be thought of as an ecological approach to meaning.

The technique can be called grammatical investigation. In Wittgenstein's specific sense of the term *grammar*, the inquiry has us clarify the meaning of a concept by having us look at how the concept is generally used in ordinary natural language. That is, instead of thinking of a concept as a representation of a natural fact, we think of a concept as an instrument which has certain uses. Thus, the technique can also be thought of as a kind of phenomenology – conceptual phenomenology – which looks at concepts as tools to be examined, as lenses to be pointed at different things, peered through and projected imaginatively into new contexts. In this sense, a Wittgensteinian philosophy of sight is itself a kind of seeing.

The plan for our enquiry is thus as follows. I begin with a close reading of Wittgenstein's remarks on psychological and, in particular, visual-perceptual concepts.[3] My interpretation focuses on his treatment of the phenomenon of aspectual seeing, based primarily on his famous discussion in section xi of Part Two of *Philosophical Investigations*. Having demonstrated this technique for the elucidation of conceptual grammar in the first chapter, I proceed to employ it dialectically, in a quasi-Socratic sense, within various epistemological contexts, including naturalistic research into early vision processing; the phenomenology of subjective experience; the causal theory of perception and naturalistic theories of mind/body supereminence; the humanistic debate about visual studies as a cultural-theoretic approach to perception, and finally, the epistemology of aesthetic experience. Each of these domains reveals its own intricate field of conceptual grammar. Held together in the ways that Wittgenstein's method facilitates, they constitute interwoven glimpses of a much larger expanse of meaning: the grammar of sight. The vision of this expanse opens up space for further illumination and understanding. This is not a theory; it is an impetus for epistemological anarchy: for an open-ended, epistemologically nuanced art-science of seeing.

A thumbnail sketch of the first chapter serves to illustrate the method. In the enticing and obscure nether region of Part Two of *Philosophical Investigations*, Wittgenstein's theoretical eros settles upon a detailed examination of the logical behaviour of two concepts that he refers to as *noticing an aspect* and *continuous seeing-as*. The terms pick out experiences that have long puzzled perceptual theorists and which have served as the basis for theories of various sorts, but it is not clear just what Wittgenstein's interest is, hence the difficult hermeneutical problem of evaluating his remarks. Now on my interpretation, the focus of Wittgenstein's discussion concerns what I call the *raggedness* of the concept of seeing, which has to do with the diverse criteria underlying our employment of the concept. Different senses of the concept of seeing raise a question as to how these different uses are justified. The question *Is aspectual perception a case of seeing or of thinking?* throws us back onto the actual criteria employed to draw this distinction in workaday natural language. It points to the instrumentality of distinctions, the reasons why it matters, for purposes of communication, to call something an instance of seeing rather than of thinking or interpretation. The questioning of the basis of the distinction reveals what the question tends to overlook: the grammar of the concept of seeing. Calling attention to these structures reveals a conceptual articulation much richer semantically than the explanatory models adopted to account for them would suggest.[4] In turn, the grammatical structure sheds light on the interplay between empirical hypotheses and linguistic conventions; between beliefs about perception that could turn out to be false (that can be verified in principle), and elements of our understanding which are neither true nor false, but which are adopted simply because they are logically connected to talk being *about* seeing (as opposed, say, to thinking). As I make the point in the first chapter, the phenomena of aspectual seeing seem to force upon us the adoption of certain explanatory models, as ways we *must* think about seeing and visual meaning if these concepts are to be understood correctly. However, insofar as these models introduce conceptual innovations, specifically, introduce new criteria for applying these concepts, they are not merely offering a form of explanation. They are altering the very explanandum. For example, in the case of aspectual seeing, the phenomena have typically been taken to necessitate a reconstruction of seeing as an inherently interpretive process. But on my interpretation, Wittgenstein's grammatical remarks undermine the widely held view that all seeing is interpretive by showing that the interpretive model distorts the grammar of the concept by introducing artificially restrictive (or pseudo-precise) criteria for what is to count as a description of what is seen. Against the assumptions of this model, I detail the raggedness of the concept of seeing by examining the diverse ways in which *see* is used or, what amounts to the same thing, the diverse things that count as explanations of the meaning of sight.

The interpretation offered in Chapter One establishes the thematic and methodological framework for the rest of the study. Thematically, this interpretation of Wittgenstein yields the approach to the analysis of visual meaning which will be employed throughout our inquiry. This approach is shaped by two senses of the term *meaning*. The first – that meaning is use – stems from the general approach to the philosophical study of language in *Philosophical Investigations*.[5] This should not be construed as a thesis about the nature of linguistic meaning, in the sense that one might speak of a use theory of meaning.[6] Rather, it should be understood as a remark concerning how questions about the meaning of a word should be understood (what they should be understood to be asking about), and how those questions should be addressed.[7] The second sense of the term has to do with cases where we speak of experiencing the meaning of a word.[8] This sense is illustrated, for example, by moments where understanding suddenly dawns on us, where we speak of 'grasping' the meaning of the word in a flash. Visual meaning in this sense refers to cases where we speak of experiencing the meaning of a picture or an image.[9]

Framing my approach to the study of visual perception in terms of visual meaning serves to highlight a methodological issue that will occupy us, namely, the relationship between theoretical work on perception and studies of the grammar of visual-perceptual concepts. While I shall be examining theoretical work on visual perception, the aim of these examinations is neither to offer my own theory, nor simply to attack their explanatory adequacy. Least of all do I wish to argue, as some logical behaviourists and self-described Wittgensteinians have been read as doing, that a theory of visual perception is impossible or makes no sense.[10] My target will be descriptive inadequacies of a particular sort. I shall be keen on exposing ways in which the constructive efforts under examination distort the logical grammar of our ordinary perceptual concepts, and do so by introducing a pseudo-precision into our understanding of their meaning. As I shall diagnose it, this pseudo-precision results from the fact that both rational–scientific, as well as humanistic–sociological reconstructions of perceptual concepts typically introduce new criteria for applying these concepts in the guise of explaining their meaning. The result is pseudo-precision in the sense that what appears to be the discovery of deeper logical structure turns out to be a form of linguistic stipulation; a stipulation which conceals the criteria *already* in place structuring our employment of the concepts. One could pose this issue as a question concerning how one hears, or ought to hear, the appeal to ordinary word use in light of theoretical questions about the nature of seeing and of visual meaning.

So what's the point of all this? As noted above, my interest with Wittgenstein is not exegetical but philosophical. In part, it lies in developing some under-appreciated implications that Wittgenstein's work has for understanding visual perception.[11] The explosion of research into perception in recent years, in the sciences as well as the humanities, calls for interesting and fruitful ways to evaluate the epistemological virtues and liabilities of the manifold frameworks, theories and vocabularies swirling about in discursive space. The approach I develop here on the basis of Wittgenstein may offer some help towards that end, hence towards appreciating what I referred to at the outset as the complexity of the artichoke.

Ultimately, appreciating the artichoke is not just an end in itself, but a part of the larger task of philosophy. On the view that emerges in the course of this study, this task is the enhancement of human freedom, construed in a quasi-ecological sense as an understanding of the unique possibilities for individuality and creativity within a system of semantic interdependency. This is not ecology in the biological sense, it is an ecology of meaning where the interdependencies involve not the flow of nutrients and energy but the constitution and sustainability of meaning through time. This interpretation runs seriously counter to the standard view of Wittgenstein as a purely destructive thinker. On one standard view, Wittgensteinian philosophy is a purely negative or critical activity, aimed at exposing a particular kind of deep ungrammaticality or nonsense in our thought. But as I hope to demonstrate in what follows, his animus is directed less against philosophical abuses of language than against certain mechanistic assumptions about meaning and, therefore, about human life. While that standard interpretation captures one significant strain of Wittgenstein's thought, it ignores another that is equally important, and not widely recognized. To use a distinction coined by Stanley Cavell, that approach emphasizes Wittgenstein's distrust of technical or philosophical discourse, while ignoring his equally conspicuous trust of ordinary human speech.[12] The distinction can be illustrated by different ways of construing the epistemological status of Wittgenstein's *descriptions*. It follows from Wittgenstein's view of meaning as determined by use that descriptions must be understood as 'instruments for particular uses' rather than, for example, as pictures of facts, as he conceived of them in his early work.[13] Now the first view tends to emphasize the negative significance that Wittgenstein's descriptions carry for the problems they are meant to clarify.

> We must do away with all *explanation*, and description alone must take its place. And this description gets its light, that is to say its purpose, from the philosophical problems. These are, of course, not empirical problems; they are solved, rather, by looking into the workings of our language, and that in such a way as to make us recognize those workings . . .[14]

On the second view, the emphasis is on the *light* that is shown on the descriptions, or as I put it, the light that is shown *through* the descriptions, *by* the philosophical problems, *onto* our ordinary speech. Because language is an extension of life itself, this light ultimately has ethical significance. In the epilogue, I shall develop this thought by pointing out some analogies of Wittgenstein's philosophy to ecology as a normative science of interdependency.

1

The concept of seeing

The concept of 'seeing' makes a tangled impression. Well, it is tangled. I look at the landscape, my gaze ranges over it, I see all sorts of distinct and indistinct movement; this impresses itself sharply on me, that is quite hazy. After all, how completely ragged what we see can appear.[1]

A reading of Wittgenstein's discussion of aspectual perception

What does it mean, to see? What does Wittgenstein have to teach about this question?

Wittgenstein's investigation of aspectual perception in the second part of *Philosophical Investigations* is as suggestive philosophically as its aim is obscure. This obscurity naturally lends support to various interpretations. For instance, Stanley Cavell takes it for granted that interpretation is 'the principle topic of the chief section of what appears as Part Two of the *Investigations*'.[2] According-ing to Jaakko and Merrill Hinttikka, the discussion serves as a particularly poignant illustration of Wittgenstein's general interest, in his later work, in showing how one can talk about phenomenological objects in a physicalist language.[3] On the other hand, Stephen Mulhall, who has written the only book-length commentary on aspectual seeing, takes the main point of Section XI to be that all seeing must be conceived of as continuous aspect perception,[4] while Arthur Danto has voiced a hunch, common to many readers, that Wittgenstein's treatment of the duck-rabbit (see fig. 2, p. 16) implies some form of linguistic idealism.[5] While each of these interpretations offer important insights into the philosophical significance of the discussion, their focus on the peculiarity of phenomena can prompt neglect of the extent to which the whole discussion is shaped around questions regarding the concept of *seeing* gener-ally. On this point, it is not unimportant to note that the whole discussion of seeing aspects is introduced as an illustration of a grammatical distinction between two senses of the word 'see' and, correlatively, a distinction between two objects of sight. In the only remark in which he explicitly refers to the phi-losophical significance of aspectual seeing, Wittgenstein asks: 'What is the philosophical importance of this phenomenon [i.e. aspect seeing]? Is it really so much odder than everyday visual experiences? Does it cast an unexpected light on them?' And answers: 'In the description of it, the problems about the concept of seeing come to a head.'[6] As I shall interpret it, the connection between aspect seeing and the 'problems about the concept of seeing' is that the former serves to reveal the *raggedness* of the concepts of *seeing* and *what is seen*.[7]

The characteristic of raggedness has do to with our *criteria* for making judgements about seeing. For Wittgenstein, criteria are connected to our claims to knowledge. We must often appeal to evidence to support a knowledge claim, to answer the question 'How do you know?' Criteria are not evidence that something is the case, or that an object is of a particular kind. They are what determine what is to *count* as evidence in the first place, and so what kinds of claims do and do not call for evidence.[8] In this sense, criteria tell us 'what kind of object anything is'.[9] While evidence can succeed or fail to support a knowledge claim, criteria can only be said to be satisfied or fail to be satisfied, and if there is doubt about whether they are, then the case must be in some sense non-standard.[10] It is precisely the point of a grammatical investigation, which is to say, an investigation that takes the form of asking 'Under what circumstances do we say . . . ?', to show that our use of a concept is governed by criteria. In this sense, to elucidate criteria for the concept *see* is not to discover any new facts about its meaning, it is to tell us what we already know, and cannot fail to know, about what it means to see. Criteria illustrate what it is we know in knowing how to use the English word 'see'.

In speaking dogmatically here about how we are to understand the notion of a criterion, I do not mean to deny the obscurity of the notion, or to assert that 'commonsense' gives us immediate access to its import. It is a *claim*, and perhaps Wittgenstein's most important and controversial claim, that his grammatical investigations uncover 'criteria' underlying our employment of concepts. It is a methodological assumption of this project, however, that understanding what a criterion is requires understanding the force of the appeal to criteria in the context of philosophical reflection on the meanings of concepts. On this issue of how to understand the notion of a criterion, I will thus be adopting a view asserted by Cavell when he says:

> You cannot understand what a Wittgensteinian criterion is without understanding the force of his appeal to the everyday (why or how it tells what kind of object anything is, for example); and you cannot understand what the force of Wittgenstein's appeal to the everyday is without understanding what his criteria are.[11]

This assertion is not viciously circular. It only reflects Wittgenstein's emphasis on examining use to clarify questions about meaning. In what follows, this emphasis will be reflected in my dialectical approach to the problem of seeing.

It is because the criteria for the concept of seeing are diverse that the concept is ragged. As I shall try to show, what is philosophically interesting about the phenomenon of raggedness emerges when it is employed dialectically against attempts to rationally reconstruct the concept of seeing for purposes of building a theory of visual perception. I shall focus on two ways in which the concept of seeing is ragged. The first sense (section two below) has to do with the criteria for what is to count as seeing. This sense is connected to the idea that there are various senses of 'see', or various things to be said in saying that someone *S sees p*. This observation is directed against what I shall call the *Socratic model* for explaining the meanings of concepts. On this model, the assumption is made that our ordinary uses imperfectly reflect a deeper essence, or a focal meaning, which signifies the true, normative meaning of a word. The focal or unitary meaning is the *what* that Socrates' question 'what is it?' asks for. On this view, the ways in which we use a word are vague hints of what it is that we understand in understanding how to use a word correctly.

For our purposes, one of the general lessons to be learned from Wittgenstein's sustained investigation into aspectual seeing is that the tangled impression that the concept of seeing initially gives us in the course of reflecting on its meaning does not expose our ignorance of an underlying essence, but rather manifests the intricacy of ordinary grammar. What our competence with ordinary grammar does not involve as such, is the ability to describe this grammar, for example, the ability to state our criteria; herein lies one source of the idea that there is something essential that we do not know. Raggedness in this sense suggests problems with the idea of giving an analysis of the concept of seeing, for example, an explanation of what it means to see in terms of truth conditions for statements employing the term 'see'. The grammatical investigation of seeing aspects relates to this sense of raggedness in the following way. While the experience of noticing an aspect itself suggests a need to draw a distinction between literal and figurative senses of 'see', a sustained investigation into the phenomena undercuts the assumption that our various uses of the word are *merely* vague approximations of some truer meaning.

The second sense of raggedness (section three below) has to do with our criteria for what is to count as a *description of what is seen*. I can describe what I am seeing in various ways. At the same time, the same description, for example, 'the moon is rising high', can count as an accurate description of what is seen on two different occasions despite there being differences in other respects between the objects of vision. Such facts naturally suggest the idea that all of our ordinary ways of expressing what we see are vague approximations of what we in fact see. In turn, this vagueness implies some conception of what a *precise* specification of our visual experience would be.[12] I shall call this line of thought the *interpretive model*, since the vagueness of ordinary expressions of visual experience is connected to the idea that the percepts they *prima facie* express are interpretations of what we *directly* see, or what is seen in the strict sense. Contra the interpretive model, raggedness counts against the idea of there being some one description, on an occasion for offering a perceptual report, that is ideal with respect to its evaluative properties. Thinking about the media of painting, we might be inclined to assume that descriptions of what we see, in the strict sense, must employ a range of concepts limited by the intrinsic, or purely 'visual' character of our visual experience, for example, to concepts of colour and shape. Of course, what we ordinarily call a 'description of what is seen' is seldom so limited. I often describe what I see by describing the object, event, process, or state of affairs that I am looking at; an act which only on rare occasions involves speaking merely of colour and shape. But while the experience of noticing an aspect, or aspectual changes, suggests a distinction between direct and indirect, or phenomenal and physicalist descriptions of what is seen, closer inspection of the criteria for counting a description as direct calls into question any simple dichotomy.[13] In section four, this point will be further illustrated by considering the concept of continuous aspect seeing. I shall offer criticisms of two interpretations of the concept of continuous seeing-as in order to develop some implications of raggedness. Finally, in section five, I shall briefly outline a third sense of raggedness; the sense in which there are diverse forms that explanations of seeing can take. This discussion will segue to the remaining chapters.

Problems with the 'what is it?' question (Seeing aspects)

The concept of noticing an aspect is introduced in terms of a distinction between two uses of the word 'see'.

> The one: 'What do you see there?' – 'I see this' (and then a description, a drawing, a copy). The other: 'I see a likeness between these two faces' – let the man I tell this to be seeing the faces as clearly as I do myself.
> I contemplate a face, and then suddenly notice its likeness to another. I see that it has not changed; and yet I see it differently. I call this experience 'noticing an aspect'.[14]

For our purposes, there are two important differences between these uses. The first is an intuitive or felt difference between the experiences of seeing a face and of seeing similarity. One might characterize this difference by saying that the similarity is not there to be seen in the same sense as the faces are. I cannot, for example, point to the similarity or picture it in the way that I can point to or picture the face. But that expression only gestures at that difference and does not say what it might be. In explaining that difference one might say that the similarity is 'constructed' or 'inferred' from what is seen in the strict sense of 'see', i.e. the faces.[15] Or one might say that the similarity is seen, but must be understood as a property of my visual impression, rather than an objective feature of the objects seen, i.e. the faces. After all, there are various ways in which one might see the faces as similar, but are there various ways in which the faces can be seen as faces?

A second difference concerns the fact that the similarity dawns on one, and that it is something that one *notices*. Unlike the face, the experience of similarity can come and go. The similarity can be noticed or go unnoticed. One cannot draw a picture of a face without seeing that it is a face.[16] On the other hand, one could, for example, fail to notice it even after producing an 'exact' copy of what one is looking at: 'The one man might make an accurate drawing of the two faces, and the other notice in the drawing the likeness which the former did not see.'[17] Now we can think of cases in which our noticing that two faces are similar would mean that the faces themselves had actually altered. For example, imagine two digital faces on a computer screen which are being manipulated. At some point changes in one face might give it a likeness to the other. But in the case above, where the faces are not themselves changing, the change in one's impression of the faces, before and after noticing the similarity, cannot be attributed to a corresponding objective transformation of the faces. At the same time, the change of aspect is not like a subjective change of local perspective, as when one shifts position to get a clearer view, or moves in to get a closer look. In that case, changes in one's visual impression correspond to objective changes in one's spatial relation to the object of vision. By contrast, one does not have to *do* anything in order to see an aspect. Or rather, it is not clear what one has to do, or what has to happen in order to see it. Now, these differences raise some general philosophical questions about the concept of seeing. The experience of noticing an aspect leaves us with a puzzle about what is to count as a genuine case of seeing, and also about what we really *mean* when we speak of seeing, for example, a likeness between two faces. This puzzle is embodied in how we express the experience of noticing an aspect. We say 'I *see* that it has not changed; and yet I *see* it differently.' The term 'see' is used twice in the expression, but used differently, with a different meaning. One might say that there is a sense in which it is true, and a sense in which it is false that my visual impression has changed.

What the puzzlement appears to expose is a confusion regarding the grounds for finding it appropriate, and at the same time inappropriate, to speak of seeing in this context. If my inclinations to use the concept of seeing to express my experience are conflicted, a cognitive failure of sorts is suggested: I do not know (understand) what it really means to see. I have learned the grammar of the word 'see', and so I know how and when to say things like 'Did you see how tired he looks?' and 'We see things the same way'. Moreover, we can describe what we see, and do it in all of the ordinary ways that people need to be able to, with greater and lesser degrees of articulateness. But what we do not seem to understand is why we talk this way. The realist intuition underlying this felt explanatory need is that our ways of speaking about seeing, *inter alia* our ways of describing what we see, must be answerable to how things are in the world – both the extradermal world we live in, as well as the intradermal world of our psychological constitution. That is, they must be if our employment of psychological concepts is to be non-arbitrary, if it is to be grounded in reality. On the interpretation I am developing here, the investigation into aspect seeing serves to support the idea that grammar is, in an important sense, *arbitrary*.

The rules of grammar are arbitrary in the sense that there is no specifiable end that could be used to determine how they might be justified as they stand, or revised to better serve their end. Consider the difference between grammatical and culinary rules.

> ... 'cookery' is defined by its end, whereas 'speaking' is not. That is why the use of language is in a certain sense autonomous, as cooking and washing are not. You cook badly if you are guided in your cooking by rules other than the right ones; but if you follow other rules than those of chess you are *playing another game* ...[18]

One way that my investigation provides support for this idea is by attacking one important motivation for assuming that the grammar of our psychological concepts needs to be grounded in the objective nature of psychological phenomenon. That motivation has to do with the misguided intuition – one which is encouraged by the phenomena of seeing aspects themselves – that our ordinary competence with the word 'see' offers us no genuine understanding of what it means to see.

Now the explanatory models we will be examining enter our thinking on visual perception in the following manner. The idea that I do not really understand what it means to see (what 'see' means) raises a methodological question. If I am unable to state what it is that I mean in speaking of seeing, how am I to find out? Much turns on how one construes this apparent inability. One might quite naturally interpret this hesitancy in applying the concept of seeing as evidence of a cleavage between our ordinary understanding of seeing, as embodied in our linguistic competence with the word 'see', and the underlying nature of seeing. Just as ordinary linguistic competence in using the term 'water' does not suffice as knowledge of the chemical structure H_2O, one might conclude that the reason for our uncertainty in applying the concept of seeing is just our ignorance of, for example, the physical process which causes our visual experience. One might describe this by saying that while ordinary speakers of English understand the meaning of 'seeing', they do not know what seeing is, what 'seeing' ultimately refers to when used to state truths.

If what seeing means is to have an inner visual experience, then to resolve the questions about aspect seeing, I must *introspect*, or carry out a phenomenological clarification of my inner experience. On this view, my experience itself must provide the criterion to be used in deciding whether I really do see something different, for example, when the Necker cube shifts (fig. 1, p. 14),[19] when the duck-rabbit becomes a duck (fig. 2, p. 16)[20] when I suddenly see the solution to a picture-puzzle,[21] or whether I really see the arrow passing through the neck of an animal.[22] The other approach is to undertake an analysis of the neuro-visual process. In this case, the premise is mentalistic and individualistic. To understand what it means to see is to construe visual experience as an intentional mental state, the content of which can be specified in terms of the underlying physical states of the perceiver (for example, retinal stimulation, functional states, behavioural output), or as supervening on states so defined.[23] The question about how to account for aspectual perception is thus to be decided on the basis of a neurophysiological criterion.

Wittgenstein tells us that he is not interested in the 'causes' of aspect perception, but rather in the concept of 'noticing an aspect' and its place among the 'concepts of experience'.[24] Elaborating on this, he argues that a physiological analysis would not help us decide whether, and in what sense, aspect seeing is a genuine case of seeing; any such analysis would introduce a *new* criterion for what is to count as seeing.[25] From the standpoint of the puzzling phenomenon of noticing an aspect, this new criterion can tell us nothing about why we are hesitant in applying the concept 'see', since that hesitation rests on criteria *already in our possession*. On Wittgenstein's account, our hesitancy does not manifest a cognitive failure but is, rather, a case of our being entangled in the grammar of the concept of seeing. The grammatical differences between the two senses of 'see' noted above do not call for a clarification of the meaning of 'see', they *illustrate* that meaning. Thus, there is a sense in which to ask what explains our inclinations to speak of seeing here is to have already passed by the relevant phenomena. On this view, our confusion is akin to the confusion of someone who cannot draw a map of his neighbourhood. Just because he cannot offer a diagram of what is where, does not mean that he does not know his way around. Moreover, to insist that someone who understands the lay of the land must be able to draw a map is, *pace* Socrates, to overlook our criteria for ascribing to someone such understanding. Being able to make a map and knowing one's way around are distinct abilities.[26] After all, maps need to be interpreted.

Now, in order to clarify what it is that we already understand about seeing – which nonetheless engenders our confusion in the case of noticing an aspect – the criteria for the senses of 'see' engendering our confusion must be elicited. In section xi, Part Two of *Philosophical Investigations*, Wittgenstein proceeds to elicit some of these criteria by examining what we are inclined to

distinguish seeing from. We can imagine the Necker cube appearing in different contexts in a textbook in which it represents different objects (see fig. 1).
In each case we would say that we *interpret* the figure differently.

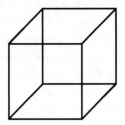

Fig. 1

But 'we can also see the illustration now as one thing now as another. So we
interpret it, and see it as we interpret it.'[27] That is, unlike simply seeing a
face, seeing a likeness or seeing the aspectual switch of the Necker cube suggests some kind of interpretive seeing. The way we express the experience indicates that it is both like and unlike seeing a face. The puzzle could be put in
terms of a distinction between *really seeing* something different versus merely
describing what I see in a different way. In the case of seeing aspects, the problem is that we are pulled in two different directions by the concepts in our
possession, i.e. *seeing* and *interpretation*. We want to say both that my visual
impression has itself altered, and also that only my way of describing what I
see has changed, that a new description has suddenly suggested itself.

> But how is it possible to *see* an object according to an *interpretation*? The ques-
> tion represents it as a queer fact; as if something were being forced into a
> form it did not really fit.[28]

It is this sense, in which neither the concept of seeing nor that of interpretation
fit the phenomenon, that illustrates just how an examination of the concept of
noticing an aspect sheds light on the concept of seeing in general. It does so
because it offers an opportunity to reflect upon the concept of seeing by
asking why that concept does not quite fit in this case, as opposed to the case
of seeing a face. What is it about the concept of seeing that makes it fit and yet
fail to fit here?

> ... is this a special sort of seeing? Is it a case of both seeing and thinking?
> Or an amalgam of the two, as I should almost like to say? The question is:
> *why* does one want to say this?[29]

Construed as a question about criteria, this question asks us to consider the circumstances under which we would ordinarily express our experience, or ascribe to someone else a perceptual state, in terms of seeing as opposed to interpretation. In what circumstances does it matter that I speak of one rather than the other? What is implied by the use of 'see' as opposed to the use of 'interpret'?

Noticing an aspect as an instance of seeing

Let us consider some reasons for calling the noticing of an aspect a genuine case of *seeing*. (a) One reason is that genuine changes in visual experience are typically ones that we can express or communicate.[30] In contrast, the case of merely describing or interpreting what one sees differently leaves one's visual impressions unmoved. That is to say, in the case of interpretation, I am *only* describing what I see differently, not really having a different visual impression. The case of the Necker cube found in different places in a text book, which Wittgenstein uses to introduce the concept of interpretation, offers nothing we can point to or describe as a change in what is seen. For example, one might say that interpreting the Necker cube alternately as a picture of a 300lb block of ice and a crystal ring box requires *imagination* since it cannot literally be seen that way. But if someone says that he *sees* the figure change from one to the other, we are justified in asking 'What visual changes are you alluding to?' *Ceteris paribus*, someone's being able to say something about how his visual impression (figure) has altered is implied by his saying that his visual perception has altered. In that sense, someone's being able to describe what has changed in his perceptual experience is a *criterion* for that change's counting as a *visual* change, as opposed to a change in interpretation or conception. If we look at how we ordinarily distinguish, even in our own case, between merely finding a new description for what we are looking at, and having a genuinely different visual impression, how we are inclined to describe what we see plays a criterial function as well.

> And is it really a different impression?' – In order to answer this I should like to ask myself whether there is really something different there in me. But how can I find out? – I *describe* differently, what I am seeing.[31]

This does not mean that being able to describe the change is a condition for the truth of statements ascribing such experiences.[32] We can, after all, find ourselves at a loss as to how to express or describe such changes.[33] But if we were *always* at a loss, ascriptions of the experience of visual change would lose their meaning, and along with them, the point of the distinction between seeing and interpreting.

(b) The preceding point can be given a more general characterization. Ordinary criteria constitutive of the distinction between seeing and interpretation typically include our linguistic (and non-linguistic) reactions to our experience. We decide for the most part on the basis of fine shades of behaviour whether someone is seeing something as opposed to merely interpreting it.[34] To speak of 'deciding' in this context is not phenomenologically felicitous, but it does capture the sense in which we do employ criteria in making psychological ascriptions. I *decide* that the car in front of me is going to turn right at the intersection because he has put on his turn signal. But that just means that I act appropriately, for example, I slow down. As opposed to interpretation, someone's being able to see something a certain way is often indicated by her having a certain facility with what she is looking at. For example, someone's seeing the duck-rabbit as a rabbit takes for granted that *this* is an eye, *those* are ears (see fig. 2).

> ... if asked 'What's that?' or 'What do you see here?' I should have replied: 'A picture-rabbit'. If I had further been asked what that was, I should have explained by pointing to all sorts of pictures of rabbits, should perhaps have pointed to real rabbits, talked about their habits, or given an imitation of them.[35]

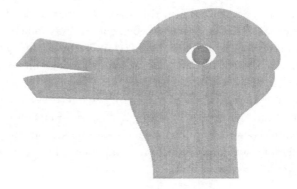

Fig. 2

If there is a question as to whether someone's smile is an expression of, say, compassion as opposed to malice, there is no question as to whether the shape of the mouth and lips is one facial expression among others, as opposed, for example, to being part of the immobile anatomic structure of the skull.[36] To take another example, we would say an engineer, intimately familiar with a certain device, can *see* what elements of a schematic drawing of it correspond to parts of the device. A non-engineer looking at the drawing will not 'see' *that* as this part, but will have to interpret. This will be shown by a certain lack of facility in following, or being able to give an explanation of, the drawing.[37] That is to say, one thing we could mean in ascribing to the non-engineer an interpretive act, as opposed to a direct perception (seeing) of the schema, is that the possibility of being mistaken is implied by the former, but not in the latter.

This sense of 'see' is sometimes identified as the *achievement sense* of the word, which is distinguished from the sense in which it could be true of some perceiver S that he had seen *p* despite his not having recognized it. But it is misleading to qualify this sense as special, or even as being a specific meaning of the word 'see', as opposed to a way that the word is used.[38] On the other hand, it is also misleading to speak of a sense of 'see', in which we can be said to see something without recognizing it, as a 'minimal' sense of the term, as if there were something about what seeing really means which is left out of that understanding. Paul Valery defined seeing as 'forgetting the name of the thing seen', and anyone with an interest in visual perception can understand why that criterion for seeing is intuitively compelling.[39] Forgetting the name of what you are looking at suggests forgetting what you already know about how something looks and so what you do not need to notice; hence what you are blind to. That would suggest the sense in which the so-called *minimal sense* of seeing could be considered to be a richer kind of experience than ordinary 'knowing one's way around'. But offering definitions is precisely *not* what Wittgenstein is interested in. Definitions can in fact get in the way of understanding what the concept means. That is why Wittgenstein says: 'Our investigation does not try to *find* the real, exact meaning of words; though we do often *give* words exact meanings in the course of our investigation.[40]

(c) Another reason why we might be inclined to call aspectual perception a case of seeing is indicated by talk of an aspect's 'dawning' on us. Sometimes, seeing an aspect is something that *happens* to us, analogous to the way a red stop sign comes into view when turning a street corner. It is not something we do, but a state we find ourselves in.[41] Accordingly, what we are truly seeing, *inter alia* what we can truly be said to be *seeing*, cannot change suddenly, while an interpretation can suddenly shift.[42] This feature of some instances of aspectual seeing is connected to the fact that interpretation involves the possibility of alternative perceptions, and so doubt about whether what is perceived is what it is perceived to be. If I speak of *interpreting* someone's facial expression, that generally means that I do not know whether she is, for example, arrogant or insecure, angry or depressed. But in the case of aspectual perception, there is no sense in speaking of being wrong or right about, for example, whether I am seeing the duck aspect or the rabbit aspect: ' "I am seeing this figure as a ..." can be verified as little as (or in the same sense as) "I am seeing bright red".'[43] This does not mean that I cannot be wrong about what I am seeing, or that if I turn out to be wrong about having seen something that I therefore cannot be said to have seen it. Because criteria for the concept of seeing are defeasible, they cannot be construed as truth conditions for statements about seeing. I could say that I can see that the car in front of me is going to turn right because the driver just put on his right turn signal, but his putting on his right turn signal is neither a necessary nor a sufficient condition for my statement's being justified. I might reasonably decide that the right turn signal of the car in front of me, which has been blinking for the past five miles, does not indicate the driver's intention to turn at the next intersection. In that case, the appropriate circumstances within which turn signals function to communicate the intentions of the driver are lacking. Moreover, the driver may want to confuse me, or he may have no idea himself what turn signals mean. But the possibility of error in my ascription does not mean that every ascription is interpretive, or merely hypothetical. If the driver succeeds in confusing me, it will only be because I read the turn signal in accordance with its conventional meaning. That turn signals can be used to mean what they do depends on the vast majority of their uses being related unproblematically to unsurprising outcomes, *inter alia* on drivers learning to respond to traffic signals in the usual ways they do.

Noticing an aspect as an instance of interpretation

Now, if we are inclined to speak of noticing an aspect as a case of seeing, we are also hesitant. With respect to the characterization of seeing as a state, aspectual perception is a state in a different sense from, for example, the visual experience of a red stop sign. While I can *try* to see the duck-rabbit as a rabbit, or try to get the Necker cube to shift its aspects, I cannot try to see a stop sign as red. While aspect perception is like seeing a red sign in that it is a state we are in, a state that can suddenly change without our doing anything, it is also related to an act of will.

> 'Now I see it as a . . .' goes with 'I am trying to see it as a . . .' or 'I can't see it as a . . . yet'. But I cannot try to see a conventional picture of a lion *as* a lion, any more than an F as that letter. (Though I may well try to see it as a gallows, for example.)[44]

The intuitive idea that perception is a form of cognition and, as such, is responsive to how things are in the world, underlies part of our hesitation here in speaking of seeing. If seeing is informative because it is responsive to the world, then interpretation is distinguished as being an active process, as a procedure applied to what is given. As active, interpretation is something we will to do, as opposed to something that happens to us. This distinction between active and passive illuminates another element of our hesitation. It was noted that when an aspect dawns it can seem like one is experiencing a new perception. When we try and succeed in noticing an aspect, the aspect at some point suddenly 'dawns' on us. Thus, while we can try to see it, we do not have complete control over the moment that the aspect dawns. Like a scale that is being tipped, once the balance shifts no more tipping is required. The scale shifts as though of its own accord, like the way a new object comes into view.

I began with the suggestion that Wittgenstein's investigations of aspectual seeing aim to reveal the raggedness of the concept of seeing. We are now in position to appreciate the first sense of raggedness mentioned above, which concerns the implications of the fact that there are diverse senses of 'see', or diverse ways in which 'see' is used. We saw how the puzzle with noticing an aspect concerned a certain hesitation about whether the change involved counted as a genuine perceptual change. Examining the ordinary criteria for drawing a distinction between seeing and interpreting revealed some reasons for our hesitation. More importantly, it showed that the concept of noticing an aspect is puzzling precisely because it straddles a distinction that, in other contexts, is easy to draw: 'Is it a *genuine* visual experience?' The question is: in what sense is it one? Here it is difficult to see that what is at issue is the fixing of concepts. A *concept* forces itself on one …[45] There is nothing inherently strange about the idea that no hard and fast distinction can be drawn between seeing and interpretation, or that there are some senses of 'see' which bear logical connections to other concepts. The assumption that makes it seem strange is the assumption that, as Charles Travis puts it, the world divides up in an occasion-insensitive way into items *x* and not-*x*, or that the fully analysed sense of a term must be *determinate*.[46] On this view, only if there is some fact of the matter that decides, independently of our particular employments of a concept, whether or not a given case counts as an instance of a concept can our hesitancy in applying a given concept be interpreted as a cognitive failure on our part.

This sense of cognitive failure is part of what gives Socrates' *what-is-it?* question its punch. It is commonly observed that ordinary discourse is *vague*. On a standard view, the vagueness of a term has to do with there being no sharp boundaries between what does and what does not fall under its extension. Thus, for example, the predicate *red* is vague in the sense that there are colours which are not definitely red, and yet not definitely some colour other than red either. On an epistemic interpretation, vagueness is a type of ignorance, specifically, our ignorance of the true limits of a predicate's extension. The intuitive force behind this interpretation is that it saves us from having to attribute vagueness to the world, so-called *ontic vagueness*.[47]

I have argued against this view by showing that what *appears* to be a form of ignorance exposed by the phenomenon of aspect seeing is in fact an expression

of grammatical intricacy. If there is something we are ignorant of in this context, it is not the essence of seeing, but how to draw a map of the grammar that
we have already mastered.[48] But neither does the raggedness of the concept of
seeing simply amount to locating vagueness in the term 'see'. Vagueness is
relative to some notion of what precision would mean, and there is no support
in what I have said for the inference that ordinary usage is defective. To the
contrary, a proper understanding of the phenomenon of raggedness tends to
undercut the idea that it so much as makes sense to judge ordinary usage as
vague. The appearance that raggedness amounts to vagueness stems from the
fact that, without appropriate surroundings, the words 'S sees p' express no
definite thought, which is to say, no thought with a truth condition definite
enough to establish as fact whether the thought is true or not. That appearance is undermined by observing the ways that our use of 'see' is governed by
criteria, and how those criteria are elicited by considering what we say when.
Raggedness does not concern the concept's being underdetermined with
respect to its meaning, but rather the fact that the use of the concept cannot
be codified in the form of a particular rule for applying it.

To return to the issue at hand, conceptual raggedness is not some exotic feature of psychological concepts which requires its own special phenomenology
to be discerned. Rather, what Wittgenstein's grammatical investigation
reveals is the ordinary linguistic facts about what 'see' means, which certain
kinds of philosophical questions can cover over in the very attempt to clarify.
Consider, for example, some ordinary ways we might complete the sentence
'I can see . . .' in the presence of a green lawn chair.

I can see . . .   *that* (pointing to the chair).
              the green chair.
              that the chair is green.
              the face in the chair.
              why the chair would be more comfortable with a pillow.
              what they were thinking when they designed the chair.
              that you wouldn't like the chair.
              what you mean about the chair's being whimsical.

One can be misled by talk of different *senses* of the term 'see', for example, if one
said that the concept of seeing has many different meanings. To speak of a
word as having different meanings is to suggest the possibility of enumerating
those meanings, as properties of the concept. But the different senses of the
word are just different ways in which the word is used. Take, for example,
the statement 'I can see the similarity between the chairs'. This sentence
cannot be identified as expressing a particular meaning or sense *as such*,
because that same sentence could be used to say different things. For example,

the sentence might be used to speak of the chair's having the same colour, or the same material or shape, or to express the same principles. If the concept of seeing is ragged in this sense, such that there are a diversity of things to be said in saying that S sees p, then the asking of the question may have already decided what the answer is.

In speaking of the uses above as exhibiting different senses, I mean something quite ordinary. For example, if I say that the chair is green, I can point to its colour, but I cannot point to it in the same sense as I point to the chair's being well designed. Again, in some of the uses above but not others, I might be able to substitute 'understand' for 'see', as in 'I can understand what they were thinking when they designed the chair' without changing the meaning of what I said. Now while fully acknowledging that there are different senses of 'see', one can nevertheless be tempted, for various reasons, to draw a distinction between true and false, or literal and figurative senses, on the basis of some conception of what it is about the genuine senses which accords with the meaning of the concept. Or one might think that all the senses must share some common feature if they are to count as genuine senses of 'see'. Or one might think that 'see' can only mean something determinate if it means one thing in particular, where the latter is taken to be incompatible logically with its having various senses. When Wittgenstein says that ideas about how things must be explained can make us overlook or distort what it is we are trying to explain, one thing he has in mind are just those ways we are led to introduce distinctions, for example, about what is to count as a genuine case of seeing, which do not reflect the intricacy of the grammar of the concept. If our hesitation in applying the concept of seeing to the case of aspectual perception rests on our rules for applying this concept, then our hesitation is caused neither by a cognitive failure on our part, i.e. on our failure to grasp the rule for applying the concept, nor by a problem with the concept of seeing itself, for example, its being vague or ambiguous. It is not some underlying essence that reveals our ordinary distinctions between seeing and interpreting to be inadequate or misleading, but our *assumption* that there must be some underlying essence, which causes us to see these ordinary uses as incomplete and vague.[49]

Not all seeing is interpretive (Descriptions of what is seen)

The second sense in which the concept of seeing is ragged has to do with the range of things that can count as descriptions or expressions of what we see. As we saw, the issue raised by the experience of noticing an aspect concerned the basis of the distinction between seeing and interpreting. But aspect seeing motivates another way of thinking about the relation between seeing and interpretation, what I shall refer to as the *Interpretive* model. The way that aspects appear to supervene on some underlying visual image or pictorial representation suggests the thesis that cases in which we would ordinarily distinguish between seeing and interpreting are not exceptions to ordinary seeing, but instances when the normally covert *interpretive* character of seeing in general is exposed. Methodologically, this thesis calls for clarification of the *concept of what is seen* through a systematic process of *deinterpretation* in which what is immediately given (sensation) to our sense organs is separated out like a precipitate from our full-blooded visual experience (perception). Deinterpretation is required, that is, if we are going to offer an account of *what is involved in seeing*. In debates among philosophers and psychologists about the interpretive character of visual perception, disagreements about how and whether such a reduction can be carried out can be said to conceal a shared premise: that all seeing is interpretive. So there is a sense in which reflecting on our ordinary understanding of what it means to see, quickly leads one to the conclusion that we seldom, if ever, merely see anything, or that what 'see' means is much more complicated conceptually than its surface grammar suggests.

However, if aspectual seeing, in particular, the concept of continuous aspect seeing, encourages this thesis, Wittgenstein's examination of the grammar of aspect seeing shows the move to betray a confusion. There is a mistake, that is, in thinking that explanations of aspectual seeing might reveal to us that the ordinary distinction between seeing and interpreting is unwarranted, even false. Of course, there may be uses of 'see' which involve logically the positing of a perceptual relation involving an interpretive element. Wittgenstein's investigation only attacks some typical ways in which aspectual seeing encourages the confused idea that all seeing is interpretive; it attacks some typical ways the thesis that 'all seeing is interpretation' is understood.

Just as there are reasons that incline us to deny that aspectual seeing counts as a genuine case of seeing, so too are there reasons inclining us to deny that descriptions of what we see that refer to aspects are genuine or direct descriptions of what is seen. Descriptions referring to aspects can be construed as indirect in the sense that they do not use concepts with a purely visual reference. Speaking of the Necker cube, Wittgenstein voices the temptation:

> Here perhaps we should like to reply: the description of what is got immediately i.e., of the visual experience, by means of an interpretation – is an indirect description. 'I see the figure as a box' means: I have a particular visual experience which I have found that I always have when I interpret the figure as a box or when I look at a box.[50]

The distinction between concepts with and concepts without a purely visual reference is suggested largely by the ways in which aspectual changes cannot be accounted for by attributing them to changes in the object or figure seen. That what is seen can change without a physical change in the figure suggests the distinction between the object seen (the physical marks on the paper called 'Necker cube') and the visual impression (the impression I have when I say 'Now *this* side is in front'). The change is then ascribed to my visual impression. Concepts referring to properties of the visual impression can thus be understood to have a non-visual reference, in the sense that they only refer indirectly to the actual figure. By contrast, purely visual concepts will be understood to refer to properties of the figure upon which my visual impression supervenes.

Wittgenstein's example, above, distinguishes between 'I see a box' and 'I see *that* figure,' but the distinction is easily extended to other cases. One can distinguish between the duck-rabbit figure and the visual impression of a duck, between 'I see a happy face' and 'I see a figure with a line shaped like *this*' (pointing to the smile), or between 'I see his hesitancy' and 'I see his face in *this* position'. In the case of the Necker cube, this would mean that, in contrast to an ordinary description of what we see, which referred to one spatial organization rather than another, a direct description – that is, a description in the true sense of 'description' – would refer to what is seen only in terms of properties inherent in the visual look of the stimulus. Deinterpretation is thus required in order to separate out the inherent properties of the visual stimulus from those properties of our visual impression.

The suggestion, which will turn out to be problematic, is that the aspect is an interpretation (or a judgement, or a conceptualization) of something else which is *directly* perceived, something which does not call for interpretation, something which is unambiguous. Descriptions referring to aspects that change suggest themselves as ambiguous in the following sense. While the perceptual report 'the rose is red' can be explained by pointing to a colour sample and saying 'the rose is *this* colour', a report about an aspectual change cannot simply refer to a copy of the figure.

> ... when we have a changing aspect the case is altered. Now the only possible expression of our experience is what before perhaps seemed, or even was, a useless specification when once we had the copy.[51]

That is to say, if someone asks me to describe what I am seeing when the aspect switches back and forth, it is not enough to simply offer a copy of the figure. That is, a copy of the Necker cube figure does not express the aspectual change *in the same way* that a copy of an ordinary square expresses what I see. Rather, I may attempt to convey the aspect seen by embellishing the copy, by making a model, or altering visually the 'exact image' like this:

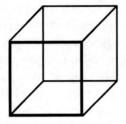

Fig. 3

Unlike a description in terms of the physical characteristics of the cube, however, this expression above is actually a modification of the copy; in order to suggest the aspect seen the expression must actually modify the exact copy. Moreover, the figure above is ambiguous in the sense that it could also be misunderstood. For example, emphasizing the square with a heavier line does not stop the aspect switch from occurring. Puzzle pictures offer another example.

> I suddenly see the solution of a picture-puzzle . . . My visual impression has changed; – what was it like before and what is it like now? – If I represent it by means of an exact copy – and isn't that a good representation of it? – no change is shown.[52]

The suggestion is that in order to describe the picture of the face I need to 'refer beyond' what I see there. In moving beyond what is seen, in the strict sense of 'see', I am thus interpreting the object-stimulus. The problem is that I cannot describe precisely what I am seeing without offering an exact copy of the puzzle, while an exact copy does not convey the solution.

Now, if the experience of noticing an aspect suggests that aspects are not part of what is truly seen, *inter alia* that descriptions referring to aspect-features are indirect because they involve non-visual references, the suggestion is easily generalized to include all ordinary cases of seeing and all ordinary descriptions of visual experience. The concept of continuous aspect seeing supplies the link: 'The picture might have been shown to me, and I never have seen anything but a rabbit in it.'[53] While aspectual changes dramatize the sense in which the aspect is not itself part of what is seen, or is so in a way different from the physical object, the concept of continuous aspect seeing suggests that ordinary cases of seeing which exhibit no apparent visual ambiguity nevertheless involve an act of interpretation which fixes their visual meaning.

Like the concept of noticing an aspect, that of continuous aspect seeing is developed by Wittgenstein in terms of the criteria for ascriptions of the experience. If a criterion of the former was its distinctive expression – the avowal that speaks of the image as changed while looking the same – criteria for the latter concern the ways in which someone's taking for granted the identity of the object (figure) under a particular aspect are manifested. In the case of the duck-rabbit, a criterion for someone's continuous aspect perception of the figure as a rabbit is just his taking for granted that the figure is of a rabbit: 'If I heard someone talking about the duck-rabbit, and *now* he spoke in a certain way about the special expression of the rabbit's face I should say, now he's seeing the picture as a rabbit.'[54] Such behaviour expresses an absence of hesitation that is grammatically connected to an absence of ambiguity in the visual experience.

> I may, then, have seen the duck-rabbit simply as a picture-rabbit from the start. That is to say, if asked 'What's that?' or 'What do you see here?' I should have replied: 'A Picture-rabbit.' If I had further been asked what that was, I should have explained by pointing to all sorts of pictures of rabbits, should perhaps have pointed to real rabbits, talked about their habits, or given an imitation of them.
>
> I should not have answered the question 'What do you see here?' by saying: 'Now I am seeing it as a picture-rabbit.' I should simply have described my perception: just as if I had said 'I see a red circle over there.' – Nevertheless someone else could have said of me: 'He is seeing the figure as a picture-rabbit.'[55]

Not being aware of the bivalent meaning of the duck-rabbit figure, I have no basis for a distinction between the object seen and my visual impression of the object. The concept is further illustrated by Wittgenstein in terms of pictorial representation: continuous seeing of something as *x* is analogous to seeing of something as a picture of *x*.

> How would the following account do: 'What I can see something *as*, is what it can be a picture of'?
>
> What this means is: the aspects in a change of aspects are those ones which the figure might sometimes have *permanently* in a picture.[56]

Here, an analogy is drawn between seeing the similarity of two faces, seeing the cube as three-dimensional, and now: the relationship between a line drawing (as a physical object, a certain pattern of pencil lead on white paper), and what the drawing is a drawing of, for example, a happy face.[57]

These considerations offer another way to grasp the concept of continuous aspect seeing. We can draw a distinction between a picture and what a picture is of, but we can also think of the ways in which we see through pictures to what they are of. Speaking of simple line drawings of human faces, Wittgenstein remarks that:

> In some respects I stand towards [a picture-face] as I do towards a human
> face. I can study its expression, can react to it as to the expression of the
> human face. A child can talk to picture-men or picture-animals, can treat
> them as it treats dolls.[58]

The suggestion that we are not ordinarily aware of the process of interpretation is sometimes illustrated with the analogy to painting. The very fact that a
painter needs to learn how to translate, and not merely transcribe, three-
dimensional spatial relations and forms onto a two-dimensional surface, confronting all of the related problems of perspective, foreshortening, etc., would
seem to demonstrate the necessity for a similar process of translation in the
case of ordinary visual experience.[59] In deinterpreting our visual experience,
we are thus led to distinguish those elements of the pictorial representation
which are not themselves represented; those elements which, as we might say,
can be described in a purely metrical vocabulary of colour and shape. The
same arrangement of colour and shape can be taken as a picture of different
objects or states of affairs. The thesis under attack – that all seeing is interpretation – can now be given a sharper formulation: all ordinary seeing is continuous aspect seeing.

Correlated grammatically with the distinction between seeing and interpretation is a distinction between direct and indirect descriptions of what is
experienced. The expression of an interpretation is an indirect description.
For example, on this view, a description of the look of someone's face as pensive, or of two faces as being similar, is an indirect way of expressing what I see.
They are indirect in the sense that they are constructed using concepts that do
not have a purely visual reference.[60] As such, they betray an ambiguity of
meaning which is covered over in ordinary usage where, for purposes of communication, they typically count as direct or genuine descriptions. In contrast, a direct description would only refer to what it is about the face that
makes it count as being pensive, or only what it is about two faces which gives
me the impression of similarity. Implied by this line of thought is that most
of what ordinarily counts as a description, a direct or complete or accurate
description, of our visual experience are in fact indirect approximations.
If 'what I can see something as is what it can be a picture of', then any description referring to elements of our visual experience which could be represented
in a picture fails to directly express what we see.

Now when Wittgenstein speaks of the raggedness of the concept 'description
of what is seen', what he is attacking is the suggestion that what ordinarily
counts as a genuine description of our visual experience is indirect or covertly
ambiguous in the above sense: 'There is not *one genuine* proper case of such
description – the rest being just vague, something which awaits clarification,

or which must just be swept aside as rubbish.'[61] If aspectual seeing encourages the interpretive conception of visual perception, it does so in part by making us forget about the ways in which the distinction between a direct and indirect description is ordinarily constituted. That is to say, the interpretive conception trades on overlooking our ordinary criteria for distinguishing between direct and indirect descriptions. As such, Wittgenstein's argument consists in assembling reminders.[62]

Consider his response to the claim that 'I see the figure as a box' is an indirect description. Wittgenstein's first response is to characterize the comment about the indirectness of 'I see the figure as a box' as a statement about its semantics: ' "I see the figure as a box" means: I have a particular visual experience which I have found that I always have when I interpret the figure as a box or when I look at a box.'[63] Wittgenstein then goes on to offer a remark that is at first counterintuitive: 'But if it meant this I ought to know it. I ought to be able to refer to the experience directly, and not only indirectly. (As I can speak of red without calling it the colour of blood.)'[64]

The remark is counterintuitive in the sense that it is not obvious that we *should* be able to refer to the 'experience' directly. For example, it would be very difficult, if not impossible, to translate a statement about the likeness between two faces into statements about the physical characteristics of the faces that underlie my description of them as similar. The antecedent of Wittgenstein's remark is decisive: I should be able to refer to the experience directly *if* the statement really means this. This would imply that if I cannot offer a more direct description – as 'I can speak of red without calling it the colour of blood' – then this cannot be what the statement really means. A description translating references to cubes or ducks into references to colour and shape would not be a more precise description; it would be a *different* description altogether, the expression of a different visual experience.

Ceteris paribus one would not ordinarily call descriptions such as 'I see the similarity between the two faces' 'indirect', unless there were some reason, obvious enough to the speaker, which would both justify the judgement, and at the same time require the speaker to offer an explanation or justification of his choice of words, in the form of a more direct description of what he sees. Having described the fruit as the 'colour of blood', I could explain or justify myself by saying, 'I mean that the fruit is red'. But if there is no more direct way of describing what I see, then there is no reason to assume that that expression harbours a tacit ambiguity.[65] The point is, however, that the phenomenon of aspect seeing can cause us to overlook the extent to which we *already* have criteria for deciding when a description is indirect, or when one is justified in asking for a more precise specification. For example, take the question 'How did Wang look?' One might respond by reporting that Wang looked stressed-out. If I were pressed on it, I might be able to proffer a more precise description of his appearance of being stressed-out. For example, I might say, 'I mean that he had a distant look in his eyes and his motions were stiff.' But I may not be able to specify what I meant. To say that all of our ordinary descriptions are indirect, however, is to say that there is *always* a more precise description that corresponds to what we mean to report. That is like saying: we seldom say what we mean when we express what we see. But why should one accept that?

Consider, for example, instances when looking at a drawing of someone I know, I exclaim: 'That looks *exactly* like him!' If there is no question of the drawing resembling the person in every respect, is my expression false or ambiguous?[66] One could of course introduce a criterion for exactness that would render the drawing an imperfect approximation to the person's appearance. However, nothing about what 'exact description' means could be used to justify that criterion of exactness. That is because the meaning of 'exact description' is constituted in part by certain ordinary perceptual reports (i.e. 'It's a rabbit') counting as genuine descriptions.

In overlooking ordinary criteria for fixing evaluative properties of expressions of visual experience, the interpretive model also overlooks the extent to which such properties are fixed by the circumstances surrounding the expressions. As we saw above, the distinction between concepts with and without a purely visual reference suggests that ordinary reports referring to aspectual features of what is seen are structurally defective as direct descriptions. In an obvious sense, however, nothing about how a description is structured can decide in itself whether it is an accurate report of what is seen. For example, I am trying to describe the shape of a fruit. I say, 'It's shaped like *this*' (drawing a figure with my finger in the air). We can imagine specific contexts in which a gestural description would be informative, and contexts in which it would be, say, an exaggeration. This shows that there are not only different ways in which the expression could be measured for its accuracy, there are different things that 'accurate' or 'exact' could mean. What does determine the evaluative properties of an expression of visual experience is something that can only be clarified by considering the circumstances under which it makes sense to draw a distinction between an adequate and an inadequate description of what we see.

> Then is the copy of the figure an *incomplete* description of my visual experience? No. – But the circumstances decide whether, and what, more detailed specifications are necessary. – It *may* be an incomplete description; if there is still something to ask.[67]

In this sense, the concept of a description of what is seen is ragged.

How grammar expresses essence (Continuous seeing-as)

As we saw above, Wittgenstein argued that if we cannot offer a more precise description of our visual experience – as we can when we call something the colour of blood – then our description cannot be said to be referring to that experience. Now one might object to Wittgenstein's rather cursory dismissal of the idea that 'I see the figure as a cube' is an indirect description of the Necker cube by arguing that ordinary language lacks the expressive resources to capture what we really see. After all, still-life painting requires considerable training. Moreover, theorists asserting the need for a phenomenal or phenomenological language have typically done so by pointing out that a language designed to speak about physical objects, as natural language is taken to be, is not especially suited to describing visual impressions. As I noted above, Jaakko and Merrill Hintikka interpret aspect seeing as a possible counterexample to Wittgenstein's thesis that our primary language is physicalistic, and that natural language cannot be analysed, as some logical positivists once thought, into a sense-datum or phenomenal language referring only to phenomenological entities. What Wittgenstein's grammatical analysis of aspectual seeing throws into question, however, is the assumption that it so much as makes sense to speak of referring to the same experience expressed in terms of aspects independently of reference to aspectual features. It makes no sense to say that someone sees the rabbit aspect of the duck-rabbit without knowing what a rabbit is.

> Would it be conceivable that someone who knows rabbits but not ducks should say: 'I can see the drawing as a rabbit and also in another way, although I have no word for the second aspect'? Later he gets to know ducks and says: 'That's what I saw the drawing as that time!' – Why is that not possible?[68]

Here it is easy to see that the problem is not merely a technical one of being able to construct a language with the appropriate concepts and grammar to refer only to our visual experiences. Rather, the hypothetical reduction is not possible for conceptual reasons. A reduction to some supposed deeper level of analysis would no longer be an explanation of the same concept. In an analogous way, the rules of chess could not be reduced to a more precise formulation. Wittgenstein indicates the character of this grammatical impossibility by referring to reports of the experience of seeing something as something, not as descriptions but *expressions*. One does not ask whether an expression could be reduced to what it is the expression of.[69]

This consideration of expressions offers another view on the phenomenon of conceptual raggedness. If the ways we typically respond to the experience of an aspect, for example, by uttering 'Now it's a rabbit!', or 'It's a rabbit', are primitive or unanalysable moves in the language-game that such expressions function within, then the uttering of them serves a criterial role in ascribing such experiences. The inclination to use such an expression is not simply inductive support for a perceptual ascription; the expression is individuative of the experience. Because the ways we express what we see are diverse, seeing itself is polymorphous: the term 'see' is ragged.

Let us now return to the concept of continuous seeing-as. Earlier, I suggested that Wittgenstein used the concept of continuous seeing-as to elaborate the confusions that the phenomenon of aspect seeing gives rise to: namely, the thesis that all seeing is interpretation. I then suggested that the concept of continuous aspect seeing serves to illustrate a conceptual problem with that thesis by attacking the idea that everything I see I always see *as something*. I shall quote again the passage where Wittgenstein identifies the concept of continuous seeing-as: 'And I must distinguish between the "continuous seeing" of an aspect and the "dawning" of an aspect. The picture might have been shown me, and I never have seen anything but a rabbit in it.'[70] One important difference between these concepts is that while the noticing of an aspect counts as an experience of sorts – as we saw, largely due to the ways we *react* to it – the notion of continuously seeing an aspect does not quite fit into the category of being an experience. One cannot make sense of continuous seeing-as in terms of a perpetually dawning aspect, almost like the circular motion of a body about a fixed point. In fact, it seems more accurate phenomenologically to talk of continuous seeing as a kind of blindness stemming from taking something for granted. Someone who has always seen the duck-rabbit as a rabbit cannot be said to have the experience of the dawning of the duck aspect, since she is by definition unaware of the ambiguity of the figure. But if not that experience, then neither the experience of the dawning of the rabbit aspect, since that experience is logically connected to the former. In experiencing the dawning of the rabbit aspect, one is seeing how the figure can be seen *also* as a rabbit. At the same time, one could say that one is seeing how the rabbit can be seen *as a rabbit*, and in a different sense *as the figure*.

Now if continuous aspect seeing is not an experience, how is the concept applied? What are its criteria? For one, my identifications of what I am seeing will not imply that the description I give is based on a point of view or interpretation.

If I had seen the duck-rabbit simply as a picture from the start, I should not have answered the question 'What do you see here?' by saying: 'Now I am seeing it as a picture-rabbit.' I should simply have described my perception: just as if I had said 'I see a red circle over there.'[71]

That is, I should not have said that 'Now I am seeing it as a rabbit' because that concept implies that there is an ambiguity in the visual meaning of the figure. The mistake here, however, is to think that in not perceiving the ambiguity, there is something that is being concealed from me. That may be the case, but the mistake is to think that it *must* be the case. The mistake arises from thinking that the rabbit aspect – the aspect I am taking for granted – is somehow blocking my perception of the duck aspect. To the contrary, it may be the case that I just do not know what rabbits are, for example, that I have no stereotypes of what rabbits are supposed to look like.

One might put the point in Gricean terms of the contextual implicature of the concept of seeing-as. Since expressions referring to seeing something as something typically imply an interpretive ambiguity in what is seen, such expressions cannot be used meaningfully in contexts where no such ambiguity is perceived, just because doing so violates the grammar of their implicature. If I say 'Now it's a face for me', you are justified in asking me what change I am alluding to, just because that is part of what is conventionally implied by my use of such an expression.[72] One motive behind Grice's notion of contextual implicature is to show that the semantics proper of certain (e.g. observational) statements can in fact be detached from facts about the occasions for particular speakings of them. On such a view, the oddness of speaking of seeing a fork as a fork does not indicate that nothing intelligible is being said, but only that the conventional reasons for speaking thus are not present.[73] Wittgenstein goes further, however.

> It would have made as little sense for me to say 'Now I am seeing it as . . .' as to say at the sight of a knife and fork 'Now I am seeing this as a knife and fork.' This expression would not be understood. – Any more than: 'Now it's a fork' or 'It can be a fork too.'[74]

And again: 'One doesn't "*take*" what one knows as cutlery at a meal *for* cutlery; any more than one ordinarily tries to move one's mouth as one eats, or aims at moving it.' This criticism goes further in the sense that Wittgenstein is not merely attacking the appropriateness of the expression, he is suggesting that using the concept of continuous seeing-as in that way distorts its semantics proper. There are various things that we could understand 'Now it's a rabbit' to mean. For example, it may mean that the figure no longer looks like a duck (or no longer looks like a rocking-chair, or a corporate identity logo, or a meaningless doodle, etc.). That is to say, there is no unique state of affairs that 'Now I'm seeing it as a rabbit' describes. Once considered independently of the contexts where it would make sense for me to express such an ambiguity, the expression no longer has a determinate sense.

The analogy to eating and moving one's mouth is particularly helpful here. The act of eating does not involve our consciously aiming to move our mouth in a certain way. It is empty verbiage to say that all eating is eating with one's mouth, or that all chewing involves moving one's jaw up and down. Conceiving of eating in such terms over-intellectualizes the activity of eating. Conceiving of seeing in such terms over-intellectualizes our relation to perceptual input. It does so insofar as it presupposes that our behaviour towards the figure, i.e. the various ways that our taking its identity as a rabbit for granted is manifested and the various ways that we react to it, can be reduced to a perceptual content specifiable independently of those ways. One might say that it presupposes that there is a level of description, revealed through deinterpretation of our visual perception of, for example, a rabbit, which can be specified independently of our expressive reactions to the visual image of a rabbit. But insofar as typical or stereotypical reactions to what we see serve a criterial role in ascribing such experiences, there is no more precise articulation of the meaning.

Nevertheless, there is a great temptation to assume that there is a seeing-as relation inherent in every visual experience. This temptation arises largely from misconstruing an interesting criterial asymmetry between first-person and third-person ascriptions of continuous seeing-as. Even though it might not make sense for me to speak of seeing the figure as a rabbit, 'Nevertheless, someone else could have said of me: "He is seeing the figure as a picture-rabbit." '[75] The asymmetry concerns the fact that it can make sense (i.e. be in accord with the meaning of the concept of continuous seeing-as) to say of someone that she is seeing the duck-rabbit as a rabbit in cases where it does not make sense for her to avow that experience herself. What this asymmetry suggests is that, irrespective of our ordinary reasons for drawing a distinction between seeing and seeing-as, there is a deeper sense in which the concept of seeing something as something applies unqualifiedly to visual experience in general. It suggests that our perception of even the most ordinary of objects is tacitly shaped or informed in various ways by aspects. It is plausible to see this picture as a shared assumption of many theories of perception which are radically opposed in other ways. For example, one might say that while realists about perception emphasize the countability and identifiability of these aspects, those drawn to hermeneutical conceptions of perception emphasize the sense in which the ways of seeing things that can be ascribed to us, irrespective of the ways we can become aware of or express, are innumerable, and that the process of deinterpretation is interminable.

Continuous seeing-as is ill-conceived, however, when it is applied *in an unqualified way* to all visual experience. While it makes sense to speak of someone innocent of the duck-aspect seeing the figure as a rabbit, it makes no *prima facie* sense to say of him that he is seeing a spoon as a spoon. There are conceivable reasons we might have for ascribing to such a person the concept of continuous seeing-as. For example, we might make that ascription if we know that he has the concept of a duck and will see the duck aspect when it is pointed out to him. That situation is unlike the case of seeing cutlery where there is no clear sense in speaking of seeing the spoon as a spoon. Things may of course change to render that expression a meaningful one. For example, we could imagine a conceptual sculpture involving ordinary spoons, but constructed in such a way that the spoons appear to be anthropomorphic figurines or alien seed pods. In that context, we can imagine saying of someone who does not understand the sculpture, 'He's seeing the spoons as spoons'. Nothing about this ordinary grammar forces on us the thesis that all seeing is seeing-as, however. In suggesting that whenever I see an object, I see it as the kind of thing it conventionally counts as being, I am using the expression 'seeing x as x' outside of the contexts within which it is used to say something.

In the sculpture example, one can understand what could be meant in uttering 'He's seeing the spoons as spoons'. For example, it might mean that he does not yet see what the sculpture is about, or that he is noticing what the sculpture is made out of, or he's just discovered what happened to his missing spoons. But when we speak of seeing an ordinary *spoon as a spoon*, for example, while looking for something to stir my coffee with, the lack of the ordinary background circumstances within which the seeing-as expression is employed undermines its meaning. Like a pawn from a chess set being used as a piece in a different game, the absence of the ordinary context leaves the use of 'I am seeing the x as an x' undetermined. A pawn only does what it ordinarily does when functioning as a piece in a game of chess. The expression 'I am seeing the x as an x' can only be used to say what it ordinarily does when functioning within the game of, for example, describing what sculptures are made out of. A pawn can, of course, be used in a different game, but then how it is to be used must be specified in terms of the rules for that game, and the same is true with seeing-as locutions.

Hermeneutical phenomenology and grammar (Stephen Mulhall)

This interpretation of Wittgenstein's analysis may sound off-key. Wittgenstein has often been taken to be arguing just the opposite; namely, that all seeing is continuous seeing-as. In turn, that 'thesis' has been taken to carry various implications for how we understand traditional epistemological and semantical questions about seeing. A case in point is Stephen Mulhall's inspired interpretation, which takes the aim of the discussion in section xi of Part Two of *Philosophical Investigations* to be precisely the thesis that all ordinary seeing is continuous aspect perception.[76] As he argues, the philosophical importance of the concept of continuous seeing-as stems from the way that it

... highlights a set of relations which must manifest themselves in contexts other than this specific one. This conclusion follows from the fact that any particular experience of aspect-dawning, in making us aware that we can see a given entity as a new kind of object, thereby highlights the fact that we are already regarding it as a particular kind of object.[77]

For example, while looking at a traditional landscape painting, I might experience the dawning of its material aspects. What before was a cloud suddenly appears as a brush stroke or a bit of paint, without any representational content. Expressing that experience, I might say, 'I am seeing it as paint now', or 'Now it looks like a brush stroke'. According to Mulhall, the very possibility that the physicality of the painting can suddenly dawn on me implies that my experience of the painting was *already* structured in terms of, or 'informed by', a set of aspect concepts; the concepts which determine *that* to be a kind of object, namely, a painting.

> ... even if seeing a painting as an array of color-patches is a particular sort of experience – is one unusual way of perceiving the painting – it necessarily involves perceiving a painting, and thus exemplifies the relation between 'painting' concepts and experience which applies to the whole domain of paintings even when no experience of aspect-dawning is at stake.[78]

In turn, Mulhall takes this fact to illustrate a universal relation between concepts, the world and experience. That we must extend the concept of continuous seeing-as beyond the ordinary range of meaningful usage is suggested by our ordinary capacity to take things for granted perceptually.

> Aspect concepts are ... any set of concepts determining any kind of object, i.e. determining what it is for an object to be an object of a given kind. If one adds to this the fact that when people – language-users – perceive and encounter particular objects, those encounters will necessarily involve a set of concepts which determine those objects as objects of a particular kind (otherwise it would make no sense to describe what takes place as (e.g.) someone perceiving some particular thing), it follows that a study of continuous aspect perception can legitimately be viewed as a philosophical investigation of human relationships with objects or phenomena *in general*.[79]

Now Mulhall's interpretation is directed against the classical empiricist idea that we do not directly perceive objects but only sense-data, or that we perceive, in the *strict sense* of 'perceive', such entities as pictures, words and people as mere material objects. Mulhall is correct on this point, if one takes Wittgenstein to be arguing that descriptions of what we see in terms of aspects,

such as 'It's a duck', cannot be analysed or translated into descriptions referring only to material properties of the objects of vision, for example, colour or
light intensity. Where Mulhall goes wrong, however, is by interpreting Wittgenstein's attack on that picture as the affirmation of a different picture.
According to Mulhall's interpretation, it not only makes *sense* to say of someone, under normal circumstances, that he is seeing the painting as a painting;
analysing why it *does* make sense uncovers what can only be called a metaphysical truth about human relationships to objects in general. But this is a misleading way of picturing our grammatical conventions. For example, Mulhall
argues that it is *false* that we encounter things as 'exemplars of objecthood
in general':

> The things I directly perceive on my desk are books, envelopes containing
> letters consisting of words and sentences, a group photograph, a lamp, a pen
> and ruler; they are not most immediately encountered simply as material
> objects of varying form and color.[80]

But is it even false to say that we encounter things as 'exemplars of objecthood
in general'? It is not at all clear what it would *mean* to do so. We might try to
imagine a use for such an expression, for example, one based on the experience
of noticing the brushstrokes of a painting. But how would we generalize that
experience to *all* things? Moreover, what does it mean to 'encounter' a thing?
Does that involve seeing it, or noticing it, or merely knowing that it is ready-
to-hand in the drawer? These questions raise a more serious problem. Mulhall
is not concerned with making sense of the idea of seeing things as exemplars of
objecthood, but rather with arguing that that idea, as a thesis about the relationship between the mind and the world, is not true. But if no sense has yet
been given to the idea of encountering pure objects in their objectivity, then
no sense has been given to the denial of that idea either. *Inter alia* no sense has
been given to the idea that all seeing is continuous aspect seeing.

In another sense, there is truth in Mulhall's contention. It is not clear, however, how important that truth is. Mulhall argues that our encounters with
things *necessarily* involve a set of concepts that determine those things as objects
of a particular kind. As he puts it, if this were *not* the case, it would not make
sense to speak of someone's perceiving a particular thing.[81] Presumably, if all
ordinary seeing were *not* continuous seeing, we could only speak meaningfully
of someone's seeing things as 'exemplars of objecthood in general', perhaps
seeing pictures as arrangements of colour and shape. But the fact that it does
make sense to speak of someone as perceiving a particular kind of thing
depends on many things. This fact is not explained, nor are ordinary uses of
'perceive' and 'see' justified, by hypothesizing a general human attitude
towards the world. It *could* make sense to speak of someone as perceiving a

particular thing, or perceiving the object as a 'this somewhat'. But for those expressions to make sense would just be for us to find a use for them; for us to imagine an occasion in which it would matter whether we used that expression rather than another.

Mulhall emphasizes in his interpretation that in speaking of the general way that we encounter objects in the world, no metaphysical claims are being made. This view stems largely from his idea that Wittgenstein's approach to philosophy 'presupposes that philosophical investigations are always and only grammatical investigations'.[82] On this view, so-called metaphysical statements bear a confusion generated when a statement about the grammar of a concept is expressed in the material mode and taken to assert something about extra-linguistic reality.[83] Hence, Mulhall can criticize Heidegger's talk of *equipmental totality* in *Being and Time* as expressing 'in material mode a grammatical point about the nature of aspect concepts'.[84] In contrast, Mulhall's own statements about 'directly perceiving things as kinds of objects rather than as pieces of world-stuff' are free from such confusion.

> In saying all of this, however, we are simply transforming expressions according to grammatical rules, connection expressions with the criteria for their application, or offering alternative characterizations of certain phenomena; no metaphysical *discoveries* can emerge from such grammatical explorations.[85]

It is not clear, however, that Mulhall adequately heeds his own methodological caveats against metaphysical pronouncements. Saying that my seeing a painting necessarily involves a set of concepts defining the painting as a particular kind of object sounds suspiciously like saying that perceiving a painting presupposes that it is a painting I am seeing. That is, it sounds as if Mulhall is simply calling attention to the fact that ascribing to someone the experience of seeing a painting, rather than, for example, seeing *merely* a piece of canvas on the wall covered with paint, involves the concept of a painting and not simply the concepts of canvas and paint. One might call this a conceptual or grammatical truth, and the value of pointing it out, as Mulhall argues persuasively, is to undermine the classical empiricist view that what we really see are sense-data. However, to go further by interpreting this grammatical fact as showing us something about our relation to the world in general seems to commit Mulhall to the same metaphysics that he accuses Heidegger of succumbing to.

It is not the character of the way that we relate to things in the world that explains or justifies the way we express our experience of those things. There is no more justification for those modes of expression than there are for the rules of chess. As I argued (section three above), the interpretive view of perception goes wrong precisely in arguing that ordinary expressions are not justified as reports of what is truly seen (i.e. sense data or 'pieces of world-stuff'). But to take this criticism as revealing a general relation of mind to things in the world is to go further by endorsing those ordinary expressions. It endorses them by taking that relation to things to justify our ways of expressing our experience. If that is *the* relation to things, then other ways of expressing ourselves – ways that do not 'take for granted' the identities of what we see – are not justified. But attempting to find a deeper basis in reality for how we speak is just to lapse into 'metaphysics', in the pejorative sense that Wittgenstein means it. It is to mistake our *need* to see things a certain way for a *necessity* in the nature of things.

The fact that 'I see a rabbit' logically implies that there is a rabbit present and visible has not discouraged perceptual psychologists from hypothesizing all manner of mediating elements, in particular computational processing, in explaining the establishment of a perceptual relation. Given that framework, it would make sense to speak of our 'human relation' to the world as a computational, or information processing relation. Can we speak of computational processes as taking for granted that things are of a particular kind? We might think of a situation where it would be useful to speak that way. In response to Mulhall's claim that we need to conceptualize ordinary perception in terms of continuous aspect seeing, or in terms of the readiness-to-hand of the objects of perception, one could say that our relation, or rather *relations*, to ordinary objects of perception are already conceptualized. That is, they are, if that just means that we have language and we can see.

It is relevant to mention here that these obscurities do not impugn the philosophical merits of Mulhall's interpretation. What is valuable about his reading is his attempt to find a point of dialectical contact between Wittgenstein's work on the grammar of perceptual concepts and figures in other traditions, in particular, Heidegger and Davidson, who seem to be addressing similar issues. It is apparent that the early Heidegger is drawn to visual phenomena similar to those that interest Wittgenstein in his investigation into aspect seeing. This passage from an early draft of *Being and Time* shares a similar sense of epistemological trust in the ordinary.

> When we say 'we see', 'seeing' here is not understood in the narrow sense of optical sensing. Here it means nothing other than 'simple cognizance of what is found'. When we hold to this expression, then we also understand and have no difficulty in taking the immediately given just as it shows itself. Thus we say that one sees in the chair itself that it came from a factory. We draw no conclusions, make no investigations, but we simply see this in it, even though we have no sensation of a factory or anything like it. The field of what is found in simple cognizance is in principle much broader than what any particular epistemology or psychology could establish on the basis of a theory of perception.[86]

The other important similarity is their shared sense of there being an internal relationship between meaning and truth. Following Husserl, Heidegger argues that perception is epistemologically trustworthy almost by definition, in the sense that the intentionality of perceiving an object just means: cognizing how something is its fleshy immediacy. There is an analogy here to Wittgenstein's argument that ordinary perceptual avowals about how things look in the world do not stand in need of a justification. A third obvious similarity between the two approaches has to do with meaning holism, where both thinkers understand the individuation conditions for meaning to comprise the larger environment. But there are grave difficulties in even comparing these two approaches. Where Wittgenstein argues that you must understand a whole form or way of life to understand a sentence of a language, Heidegger argues that the availability of an object to perception as a meaningful thing presupposes phenomenologically *a priori* structures of being as elements of the temporal unity of *Dasein*. How do we know if they are even analysing, or describing, the same phenomena?

As Mulhall sees it, the phenomena addressed by a grammatical investigation into continuous aspect seeing are the same phenomena that are conceived by Heidegger in existential–ontological terms, as expressive of a mode of being of *Dasein*. In defending Wittgenstein's approach, Mulhall argues that Heidegger's approach can be overturned by an application of Occam's razor. This amounts to showing that 'the features of human relationships with objects which we have isolated do not require the truth of [Heidegger's] metaphysical doctrine in order to be explicable . . .'[87] This approach, while a fruitful beginning to a dialectical exchange between traditions, can be said to distort the character of their respective approaches in the effort to secure neutral ground. For one, it is misleading to read the analytic of *Dasein* as an explanatory hypothesis for the readiness-to-hand of the proximate entities of everyday Being-in-the-world. The whole exercise is initiated as an attempt to answer the question of Being, and in turn, the question of the being of *Dasein*. As an application of the method of hermeneutical phenomenology, that analysis is not meant as a metaphysical hypothesis, but as a phenomenological *description*. The framework of fundamental ontology is, of course, alien to Wittgenstein's approach, and as such poses great difficulties in establishing neutral ground. Needless to say, Heidegger would not recognize Mulhall's criteria as relevant to phenomenological clarification.

On the other hand, there are dangers in attempting to locate Wittgenstein on Heidegger's map. While Mulhall accuses Heidegger of constructing 'baroque metaphysical structures' his own glosses on the broader import of Wittgenstein's grammatical investigations sound vaguely metaphysical. This is most evident in his characterization of the phenomena of continuous aspect seeing as revealing *a universal relation* between human consciousness and the world. His disregard for the criteria in place for distinguishing between seeing and continuous seeing-as, together with his talk of a distinctively 'human relation', instantiate Wittgenstein's conception of metaphysical excess as telling us how things *must* be. I submit that Mulhall is forced to talk in terms of universal relations and *general forms of encounter* because of his attempt to connect Wittgenstein's grammatical investigations with a broadly phenomenological approach to the study of perception. But talk about fundamental ways of comportment to the world is anathema to the spirit of Wittgenstein's philosophy. It is not an easy task to see just how to put these two systems of thinking, ordinary language philosophy and hermeneutical phenomenology, into a genuine *Auseinandersetzung*.

2
Theories of visual meaning

I am not more certain of the meaning of my words than I am of certain judgements. Can I doubt that this colour is called 'blue'? (My) doubts form a system.[1]

Epistemology of early vision research

In this chapter I shall develop the thoughts introduced in the first chapter by considering what significance they have for a new and highly productive context of perceptual theorizing; namely, research into early vision: an empirical research project initiated by David Marr and one rooted in the computational theory of mind. This theory of mind, which is sometimes referred to as classical Turning cognitive architecture, conceptually likens the mind to a computer which processes syntactically-structured information. The virtue of this model is that, as Jerry Fodor has expressed, it is the only remotely plausible account of the human mind which explains how mental states can have causal powers, and so serves as a way to understand the metaphysical problem of how the human mind fits into the causal order of nature. The natural extension of this theory into natural science conceives of the functional organization of this information-processing machine in terms of Darwinian evolutionary bio-psychology, an extension that is referred to sometimes as the 'new synthesis' in cognitive science.

How do the insights we derive from the meaning of sight, by Wittgensteinian analysis of natural language perceptual concepts, relate to this kind of research?

My interest here lies in showing more precisely just how the appeal to ordinary conceptual meaning can and cannot be brought to bear on hypothesis formation in the study of perception. Turning first to the work of Zenon Pylyshyn, we'll see just how theoretical considerations can motivate a reconstruction of the distinction between seeing and interpretation, and why Wittgensteinian grammatical analysis has no bearing on such a reconstruction. I'll then consider another account of early vision, given by Donald Hoffman, which is susceptible to Wittgensteinian critique. In the case of Hoffman, my criticism is directed not at the thesis of an innate visual grammar, but at the perceptual epistemology that he argues is implied by that thesis. This criticism is developed into a qualified critique of syntactic conceptions of visual meaning and, at the same time, a view of the concept of visual meaning, as relative to a system of visual grammar. I'll then suggest how this might help to clarify a related issue: a methodological question about the interdisciplinary study of vision.

One might well question the point of dwelling on what appears to be the simple fact that the meanings of words in ordinary or natural language are not well-defined. If our ordinary understanding of visual perception as it is embodied, for example, in our use of the word 'see', is polymorphous, then one might simply conclude that the perspective on visual perception offered by that understanding is simply irrelevant to serious theoretical work. As polymorphous, that ordinary conception would be irrelevant just because it does not offer us an understanding of perception as a natural phenomenon, as something thinkable within the domains of natural science, e.g. physics, biology, chemistry. For example, Noam Chomsky argues a similar point in *New Horizons in the Study of Language and Mind*. Responding to Wittgensteinian-inspired claims that certain human abilities, like language use, cannot be explained naturalistically, Chomsky argues that:

> The question is not whether the concepts of common-sense understanding can themselves be studied in some branch of naturalistic inquiry; perhaps they can. Rather, it is whether in studying the natural world (for that matter, in studying these concepts, as part of the natural world), we view it from the standpoint provided by such concepts. Surely not. There may be scientific studies of some aspects of what people are and do, but they will not use the common-sense notions human being and language speaking – with their special role in human life and thought – in formulating their explanatory principles.[2]

But what is the epistemological status of the standpoint provided by our ordinary concepts of perception? On one view, Wittgensteinian grammatical analysis reveals a level of *a priori* logical structure which constrains the scope of empirical theories of perceptual processing; in the sense that a theoretical explanation of seeing which reduces the ordinary concepts of perception to a conceptual taxonomy based on, for example, classical Turning cognitive architecture would be guilty of actually ignoring the very subject-matter that is being purportedly explained. For example, Peter Hacker argues this hard-line interpretation when he says that:

> ... the very thought that our normal psychological vocabulary of belief and desire, emotion and attitude, might be eliminable in a future psychological science betokens fundamental confusion. For with their elimination, one would arguably eliminate the very explananda of the science of psychology.[3]

The argument echoes the epistemology of various forms of post-Kantian idealism, which identify some feature of mentation, such as intentionality or qualitativeness, as incapable of empirical or causal analysis due to its logical form. This has led certain philosophers to claim that, for example, the very idea of computational psychology, which reconstructs mental states as relationships to syntactically-structured mental representations, is conceptually incoherent in principle.[4] The problem with this interpretation is that it does not heed the lesson of Wittgenstein's idea that meaning is determined by how we use concepts, hence, that meaning is determined by our interpretive practices. If computational psychology is itself an interpretive practice with its own motivations for conceiving of seeing in terms of information-processing, then that epistemological context itself must justify the concept of seeing being employed. To argue *a priori*, as Hacker does, that seeing cannot be defined as a cognitive module, is to make the same conceptual mistake that Wittgenstein identifies in his analysis of aspectual perception: namely, failing to realize that the meaning of a concept is determined by how it is used.

Seeing is not thinking (Zenon Pylyshyn)

Consider the following use. In Zenon Pylyshyn's book *Seeing and Visualizing*, he argues for a distinction between seeing and thinking (or knowing), based on empirical research into early vision, as well as theorizing within the model of computational psychology, in terms of a cognitive module which computes geometrical properties of objects and relations, and does so independently of cognition, knowledge, or anything 'quasi-inferential'. Early vision, which has to do with pre-recognitional aspects of what is perceived, establishes the borders, shapes, sizes and relative positions of objects in the world on the basis of the information coded within the light reflected from the scene. The term for this level of processing, early vision, counts as a specific cognitive module because the processing involved at this level is cognitively impenetrable.

> This system individuates, or picks out, objects in a scene and computes the spatial layout of visible surfaces and the 3D shape of the objects in the scene. It thus covers a lot of what one means by 'visual perception'. What it does not do is identify the things we are looking at, in the sense of relating them to things we have seen before, to the contents of memory. And it does not make judgments about how things really are.[5]

There are several motivations involved with distinguishing seeing and thinking in just this way, and it matters theoretically. First note, as Pylyshyn himself does, the discrepancies between how he distinguishes seeing from thinking, with the ways that Wittgenstein showed we do in ordinary usage.

Ordinary language uses terms like 'appears' or 'seems' in ways that do not distinguish plausible functions of the visual system from inference based partly on visual cues and partly on other (nonvisual) information. For example, we speak of someone 'looking sick' or of a painting 'looking like a Rembrandt.'[6]

So there is no question here: the way he is going about distinguishing seeing from thinking does not, and is not intended to, capture the ordinary logic of the concept of sight, although it does overlap and touch at points. Specifically, it captures the sense of the term when it is used to mean, for instance, that you saw something without recognizing it. What justification is there for this linguistic stipulation? In fact, the reconstructed distinction between seeing and thinking (cognition) embodies an empirical claim, cast within the framework of computational psychology, that 'there exists a nontrivial part of the overall visual process that is [cognitively] impenetrable'.[7] This 'modularity-of-vision thesis' is an empirical claim with theoretical significance in the sense that it hypothesizes that the psychological mechanisms responsible for the perception of visual form are (a) informationally encapsulated from the rest of cognition, and that (b) the visual system proper operates on principles proprietary to vision alone. The hypothesis is disconfirmable in light of a wide body of experimental research on early vision that, Pylyshyn argues, undermines the viability of the competing thesis, which hypothesizes an architectural continuity between vision. This continuity thesis, which Pylyshyn identifies with the 'new look' approach to the perceptual psychology initiated by Jerome Bruner in the 1940s, is familiar to readers of Wittgenstein because it crosses paths with approaches to the philosophy of science, such as those of Thomas Kuhn and Norwood Hanson, which take perception to be intrinsically theory-laden, and hence understand vision to be shaped by cognition, and percepts by concepts. Pylyshyn's approach begins with the long-standing observation that optical illusions often prove to be resistant to rational influence: 'It is a remarkable fact about the perceptual illusions that knowing about them does not make them disappear.'[8] According to his thesis, the resistance of optical illusions to what we know and believe about what we are seeing is explained by hypothesizing an independence of the principles of visual organization from the principles of inferential reasoning used in general cognition. This is why, for example, something we know to be physically impossible, such as an Escher staircase that ascends into itself, keeps appearing to us the way it does: the information processed by the visual system is not influenced by information from what we know about the nature of physical objects. Take the Necker cube again. On the one hand, the experience does seem to suggest a kind of reasoning, or an inferential kind of process, in which the purely two-dimensional visual information of the figure is thought about, albeit quickly and subconsciously, based on what we *know* about the geometry of cubes and of objects in general. On this view, when the Necker cube inverts itself, we are experiencing a change of hypothesis because our mind cannot make up its mind (see fig. 4). Both hypotheses are equally warranted, given what we *know* (for the most part, unconsciously) about projective geometry and physical objects, and yet they are mutually incompatible. This looks like some kind of inferential, hence, cognitive, process. So either vision is cognitive through and through, or there is no such thing as pure seeing, ordinarily understood. Now on Pylyshyn's hypothesis, this is wrong. To the contrary, the body of empirical research on the cognitive penetrability of early vision suggests that the visual system operates on a different set of principles called *natural constraints*. These principles operate by assigning labels to elements of the visual field, which, like syntactic rules, govern the ways that the meaning of the whole depends upon the identity and arrangement of the parts. Hence, these principles explain 'why it is that how you perceive one aspect of a visual scene determines how you perceive another aspect of the scene'.[9] On this view, the Necker cube is in fact a case of pure vision, in the sense that the visual system alone is responsible for the experience.

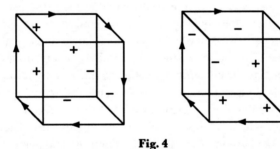

Fig. 4

The visual system does not *recognize* the form, but it provides the geometrically parsed, syntactically-labelled forms given to cognition to then recognize and think further about. Accordingly, the flip-flop experience is caused by the fact that there are two different and consistent labellings of vertexes, or places where lines intersect.

Because no concepts or knowledge of the geometry of polyhedrals is required to experience the Necker cube effect, the experience counts as a case of pure seeing, not involving cognition, thinking, or interpretation. The modularity-of-vision thesis draws the distinction between seeing and thinking differently than the more context-dependent ways that seeing is distinguished from thinking in ordinary language, but this doesn't mean that the thesis is either conceptually confused or empirically false. It just means that new conceptual criteria have been introduced, which have the meaning and justification they do in virtue of their place within the epistemological context of the theorizing.

Now, in Wittgenstein's analysis, we saw how the perception of the Necker cube sat uneasily on the conceptual edge of seeing and thinking and, as such, helped to reveal what our criteria for applying the concept of seeing are, hence the polymorphous conceptuality of sight. The appeal to use does not claim that ordinary grammar constrains what kinds of theories we can construct about perception. The claim is, rather, that certain explanatory models have no application to our understanding of that grammar. It is the assumption that certain explanatory models must be adopted in explaining the meaning of perceptual concepts that we are attacking by revealing the distortions such models introduce.

One of the lessons of Wittgenstein's investigation into seeing aspects is that when we ask the question, 'What is seeing?' we are in danger of expecting the wrong kind of answer; an answer based not on the actual meaning of the concept, but on an unexamined and uncritically adopted picture of how seeing must be explained. As we saw in the case of noticing an aspect, one mistake that Wittgenstein concerned himself with exposing has to do with misunderstanding the reasons why we were hesitant to apply the concept of seeing, giving rise to a second misunderstanding regarding what needed to be explained in order to resolve our uncertainty. While empirical questions ask about how things stand in the world, conceptual questions ask about our criteria for applying concepts, and so, in a sense, are questions about our instruments of measurement, as opposed to questions about the measure of particular entities. So, no, Wittgensteinian analysis has no bearing on Pylyshyn's account of the difference between seeing and thinking.

Does this mean that Wittgenstein's grammatical analysis has no bearing at all on theorizing about perception? Some people seem to think as much – that ordinary language is just part of the manifest image of the world, the world in terms of which human beings come to know themselves, as distinguished from the true world as understood by scientific rationality. But such a view rests on the questionable assumption that the concepts of natural human language stand in need of a justification, and in turn, that naturalistic inquiry could reveal their lack of justification, in turn supplying us with a true language, with concepts that truly fit the world. Partisans of a broadly scientific conception of knowledge and understanding sometimes argue that philosophers who purport to find conceptual or *a priori* limits to naturalistic explanation are mystery-mongers engaged in a misguided, and ultimately futile, attempt to preserve the world's enchantment against the march of naturalism. This charge can be turned on its head. If understanding is a correlate of conceptual practice, then there are various genuine senses of 'understanding' which have no other manifestation than in how someone employs a concept. Just as there are different uses of the term *see*, so too there are different uses of the expression 'explanation of seeing'. There are different things to be asked about in asking what it means to see and different ways of going about answering that question.

Seeing is constructive intelligence (Donald Hoffman)

In order to understand a context in which Wittgenstein's analysis does bear on the theory of perception, consider another account of the psychology of early vision, given by the vision researcher Donald Hoffman. In *Visual Intelligence: How We Create What We See*,[10] Donald Hoffman, a professor of cognitive and computer science at Berkeley, offers a theory of early visual perception based on the idea of a 'universal visual grammar'. Much of the book is dedicated to describing this grammar in terms of the various natural constraints which are proprietary to the operation of early visual processing in the mind/brain. In poverty-of-the-stimulus arguments directly inspired by Chomsky's theory of a universal generative grammar for natural languages, Hoffman characterizes the information-processing situation facing the neonate as the 'fundamental problem of vision', which involves the predicament that: 'The (2D) image at the eye has countless possible (3D) interpretations';[11] in the precise mathematical sense that a two-dimensional image can be projected as representing an infinite number of three-dimensional structures.[12] Universal visual grammar thus explains ordinary perceptual competences of early vision, such as perceiving the relative spatial and depth configurations of objects, in terms of innate grammatical rules that allow us to 'read' an otherwise meaningless visual stimulus. But Hoffman offers much more than a theory of early visual processing. In *Visual Intelligence*, his aim is to construct, from experimental research findings, a picture of visual perception and visual meaning that interprets the significance of that research for how we think about perception generally. The central core of this interpretation is an epistemology of visual perception that, Hoffman argues, contradicts and undermines our ordinary views of the nature and trustworthiness of perception in radical ways.

How does Wittgenstein's approach to the analysis of psychological concepts bear on Hoffman's account?

One specific kind of conceptual confusion that Wittgenstein was interested in pointing out has to do with cases in which the introduction of new criteria for conceptual meaning is misconstrued as empirical disconfirmation of the conventional criteria.

Nothing is commoner than for the meaning of an expression to oscillate, for a phenomenon to be regarded sometimes as a symptom, sometimes as a criterion, of a state of affairs. And mostly in such a case the shift of meaning is not noted. In science it is usual to make phenomena that allow of exact measurement into defining criteria for an expression; and then one is inclined to think that now the proper meaning has been found. Innumerable confusions have arisen in this way.[13]

Consider the ways in which Hoffman's thinking about the significance of early vision research may succumb to this kind of confusion. Hoffman's account shares a plot with many modern theories of perception. It is a story about how, while we used to believe that seeing was a merely passive process, new empirical discoveries about what happens when we see have revealed that seeing is a highly *mediated* process. In the classical modern, primarily Berkeleyan and Humean, attack on the traditional, primarily Aristotelian, account of perception, one finds the supposition that certain facts reveal that we cannot directly see the objects that we ordinarily believe ourselves to be seeing. The facts traditionally motivating this idea are old chestnuts such as the stick in the water that looks bent, and knowledge of the physiological structure and optical function of the human eye. After this change, our ordinary pre-scientific understanding of visual perception begins to be thought by mainstream perceptual theorists as a naive, rudimentary hypothesis, sometimes termed 'direct realism', about the nature of the perceptual relation; namely, that visual perception is a transparent or unmediated process whereby consciousness somehow reaches out and apprehends what it sees. Corresponding to this 'hypothesis' about perception is attributed an epistemological hypothesis underlying our pre-scientific view, *naive realism*, of the mind's relation to the world.

In Hoffman's account of perception, the details of the plot are, of course, different. His interest is primarily psychological, and his use of the optical figures, at the beginning of the first chapter, is his way of illustrating the theoretical problem, of which the thesis of a universal visual grammar is the solution. But while the descriptions are meant to support the hypothesis of a universal visual grammar, the terms he uses distort the phenomena in two related ways. Firstly, they conflate the distinction between properties belonging to a percept as such, and properties represented by a percept. Secondly, they overemphasize the determinacy of the percept while under-emphasizing the determinacy of the proximal stimulus. Both difficulties indicate how his hypothesis is descriptively inadequate. This inadequacy does not impugn the hypothesis as an explanation of perceptual competencies. The discrepancies noted simply reveal the sense in which the descriptions he offers presuppose the tacit introduction of new criteria for what is to count as a veridical report of what is seen.

This raises the possibility that, as I shall develop it, the *explanandum* has been shaped to fit the *explanans*, rather than the theory answering to the facts. The claim needs to be nuanced, however, since it would reflect an oversimplified understanding of scientific method to assume that naturalistic inquiry into seeing must always limit itself to how we ordinarily express ourselves.[14]

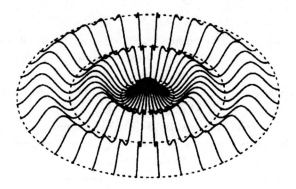

Fig. 5

Hoffman's first example is called the *ripple* (see above).[15] He first describes it as a figure on a two-dimensional surface, adding: 'But the figure also appears to be, as the name "ripple" suggests, a surface that is far from flat, and that undulates in space like waves on a pond.'[16] Hoffman emphasizes the flatness of the surface because he wants to draw a distinction between visual appearance and physical reality. What is there physically is flat, as opposed to what we see, which is not flat. For it also appears to be not flat but rippled. So there is a contradiction and this reveals, according to Hoffman, something very important about the visual process.

> Logic dictates that the ripple cannot be at once flat and not flat, so either the hand or the eye (or both) must be in error. Everyone to whom I have shown the ripple has opted to believe the hand. So assume for now that the hand is right and the figure is flat. Then your visual system has made a serious error: it has constructed an elaborate ripple in space despite ample evidence that this construction is unwarranted.[17]

The penny cannot be both circular and elliptical at the same time. This is reminiscent of traditional arguments for sense-data which involve distinguishing between properties of objects and properties of visual impressions, on the grounds that one thing cannot own both.[18] Hoffman suggests that the reader may want to check whether the surface really is flat. This might strike one as an odd thing to suggest, since there is really no question that the page is flat. It is a false suggestion that we could be in doubt here, but the suggestion is not idle.

Hoffman speaks of the visual impression of the rippledness of the ripple as object-like, as tenacious and palpable as the ink lines on the paper. Thus, he talks as if seeing the ripple diagram as rippled is the same as seeing the paper as rippled. But we must surely distinguish between seeing a pictorial representation of a rippled surface and seeing a surface that appears to be rippled. It is not as if it appears that there is something physically rippled on the page, or that the page appears rippled. Rather, it is that the figure is a pictorial representation of a rippled structure. What is the salient difference between these perspectives? Pictorial representations are not illusory. A drawing of a human face does not give the illusion of there being a real human face present. But if we might be mistaken as to the physical properties of an illusory figure, for example, the true length of the Müller-Lyer lines, there is no logical space for conflict between a picture and what the picture is of. Is there a contradiction involved in the fact that a stick figure looks like a human form, or that some pencil marks make up a picture of a leaf?

Admittedly, the ripple might strike one as a borderline case between optical illusions and pictorial representations. But this distinction is not important from the standpoint of Hoffman's argument. His initial discussion of so-called optical illusions moves on to include the representational properties of pictorial representations as an analogous phenomenon: 'This active process of vision, this penchant to construct, is key to the success of great paintings. From one perspective a painting is just dabs of pigment on canvas. But the cooperative viewer sees more ...'[19] This indicates that he subsumes cases of pictorial representation under the category of optical illusion. This subsumption is indicative of Hoffman's assumptions. For one, it shows that he is employing the phenomenon of optical illusion as a paradigm of visual perception as such. This is important for his argument in at least three ways. First, it allows him to speak of visual perceptions as object-like, in the sense of having properties specifiable independently of the stimulus. In this sense, he can speak of our visual impression as itself rippled, as opposed to being a perception of a representation of something rippled. If our visual perceptions are so structured, in the sense that they have a particular individuating structure, one can ask about the causal conditions of this structure, about the causal processes that produce this structure. A determinate construction implies a determinate constructive process. On the other hand, if visual perceptions are not essentially structured in this way, it makes no sense to ask about the causal process determining their structure. More to the point, if percepts have no object-like structure, they cannot get in the way of our cognitive contact with objects in the way Hoffman's descriptions suggest.

Secondly, the paradigm of optical illusion is used to characterize the difference between the objective stimulus and the perceptual experience as resting on an inferential or constructive activity. Optical illusions support this model because it is easier to ask why they produce the optical effect, hence, easier to specify inferential grounds independently of specifying their optical effect. Pictorial representation does not work for this purpose. Of course, one can distinguish dabs of paint from the human form they represent in a painting. But it is much harder to say how, or why, they represent, or produce in the viewer a representation of, a human form. The short answer – because they just *look* like a human form – is too short for the perceptual psychologist. But it may be the case that the form of the answer required by naturalistic psychology is, methodologically, too long for the phenomena.

Thirdly, the paradigm licenses the interpretation of visual perceptions as intrinsically illusory, as *false constructs* and *visual fantasies*.[20] This is not merely superfluous rhetoric aimed at dramatizing the science. It is an essential aspect of Hoffman's argument that visual impressions not only do not bear any logical connection to the object seen, but actually conflict with it. This conflict supports the idea of a source of visual meaning which is independent of the objective or extradermal stimulus.[21] For example, Hoffman suggests that the dimensionality of the ripple conflicts with the flatness of the paper; but everything turns on Hoffman's descriptions here. The surface of the paper is flat only on one understanding of what 'flat' means. The width of the paper can certainly be measured, and the surface of the paper would appear full of hills and valleys if looked at closely enough. 'The figure on the paper is flat' could be understood to mean different things, depending on the context. Moreover, as I noted above, 'The figure *looks* rippled' could also be understood in different ways. If it is used to mean simply that the figure represents a rippled surface, then there is no question of anything fictitious. To call all pictorial representations fictitious simply because of their representational or intentional properties is not a significant use of the term 'fictitious'. Representations can be false if they represent what is not the case, but they cannot be false in virtue of being *representations*.

These infelicities suggest that when Hoffman says our visual system is in error, he is not merely describing what we see. He is stipulating a new criterion for what is to count as what is seen. Only then can he employ a criterion of correctness and error different from our usual criteria. Just what is his criterion? If we do not need to touch the picture to perceive its two-dimensionality, in what sense is our visual system in error? Ordinarily, we would perhaps say that someone who could not see the ripple picture as representing depth was visually impaired. Naturally, a consideration of the grammar of ordinary perceptual ascriptions will offer little help if what one is interested in concerns causal mechanisms underlying perceptual experiences.

Hoffman is proceeding from the working hypothesis that the proximal visual stimulus under-determines certain of the representation features that ordinary perceptions exhibit, features such as shape and spatial structure. The easiest way to support this hypothesis is by revealing a systematic discrepancy between the structure of the stimulus and the structure of our perception. If the structure of the percept can then be shown to display a logic or syntactic structure that the stimulus lacks, the hypothesis of a universal visual grammar is provided empirical support. Accordingly, from the fact that the dimensionality of the visual impression depends neither on the object (because the drawing is *itself* not three-dimensional), nor on our *belief* that the image is really flat (since our awareness of the flatness of the paper does not dissolve the illusion), Hoffman argues that something else must account for the impression of depth. The idea is that there must be some other constraint at work, shaping our perception independently of the stimulus and of our knowledge of the real properties of the stimulus. But the three problems stated above suggest that such a thesis is precipitate.

Take another of Hoffman's examples: the 'magic square' (fig. 6a below).

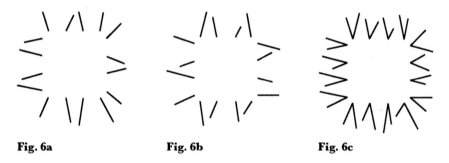

Fig. 6a　　　　　　　**Fig. 6b**　　　　　　　**Fig. 6c**

Hoffman tells us that psychological testing reveals that subjects, as a rule, see the square created by the lines as brighter or lighter than the background area. Because a photometric reading reveals no difference in light between the square and the background, the suggestion is that, like the ripple, the magic square shows evidence of a constructive activity. Neither our knowing that the square is not really brighter (if we accept the objectivity of the photometer), nor the square's itself being brighter (since it isn't), can be the cause of what we see. Hence, there is another factor which is in these ways autonomous. Again, 'Logic dictates that the figure cannot at once contain and not contain a bright square, so either the photometer or your visual system (or both) must be in error.'[22]

Hoffman argues that the magic square offers us a clear-cut example of our visual system erring. We see a brighter square in the figure but in reality there is no square. This example is more of an optical illusion than the ripple example, and so supports Hoffman's picture more straightforwardly. Still,

Hoffman's description of the character of arbitrariness and error in the visual impression is misleading in ways which support the hypothesis but distort the phenomena.

The magic of the magic square lies in the fact that (a) we see the outline of a square even though there is no square drawn, and (b) the square we see seems brighter than the surrounding area even though both areas are in reality, i.e. according to the photometer, equally bright. The first aspect illustrates the well-known phenomenon called *subjective contour*, as opposed to *objective contour*. If there is no actual square there, then where does the impression come from? Isn't this a clear-cut case of fabrication as Hoffman assumes? While the use of the terms *subjective* and *objective* is perfectly legitimate, the use does overdramatize the differences between the magic square and a 'normal' square. First of all, there is no precise point at which a drawing of a normal square, that is, a drawing of a square, becomes a 'magic square'. Consider a sequence of squares, starting with an ordinary drawing and progressing by incremental subtractions of pieces of the line (fig. 7 below).

Fig. 7

If one looks closely enough at the far left square, one will find pixels. Does that mean that there is no objective contour? Certainly not, since that would mean that there are *no* real squares, and the distinction would lose its point. What about the second leftmost square? Now we can see breaks in the outline. Does this mean that the square is 'subjective'? Calling it such might have a conceivable purpose, but it seems rather arbitrary. If one grants that the second square is a genuine square, then there is no justification for speaking of the magic square as inherently nonreal or illusory or subjective.

Certainly there is one important difference between a magic and a normal square. In the former case, it makes sense to ask questions like 'why does *this* give the impression of a square?' or 'How does this work as a picture of a square?'. What might an answer to such questions be? *Because the surrounding lines look like they are being covered over by something.* Or: *The surrounding lines look like they are being blocked by a solid object.* And we could in turn ask why they do give this impression. That is, we can point to causes for its looking like a square, *inter alia* reasons why the figure (i.e. the magic square) counts as looking like a square. But if you ask, 'Why does *this* (pointing to a normal square) look like a square?', the uninteresting answer is: *It looks like a square because it is a square.* That's like saying, 'This is a square because it looks like itself' or 'A square looks like *this* because *this* looks like a square'. So we might reformulate the question as asking 'Why is *this* called "square"?' and then it becomes obvious that there is no answer beyond 'Because that's just what "square" means'. The connection asked about is arbitrary, since the term *square* could have been used to denote something else, for example, circles.

How does this bear on Hoffman's suggestion? The magic square is plausibly construed as a limit case of the ordinary ability to perceive squares, and the latter does not suggest the constructive activity that Hoffman finds in the former. Rather, the ability to see squares is logically connected to the fact that certain figures count as squares: 'seeing a square' is just what *that* is called. At the level of ordinary discourse, this means that what it means to see a square is not something that can be characterized *individualistically*, since a reference to actual squares seen is involved in the characterization of the ability. For present purposes, I shall take individualism to be the view that, as Tyler Burge puts it,

> an individual person or animal's mental state and event kinds – including the individual's intentional or representational kinds – can in principle be individuated in complete independence of the natures of empirical objects, properties, or relations . . . [or that the] mental natures of all an individual's mental states and events are such that there is no necessary or other deep individuative relation between the individual's being in those states, or undergoing events, with those natures, and the nature of the individual's physical and social environments.[23]

This does not mean that no transductive processes are involved in retinal cells when we see squares, or that square (edge and corner) detection algorithms cannot be ascribed to various neurons in the lateral geniculate nucleus. Rather, it means that squares, ordinarily so-called, are not constructed entities, and hence, are not entities constructed by vision.

The second point about the apparent brightness of the magic square raises the difficult issue of the relativity of colour and light in the visual field. Nevertheless, a similar point can be made that the illusory aspect of the magic square only counts as illusory in reference to a background practice of reporting relative degrees of light intensity which is accurate *as a rule*. Hoffman says that our perception of the relatively greater brightness of the square is shown to be in error because the photometer does not register any difference. But why do we so much as have the idea that the photometer could correct our perceptual judgement? Why do we assume that what our eyes tell us, and what the photometer tells us, are about the same thing? After all, when we are seeing, we are not measuring photons. The question is really why we would come to identify the perception of brightness itself with the process of registering photons. The answer is that, if there were not a rough agreement between our impressions of relative light and darkness, and relatively more and less quantities of photons, we would never have taken the photometer to be a measure for light. Rather, we would have, for example, taken it as a measure of a different kind of radiation. So while the photometer can contradict what we see with our eyes, so that it can make sense to say in cases like the magic square that our eyes are deceiving us, it could not make sense to say that the photometer might always contradict what we see. If it did, then we would no longer use it as a measure of visible light. The photometer can certainly improve our judgements in some cases, rendering more accurate distinctions or degrees of light, but it cannot overturn all, or even more than a few of such judgements without losing its sense. You can fool some of the senses some of the time, but not all of the senses all of the time.

What this shows is that the photometer does not for the first time reveal what genuine brightness is, but introduces a new criterion, based on our ordinary practice of reporting perceptual differences of relative brightness. More specifically, this shows that instead of attending to the ordinary language we use to describe what we see, Hoffman has tacitly introduced new criteria for what is to count as a perception of genuine brightness. This is not only misleading epistemologically: it overlooks that there is already a grammar in place structuring what we see, which is to say, constituting the meaning of the concept of what is seen. On a related point, Wittgenstein says that: 'The point here is not that our sense-impressions can lie, but that we understand their language. (And this language like any other is founded on convention.)'[24] This is not to say that the introduction of new criteria is illicit by any means. But not understanding the move for what it is – linguistic stipulation – underwrites the epistemological and semantic confusions which the theory gives rise to. Epistemologically, the mistake lies in failing to see how the stipulated criteria are modifications of pre-existing criteria with their own modes of justification. Exposing this mistake serves to reveal that the rules hypothesized to explain perceptual competencies are epistemologically posterior to the rules governing ordinary employments of the concept of seeing. Semantically, the difficulty rests on overlooking how the semantics of visual concepts are originally constituted within ordinary practices of describing and expressing experience. But if we are considering our ordinary conceptual practices, then we see that there is an internal, or conceptual, connection between our visual experience and the objects of that experience. This connection is established when we learn language, and it is the basis upon which doubt in the truth of perceptual judgements can even make sense. The point of saying that meaning is use is that language is an instrument, that concepts are items in a system of measurement, and that there is something nonsensical about the claim that we could so much as *discover* that our ordinary understanding of what it means to see is different, or even contradictory to, what we take it to be. As if we could discover that it is empirically false that something can be measured in inches and feet, as opposed to centimeters.

To put it bluntly, it is part of the logical grammar of the ordinary concept of sight that, according to standard usage, if you can be said to see something truly, then it follows logically – grammatically – that the thing appears as it truly is. This is just what it ordinarily *means* to see something truly, and it is important to our way of life that we be able to say of someone that she sees how things are, or that she sees clearly, or that so-and-so just doesn't see it. Now, instead of simply, theoretically explaining how it is that we see, for example, a cube, Hoffmann is redefining what it means to see a cube, and then arguing that, given empirical facts, it is impossible to ever truly see a cube. While it would be pointless linguistic imperialism to say that vision cannot be redefined on pain of contradiction, it is a deep philosophical insight to see how the standpoint provided by our ordinary perceptual concepts has no less epistemological justification after active computational principles of early visual processing are discovered than beforehand.

Visual meaning as representation and as instrument

Colloquial language is a part of the human organism and not less complicated than it.[25]

Even more helpful would be to see whether the way that conceptual meaning is analysed by Wittgensteinian grammatical investigations is reconcilable with the computational-syntactic conception used by Hoffman and Pylyshyn. If the grammar of ordinary language concepts is as complex as Wittgenstein's analysis suggests, then we should not expect a single explanatory framework to capture its essence.

It is a widely-held view that conceiving of meaning as use is not compatible with syntactic views of language, which take meaning to supervene on the identity and relations between the parts of a mental representation, like a percept. This is not surprising, given the theoretical cleavage between the respective frameworks, which spans the internalism/externalism debate in semantics and epistemology, and the whole question of whether language should be thought of primarily in terms of representation, or in terms of communicative or interpretive practices, so-called 'language-games'. Of course, the debate has a parallel within Wittgenstein's own development from the *Tractatus* and the *Investigations*. On a standard interpretation, the picture theory of language, of the early Wittgenstein, is diametrically opposed to, and conceptually incommensurable with, the holistic view of linguistic meaning in his later work. Now, it is relevant to note here that this standard interpretation tends to downplay the overlap of the two approaches. It underemphasizes, for example, the fact that Wittgenstein does *also* refer to use, and even the human being as a natural organism, as factors in the constitution of linguistic meaning in the *Tractatus* (see quotation above). Moreover, in the *Investigations* he never denies that *picturing* is one function that language performs; he just argues that it is not the essential or basic function. So is there a middle path, or rather a middle view, that would allow us to see a Wittgensteinian, and what we could call a Chomskian, approach to the analysis of visual meaning as complementary, as opposed to simply reflecting different epistemic interests? I think there is. An examination of the differences between the two epistemological contexts reveals that their conceptual incommensurability turns largely on the distinction between syntax and semantics, where different concepts of *understanding*, correlated to different concepts of understanding, apply to each. On the other hand, seeing these differences allows us to also see how each level of meaning-constituting structure might fit into a larger picture of perception, and a deeper understanding of knowledge. In the spirit of Paul Feyerabend's anarchist epistemology, there is an abundance of *being* in the study of perception that requires a fine-grained, and at the same time, holistic perspective on epistemic criteria.

I have argued that Wittgenstein's grammatical analysis of ordinary concepts does not preclude theoretical reconstructions of those concepts which make them amenable to incorporation within a broadly naturalistic approach to psychology. It follows that such reconstructions must be understood, not as unwarranted *explanations* of ordinary grammar, but as *extensions* of that grammar; extensions which, at the same time, shed light on the facts of nature which make up the background conditions upon which our employment of that grammar depends. On the other hand, the theoretical account of vision offered by Pylyshyn does not claim to explain all properties of visual experience, but only those properties which fall within the pre-conceptual, and pre-inferential proprietary domain of early vision, or what he calls *vision* proper: vision as a cognitive module. That means that the syntactic structuring underlying the perception of the basic geometry, size and relative locations of objects does not involve any aspects of perception which involve *concepts*, or anything involving inference. Hence, for example, early vision does not involve the ability to *recognize* objects, but only to register their geometry, size and location, insofar as recognizing an object requires that one have the concept of that object. This leaves open the possibility that, while some aspects of visual experience are syntactically computed, and hence explicable within a syntactic model of vision, many other aspects can only be understood by reference to the perceptual practices which *extend* the informational scope of early vision. In turn, uncovering the rules structuring these practices requires uncovering the criteria constituting the meanings of the linguistic and visual concepts used to articulate those experiences: in short, just the sort of investigation Wittgenstein undertakes.

We can see how this works out in greater detail by considering the epistemology of universal visual grammar from a different angle. In Chomsky's internalist theory of language, the hypothesis of a universal generative grammar is supposed to explain how we can acquire natural language, specifically, the natural language spoken by our tribe, on the basis of impoverished and even misleading linguistic data. Universal generative grammar, or what Chomsky now refers to as an *I-language*, explains why we can learn, from the noises we hear as infants, the grammatical structure imperfectly presented by that impoverished stimuli.[26] The core idea behind the I-language is the notion of generative procedure which produces syntactical constructions, *or structural descriptions*, by mapping together phonetic, semantic, and other syntactic properties.[27] On this hypothesis, the differences between natural languages, differences which make knowledge of English virtually useless for understanding Swahili, are only surface manifestations of single, underlying language faculty.[28] Unlike natural languages, which are subject to cultural change, the underlying language faculty can be regarded as a biologically-determined function that not only 'maps evidence available into acquired knowledge, uniformly for all languages', but even plays a role in 'determining what counts as evidence and how it is used'.[29]

Now consider again the analogy of learning language with learning how to see, that there is also a universal *visual* grammar. In the case of visual meaning, the problem we face as children has to do with the poverty of the stimulus. What universal visual grammar allows us to do is not to bring structure to inherently unstructured stimuli, but to learn the syntactic form they imperfectly present via retinal irradiation. In the case of natural language acquisition, it is not as if the generative procedure of the I-language allows us to acquire language in a vacuum. If instead of our natural pre-linguistic environs, we were stimulated by meaningless noises as infants, the innate rules of language wouldn't come up with anything, since there would be no grammatical structure within the impoverished linguistic data to discover. In the case of visual grammar, this implies that if the proximal stimuli were not *already* structured syntactically, we would never be able to interpret them. We would have no experience, in the sense of no meaning-generating options to choose from. Following through with the analogy, we reach the conclusion that the impoverished proximate stimuli we encounter must *already be syntactically structured*. While in the case of Chomsky's theory of language, we come to understand the language our tribe speaks, in the case of Hoffman's theory of vision, we come to learn the language that visual appearances speak.

Now if our visual experiences already speak a language, learning to see is just learning their language. One might say that visual impressions already have meaning, but we need to learn how to understand that meaning. In Chomsky's picture, the subterranean link between the language-acquiring infant and its tribe is their common biology, their innate universal grammar. But how are we to understand the relation between the grammar of visual experience that we approach uncomprehendingly as infants and the universal visual grammar that allows us to decipher that grammar? Epistemologically, where ought the analogy to lead us?

According to Hoffman, the syntax that our brain discovers in visual sensory stimuli *is there*, like the grammar of natural languages, because the innate universal visual grammar in the brain constructed it. Whereas in Chomsky's picture, the problem of language acquisition is to figure out the language spoken by our tribe, the problem of vision acquisition for Hoffman is to figure out the grammar spoken by our own brain. Hence, learning to see is a solipsistic exercise in self-knowledge. Hoffman takes these implications seriously. The metaphysics of this picture are sketched out using what Hoffman calls the *icon metaphor*.

> The relation between what you see phenomenally and what you see relationally is like the relation between icons and software on a computer. When you use, say, that neat paint program or word processor on your PC, you interact with megabytes of software of such complexity that its creation took talented programmers many months of concerted effort. Fortunately for you, they made their software 'user-friendly' so you don't need to know its grisly innards ... The relation between icons and software is systematic but arbitrary; those icons could take many different forms and colors, as they often do from one paint program to the next, and still have the same function.[30]

The analogy is quite strange and entails Cartesian solipsism. It suggests the situation from the sci-fi thriller *The Matrix*, where apparent reality is in fact a virtual reality and genuine reality is a bunch of brain-in-vat human batteries. The difference is that in Hoffman's picture we are the victims of our own brains, which manipulate our visual experience for no particular purpose. Moreover, the illusion is unameliorable. In *The Matrix*, the prisoners can escape to look behind the veil, whereas in Hoffman's picture, the thing-in-itself is *in principle* unavailable visually: 'To construct is the essence of vision.

Dispense with construction and you dispense with vision. Everything you see by sight is your construction.'[31] Now the sceptical implications of the individualist epistemology are usually down played with the idea that, because our visual system needs to provide information necessary for survival, there is an adaptive pressure on the system to provide 'accurate' knowledge of the environment. But considerations of the etiology of these rules, as arising from the process of natural selection, do not offer any conceptual support against scepticism. On certain interpretations of the Darwinian picture, we can rest assured that our perceptions of the world are veridical, at least in a pragmatic sense of truth. If our senses were systematically wrong about how things are in the world, it is perhaps highly improbable that we would have survived. Nevertheless, Hoffman argues correctly that ' "well-adapted" does not mean "resembles" '.[32] The connection between how things appear to us and how they 'really look' is, as we have seen, while systematic in a global sense, entirely *arbitrary*. We do not know what objects really look like, but only that there is a complicated relationship between how things look *to us*, and the adaptation pressures that our ancestors faced.[33]

Now if we reject the conclusion that the syntactic structure that our visual system finds in what we proximally see is itself a product of our brain, and so reject the scepticism that goes along with it, does this imply that we adopt a dogmatic realism about visual meaning, or that we must posit a pre-established harmony between how things look in the world and how our visual system structures them? Can this approach to meaning be squared with Hoffman's internalist approach to visual meaning? It is hard to see how it could, given that one view – *externalism* – sees the connection between percept and object as internal and logical, while the other – *internalism* – sees the connection as arbitrary and causal. Externalism answers scepticism by distinguishing between the *psychological thesis*, that the *source* of all empirical knowledge is some nonconceptual, empirical content (sense-data, raw feels, stimulus meaning, etc.) directly available to the human mind, and the *epistemological thesis*, that nonconceptual empirical content is epistemically basic, as a necessary intermediary between the world and consciousness. Externalism follows from Wittgenstein's approach to the analysis of meaning because there is an internal relationship between words and the objects they refer to in the world; the objects themselves are constitutive of the meaning of the words, hence part of language itself. Private sense-data or retinal irritations cannot, and are not, used when words such as *blue* or *chair* are being ostensively defined for linguistic neonates, just because they cannot be pointed to. As such, they are not part of the meaning of the terms; if they were, then it would be difficult to explain how we could ever mean the same thing and so ever communicate.

Put differently, if it makes sense to doubt whether you can in fact *know* the true identity of an object, it must make sense to doubt whether you can doubt the true meaning of its name. But it makes no sense to doubt, for example, whether 'blue' really means something other than *that* (pointing to something blue). We might redefine the word to mean something else, but that could never mean that the first definition was false. There is an internal relationship, established by convention upon the backdrop of the natural world, between words and their referents which precludes doubt, and which is in fact the basis for being able to doubt intelligibly. So, while internalism applies to the individual's efforts to figure out the language being spoken, externalism applies to the linguistic practices which the individual is enabled to participate in because of their information-processing capacities. In the same way that a linguistic neonate cannot doubt whether it has learned the correct language spoken by its parents, the visual neonate cannot doubt that it has visually interpreted correctly the perceivables in its environs.

This gives us a way of seeing what is right in the analogy to natural language acquisition. In acquiring natural language, we are not simply learning how to use language, but rather learning how to understand a particular language; for example, English. There are innumerable other particular languages we could learn. But these different natural languages are not different interpretations of the same data; rather different manifestations of the same underlying deep grammar, differentiated by the stimulus circumstances of the language learner. Analogously, we can speak of there being natural visual languages, the grammar of which we learn on the basis of our biologically-based visual grammar. At the level of visual meaning that Hoffman and Pylyshyn are working at – early vision processing – it is safe to assume that every normal human being learns to see things in roughly the same way. It is this common fund of visual experience that perceptual psychology draws from in constructing theories of how we can learn these visual languages. But if things did not look a certain way, our visual system would never be able to learn to speak their language. We would not be able to learn that their appearing that way means thus and so, or that their being the way they are is the reason why they look the way they do. Every conceptual element of perceptual experience then depends on the grammar of a practice of seeing, knowledge of which is made possible on the basis of the universal visual grammar. And the Wittgensteinian analysis helps us to see just what those grammars are, in part by showing how they cannot be identified with something that has no conceptual relation to the practice, like a universal visual grammar.

Visual syntax and visual semantics

We could think of a perceptual practice as any conceptually-mediated, rule-governed perceptual habit, anything from seeing the Necker cube as the

Necker cube to styles of pictorial representation, to the forms of perceptual specialization developed by police detectives or botanists or cloud watchers or people-watchers or painters. Each practice, as an extension of the information-processing stage of early vision, has a grammar, elucidated through an examination of conceptual criteria, to parametrically specify what counts as, for example, a direct object of sight, and what is counted as an interpretation. Let's look one last time at the conceptual abundance of the Necker cube and consider two different kinds of visual understanding we can be said to have of it. We can then examine how they complement each other. Here's Hoffman's starting point again: 'Why do you see a cube when you view the figure? Because the figure triggers your visual intelligence to construct a cube.'[34] Accordingly, to *see* the Necker cube one way rather than another is just to *understand* what one sees, and to understand just means to *construct* a percept as a syntactic entity on the basis of innate grammar of sight. The percept has meaning just because it is syntactically structured, in the sense that the meaning is computed on the basis of the identity and relation of its parts. This model explains, for example, why it is easier to see the Necker cube as three-dimensional than it is to see Kopferman cubes as three-dimensional.

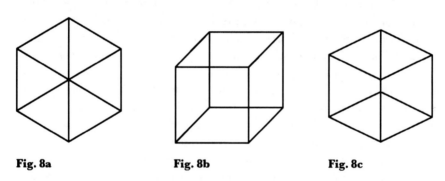

Fig. 8a   **Fig. 8b**   **Fig. 8c**

Why is it easier to see the Necker cube (fig. 8b) as a cube, that is, as three-dimensional, than it is to see the Kopfermann cubes on either side?

The rule of generic views, which is posited to explain this, reads as follows: 'Rule of generic views: Construct only those visual worlds for which the image is a stable (i.e. generic) view.'[35] In the case of the Kopfermann cubes, it is an accident of the perspective that those figures are pictured from a standpoint such that several vertices appear to overlap. Hence, while the Kopfermann cube on the left (fig. 8a) *can* be interpreted as a veridical perception of a cube, it is more difficult than in the case of the Necker cube because the rule of generic views instructs your brain to read the crossing vertices as non-accidental, as portraying a generic view of the structure in question, as a stable view which will not change structurally when seen from different perspectives. This rule explains, to take another example, why a two-dimensional picture, for example, an ordinary line drawn on paper, appears to us as a picture of a straight line, and not, for example, a circle or a squiggly line seen from the side. If the line were, in fact, a representation of a squiggly line from the side, then its appearing straight would be an accident of the perspective from which it is represented, and its appearance would change dramatically with the perspective.

The model of visual understanding is internalist and syntactic. The fact that our visual system employs this rule means that we are imposing an arbitrary interpretation on the stimulus; arbitrary because it is one three-dimensional interpretation out of an infinite number of possible three-dimensional interpretations, all of which equally fit the two-dimensional image. Because it is arbitrary, we have no epistemological justification – no 'inference ticket' – to conclude anything about what things really look like on the basis of how they appear. It is a syntactical form of understanding because the rules apply automatically, on the basis of the physical properties of the parts and their relationship. To *see* the Necker cube one way rather than another is just to *understand* the stimulus, and to understand just means to *construct* a percept, as a syntactic entity. On this view, the percept has meaning just because it is syntactically structured. Correlatively, one understands what one is seeing, just because one's visual system has applied rules of visual grammar to the proximal stimulus. On this view, there is no possibility of misapplying these rules, since the employment is a spontaneous activity. No judgement or act of interpretation is involved in the application, since the rules are applied simply on the basis of the physical properties of the stimulus. Finally, the innate visual grammar determines the individuation conditions for perceptual content locally. Each percept is individuated in terms of its internal syntactic structure. A given perception's being the perception it is depends on its having the particular structure it has. Two perceptions cannot be of the same thing if they have different structures; two perceptions sharing a common structure cannot differ in their intentional content.

These factors make the innate rules of visual grammar different in several important respects from the rules involved in the employment of ordinary perceptual concepts. Consider the rules underlying ordinary ascriptions of perceptual experience, for example, the rule for applying the concept of a picture of a cube. In what consists someone's understanding of this concept? One is inclined to say that understanding consists in internalizing a representation of a cube. But any such representation could be taken to represent various other concepts, for example, the concept of a geometric solid, a glass cube, an inverted box, a wire frame, etc.[36] Unlike the syntactic conception of understanding implied in Hoffman's theory, criteria for ordinary language ascriptions of understanding typically take the form of manifested abilities *to go on* in applying a concept in conformity with practice, as consti-tuted through criteria.[37] In contrast, the rules of visual grammar constitute a cognitive ability which is logically distinct from the employment of that ability in actual cases of visual perception. That is one reason why it is possible to give a formal account of those rules, for example, to write algorithms describing their formal properties.

This distinction is connected to another: the fact that rules for concepts in natural languages, like English, can be variously applied. Criteria fix the semantics of ordinary language concepts, but judgement is required to decide when the criteria are satisfied. Established practice in general makes the ques-tion of what is to count as a picture of a cube a non-starter. But we can imagine borderline cases in which nothing about what the concept means decides whether *that* picture counts as a picture of a cube. In contrast, innate rules of grammar cannot require interpretation. They cannot presuppose any acts of judgement since they are supposed to explain how we come to understand what we see in the first place. They are supposed to explain how judgement is possible in the first place.

Finally, in the case of ordinary perceptual ascriptions, individuation condi-tions for perceptual ascriptions are more complicated, as they depend on fea-tures of the circumstances of the ascription. For example, the same pictorial representation can be described in various ways, which are at once different in meaning, and yet accurate as descriptions of what is seen. What is to count as an accurate or valid ascription thus depends on the context. The same con-text sensitivity affects the concept of understanding. On Hoffman's account, to understand what is seen can mean only one thing in each case, namely, to apply the rules of visual grammar. In contrast, at the level of ordinary lan-guage, what it means to understand what one sees can vary widely.[38] For example, while it is typical of perceptual psychologists within the cognitive tradition to argue, against the traditional empiricist view, that vision is intel-ligent – *pace* Kant, that sensible intuition is *not* blind – seeing and understand-ing are clearly, albeit only contextually, distinguished at the level of ordinary language. From the standpoint of the latter, both the old picture and the new one are distortions of the phenomena.

This last difference is manifested in the difficulty that Hoffman's account of visual understanding has in distinguishing between the experience of seeing a cube and of seeing *that* (pointing to a cube) as a cube. Consider the following example. Two young children are watching their mother in the kitchen. She opens a cabinet to get something, leaving the drawer open in such a way that the length which the drawer extends from the cabinet is the same distance as the height and width of the drawer. The extended part of the drawer forms a cubic form.

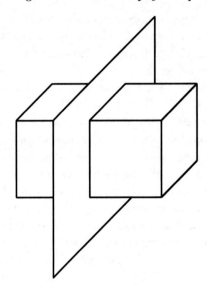

Fig. 9

If one child has learned the names of the basic geometrical shapes, we might imagine him pointing and saying 'The drawer looks like a cube'. If the other child does not have the concept of a cube, or does not see the cubic shape formed by the drawer, it would make sense to distinguish between the first child seeing the drawer as a cube, where the second child only sees a drawer or sees a cubic form. Whether we did want to say that the second child in fact saw a cube would depend on what reasons we might have for saying that. For example, it may be important that the child recognizes that some cube-shaped object fits into the drawer. Regardless, ascribing to the first child the experience of seeing the drawer *as a cube* seems to be a categorically different kind of ascription. Like the concept of noticing an aspect, it is experiencing the visual meaning of an image, in the sense of recognizing the applicability of a visual concept, i.e. the concept of a cube.

These differences between the two sets of rules reflect different conceptions of visual meaning and visual understanding. In contrast to the syntactic conception of meaning sketched above, Wittgenstein offers a way of understanding visual meaning as constituted by ordinary descriptive and expressive practices. The difference between this view and Hoffman's syntactic conception can be illustrated by considering other ways in which Wittgenstein's treatment of the Necker cube departs from Hoffman's. We saw how Hoffman explained the aspectual changes in terms of the constructive activity of perception. On that account, the aspects correspond to two syntactic objects. It is striking that for Wittgenstein, the strangeness of the Necker cube lies precisely in the fact that our impression is *not* object-like, is not like an 'inner picture'.

Unlike the perception of colour, in the case of the aspectual switch, I cannot offer someone an exact copy of what I am seeing, to communicate what it is I see. I may highlight certain vertices of the cube in order to get them to see the shift of aspects, and that might work to get them to see the change of aspects. But simply seeing the front vertices highlighted with a black pencil is not the same as seeing the change of aspect. Someone could see those highlights and still not see the aspectual change. On the other hand, if one takes the aspectual impression to be an inner object, a constructed phenomenological entity, then one is saddled with trying to make sense of a concept of organization as a distinct element in the impression.[39] For example, a change in the organization of a set of blocks can be pictured, but a change in the 'organization' of the Necker cube cannot.[40] In the case of the aspects that switch back and forth in the Necker cube, our impression is not simply of a three-dimensional form, but of how the graphic figure can be seen variously as one thing or another. We are not seeing something in addition to the figure, but seeing something *about* it.

From this perspective, Hoffman's analysis does not explain the strangeness of the phenomenon. Given Hoffman's explanatory framework, he interprets meaning syntactically, construing the aspectual change as a constructive activity. But the construct that is *there* is not there in the same way that the figure is. It doesn't seem to be located anywhere. It is as if something black and white were being filled in with the colour of meaning, but without their physical appearance changing. But calling the percept a *construct* doesn't explain the strangeness of the phenomenon. Part of the puzzle is that, while the meaning is integral to the perception, it seems to be a mistake to locate the meaning *within* the act of perception: ' "Seeing as . . ." is not a part of perception. And for that reason it is like seeing and again not like.'[41] The example of the duck-rabbit brings out more clearly the sense in which the meaning of the visual impression cannot be conceived of as supervening on individualistic facts of the perceiver. The duck-rabbit can mean different things visually, and what it can mean for a given perceiver depends on such things as whether she is familiar with ducks, rabbits, various styles of pictorial representation, etc. This kind of understanding cannot plausibly be taken to derive from purely syntactical determinations.

Consider one consequence of trying to so derive it. Chomsky has suggested that considerations regarding the speed at which children acquire words in natural language support the hypothesis that even the meanings of concepts are determined syntactically by innate lexical structure. This involves the counterintuitive idea that the meanings of all possible concepts, thus such concepts as *bureaucrat* and *carburettor* are contained innately in the language organ of the brain. The analogy to a universal visual grammar would suggest that our ability to perceive duck- and rabbit-looks is based on innate visual concepts of ducks and rabbits. Thus, even if no ducks or rabbits had ever existed, it would still make sense to ascribe understanding of how ducks and rabbits look to all human beings (or to their brains).[42]

Let's return to the issue of rules by considering a standard criticism of the idea of an unconscious rule. Using his Chinese room thought-experiment, John Searle has argued that understanding cannot be simply a matter of syntax. Syntax concerns the manipulation of formal symbols, and no manner of formal complexity can generate a semantic relation to things in the world.[43] For this reason, computers cannot be said to think, or know what the symbols mean. *Inter alia* they cannot be said to understand what information might be available to them via mechanical sensory organs. A related argument attacks the idea of an unconscious rule, by pointing to the inherent semantic indeterminacy of formal symbols.

If formal symbols are taken to represent in virtue of their internal structure, then it is easy to show that any such structure can be taken in different ways to represent different objects or states of affairs.[44] However, such arguments seem to understate the problem. At the level of ordinary language, states of understanding are logically bound up with non-individualistic criteria for ascribing them to language users or perceivers. Such criteria include, generally, how someone acts or what they say about the rules they are following. The possibility of ascribing to someone the experience of seeing the duck-rabbit as a duck involves, logically, the possibility of that person's being able to express how she is seeing the figure. This ability to explain how something is being seen instantiates the concept of following a rule. What they see does not merely conform to a particular description. Its being describable in certain terms by the perceiver plays a part in fixing the content of that experience. What someone says shows that they are taking what they see in one way rather than another; that what is seen counts for something.

In contrast to what we ordinarily think of as understanding the meaning of a word, the syntactic rules of early vision are too complex and quickly activated to have any conscious control over. This makes them strange. Our prodigious visual intelligence is supposed to be manifested in the fact that the principles used in constructing meaningful visual experiences are both profoundly complicated and at the same time, employed, in virtuoso fashion, at great computational speed. But the principles of organic chemistry used to explain the chemical processes of our digestive system are also extremely complicated. Does that imply that all creatures with stomachs are geniuses at digestion?

Of course, seeing differs from digestion in that the former, involving, minimally, the phenomenon of intentionality, is taken to have a cognitive dimension lacking in the latter. Nevertheless, the question touches on the controversy surrounding the notion of an *unconscious rule* which is central to the explanatory framework of cognitive psychology. Hoffman's account exhibits some of the conceptual tensions impinging on this notion. He concedes that talk of perceivers as *following* rules of visual grammar when they see cannot be taken literally. For example, he does not think that the rules he describes throughout the book are internally represented in some language of thought.

> They are not explicitly written down in your mind, as one might write down instructions for assembling a bicycle, but are implicit in its workings, just as the laws of physics are not explicitly written down in nature, but are implicit in its workings. You are not, in general, aware of these rules or of their role in constructing what you see.[45]

While the rules are not *in principle* inaccessible to introspection, it is implausible to assume, due to their sheer complexity, that having been discovered they might be consciously followed. So, whether or not they are consciously followed cannot matter for explaining what understanding is. At the same time, there are conceptual reasons why Hoffman speaks throughout the book of the rules of visual grammar, as in some important sense, being *followed* or *used*. The concepts of meaning and understanding are conceptually connected to the notion of following a rule, while the notion of following a rule is typically opposed to merely external conformity with a rule.

This much is, *prima facie*, fundamental to the idea of speaking a language. To use a word is to mean something by uttering it. Using a word to mean something is using it to say something, for example, to tell someone how things look. This is the sense in which to use a word implies, we might say, that the word is being used meaningfully, and hence in accordance with a rule. To take one of Wittgenstein's recurring examples, two people who randomly move chess pieces about on a board cannot be said to be playing chess, even if their movements physically resemble legitimate moves in a chess game.[46] This marks the difference between understanding what one is saying and merely parroting words. Someone who is merely parroting words does not use those words to say one thing rather than another. In contrast, when someone speaks understandingly, their meaning what they do is part of the explanation for why the person used those words.[47]

These considerations highlight some important ways in which the rules of visual grammar, as Hoffman conceives them, are disanalogous to the ordinary rules we learn to follow in learning natural languages. Insofar as these rules purportedly concern formal aspects of the input to the visual system (the retinal image), the type of understanding can be construed as syntactical understanding. On this view, to see p is to understand by its look what p is, and understanding what p is by its look just is to apply the rules of visual processing. The form understanding takes is simply the application of the syntactic rules, which results in the construction of a visual percept itself, conceived as a syntactical entity. There is nothing over and above the processes that construct these percept-objects needed to interpret them: no blind intuition needing to be conceptualized by the understanding.

There are reasons, connected to ordinary, pre-theoretical discourse, for speaking of unconscious rules for *visual grammar*, and of *visual intelligence*. We speak of the intelligent or intentional behaviour of creatures such as house-flies and frogs because of the parallels to human behaviour. It makes sense to speak of frogs as seeing flies because it makes sense to speak of frogs having purposes, beliefs and desires, however primitive. In contrast, it does not make sense to speak of trees or the moon as having desires or purposes. The ways a housefly's visual stimuli relate to its behaviour can, and have been formalized, and there is no reason to deny that aspects of human vision are capable of for-malization along the lines of Hoffman's account. There is an important sense, however, in which seeing *is* a distinctively human ability. It is distinctively human in the sense that ascriptions of human visual experience are typically bound up with the languages, linguistic and visual, that articulate what is to count as a case of seeing, and how the content of what is seen is constituted. Hoffman's icon metaphor actually inadvertently acknowledges the difference between these two senses of understanding. The virtual reality metaphor he employs implies not simply that visual experience is a virtual construction of our visual system, but that it is a virtual construction which some inner homunculus enjoys. Of course, there is no homunculus, but that shows the dif-ference between syntactic understanding of meaning and the kinds of under-standing one finds manifested in the innumerable language-games and practices of seeing which make up the domain of human culture.

3

The experience and expression of sight

Can you imagine what a red-green color blind man sees? Can you paint a picture of the room as he sees it? Can he paint it as he sees it? Then can I paint it as I see it? In what sense can I?[1]

Subjectivity, ineffability and private language

Is there something it is like, to see? Could the experience ever be described? Could it be explained or described or expressed?

It is a compelling idea that visual experience is in some important sense ineffable. How could I ever put into words, or hand gestures, or other signs, what it is like to see a red rose, to see red, *to see*? Many intuitions and theories about perception, mind and language intersect and grate against each other when one pursues answers to this question. For many, the ineffability of experience has a spiritual or ethical significance, since it shows that the significance of life outstrips our categories, or that the human soul exists because our conscious experience cannot be explained naturalistically. For others, ineffability is an affront to the verificationist principle of natural scientific enquiry and must be somehow reduced. What makes the experience of ineffability relevant for our immediate enquiry is that it has tended to suggest certain metaphysical truths about mind, as distinguished from body or physical nature, so-called. Following Christian theology, Rene Descartes famously drew an ontological distinction between thinking things and physical things, and this distinction is challenged both by Wittgenstein as well as by the embodied view of mind adopted by cognitive science, albeit in subtly different ways.

Wittgenstein's interest in language and how what we see is expressible discursively makes ineffability a central theme in his queries. Ineffability is, for instance, a way to measure the limits, and so domain of, discursive expression. The topic also serves as a way to connect Wittgenstein's grammatical analyses of ordinary perceptual concepts to another provocative part of the *Philosophical Investigations*: the private language argument. Drawing on Wittgenstein's criticisms of the now disreputable sense-data theory, I will develop an interpretation of the concept of visual qualia as a problematic response to the phenomenon of ineffability. Towards the goal of relating Wittgenstein's work on perception and language to contemporary ways of addressing these problems, my account of visual qualia will be contrasted with Daniel Dennett's verificationist attack on qualia. I am sympathetic to this approach, but I shall use Dennett's staunch denial of the idea of qualia to develop an alternative view of why the concept is conceptually suspect. In so doing, my interpretation will diverge from Dennett's understanding of the import of those pre-theoretical intuitions. Dennett tends to see the mistakes involved with the postulation of qualia to derive from misunderstandings or outright ignorance of scientific advances in the study of perception.[2] In contrast to this approach, I shall be interested in revealing the extent to which a proper diagnosis of these mistakes reveals certain conceptual truths about the relation between perception and language.[3] Arguing against a standard view that Wittgenstein denies the ineffability of experience, and so denies its most salient subjective features, I shall show that the implications of his research are considerably more nuanced. Wittgenstein explicitly states that he is not denying the existence of what is ineffable in experience, but only certain ways of making sense of those aspects theoretically.[4] In fact, there is a sense in which Wittgenstein's analysis leads one to a deepened appreciation of the phenomena after one's intuitions regarding ineffability have been shorn of traditional philosophical explanations.

The framework of the chapter is thus as follows. In the first section, the concept of ineffability is introduced in terms of a characteristic I shall refer to as 'logical privacy'. This section will focus on the possibility of visual qualia inversion. Examining Dennett's verificationist criticisms of this possibility, I shall turn to Wittgenstein's private language arguments in the next section as an alternative approach to the issue.[5] This discussion will establish two ways of diagnosing the confusion leading to the hypothesis of qualia, and thus two ways of seeing what is philosophically at stake in the matter. On my reading, the private language argument takes the form of a dialectical struggle against the intuitions of the private language interlocutor, who attempts to overcome perceived defects in how ordinary language can serve to express and describe visual experience.[6] My interpretation will serve as a basis for critiquing the sociological interpretation of the private language argument, which I identify with Kripke's reading. In the final section, I will critique a broadly naturalistic interpretation of the private language argument by examining Dennett's attempts to reinterpret the pre-theoretical intuitions about ineffability as vague perceptions of empirical facts about perception. In contrast to Dennett's notion of the 'practical ineffability' of visual experience as a reflection of its informational richness, I shall offer a view of the phenomenon of ineffability as reflecting a conceptual truth about the nature of description.[7] While not serving as a criticism of Dennett's analysis as such, I will suggest that his analysis presupposes that any limit to discursive articulation would have to be set by the information-processing properties of the perceptual and cognitive faculties of perceivers. In contrast, the ways that the concept of quale is shown to betray a conceptual confusion are just the ways in which the theoretical questions connected with qualia can plausibly be understood as questions about criteria.

The concept of visual qualia

The ineffability of visual experience is sometimes identified as a second-order property of visual qualia, where qualia are conceived of as intrinsic properties of our experience incapable of discursive articulation.[8] On the approach I shall take in this chapter, however, ineffability is not a property qualia have, or a property our experience has in virtue of having qualitative properties. Instead, ineffability is a criterion used to make sense out of the idea that our experience has something called its qualitative or subjective feel. On this view, making sense out of the idea of qualia, and so the implications of their existence for the philosophy of mind and language, does not mean arguing, for example, that they can be incorporated into a physicalist ontology or a functionalist philosophy of mind. It requires making sense of the idea of ineffability, of not being able to express what we see. Correlatively, undermining the idea of qualia means attacking the intelligibility of ineffable experience, of visual experiences, the content of which cannot be manifested in linguistic or non-linguistic behaviour. But I shall be neither defending nor denying the existence of qualia. In speaking above of ineffability as a criterion for making sense out of, or denying sense to, the idea of a quale, I mean to suggest that the debate about qualia and what they mean for the philosophy of mind and the theory of perception is shaped by deep intuitions about how language relates to experience. On my interpretation, both arguments for qualia and those against distort in different ways our understanding of how language relates to experience.

This focus on ineffability might strike one as an odd way of framing the issue of qualia. Contemporary debate about qualia has tended to focus on ontological and phenomenological questions about qualia that, while involving issues surrounding the privacy of experience, have not focused on the issue of ineffability. Consider Sydney Shoemaker's account of qualia in 'Qualia and Consciousness',[9] which I take to be representative of arguments defending a thick conception of qualia. Shoemaker argues for a conception of qualia in terms of positions on three definitive questions: the accessibility of qualia to consciousness; the character of the properties we are aware of in being aware of our qualia; and the ontological problem of accounting for qualia within a physicalistic theory of mind. (a) The first issue concerns the way in which qualia are supposed to account for our intuitions about there being a certain raw feel to experience, a certain way it is like to see a stop sign, to see the colour red, *to see*.[10] Intuitively, if qualia are supposed to constitute the way an experience is felt, a qualitative property or set of properties, that seems to imply conceptually a consciousness there to being experiencing the feel. But must qualia be introspectively available to conscious awareness? For Shoemaker, they must, although the connection does not rest on any special logical connection between consciousness and qualia. It is based on the relation between consciousness and our ordinary psychological concepts, our 'family of folk psychological states with which the notion of qualia is intimately bound up'.[11] (b) The second element of Shoemaker's account of qualia concerns the kind of properties we are aware of, in being aware of what our experience is like, and debate concerns how best to conceive the relation between 'phenomenal' and 'intentional' properties of experiences. Against 'intentionalist' positions,[12] Shoemaker argues that while intentional similarity between visual experiences (i.e. their both being *of* the same thing) is introspectively available, our awareness of intentional properties must be based on awareness of phenomenal properties.[13] (c) The third issue is the ontological status of qualia and concerns the problem of locating qualia within a broadly functionalist theory of mind and a physicalist ontology. Here, Shoemaker offers a compatibilist argument for qualia. Against thinkers who argue that qualia are incompatible with physicalism,[14] Shoemaker argues that identity conditions for qualia types can be given a functional characterization as internal sensory states mediating causal connections between stimuli and behaviour.[15]

Two reasons lead me to ignore these issues in favour of the issue of ineffability. The first has to do with a change in the debate over qualia which forces the question of ineffability to the fore. The second issue has to do with the way that Wittgenstein's approach to perception naturally raises the issue of ineffability as a problem. Considering these reasons will help to clarify my motives. In recent years, debate about qualia has shifted away from ontological and phenomenological issues – the issues shaping Shoemaker's account – and has taken up the question as to whether qualia can even be said to exist. This shift has been effected in part by Daniel Dennett's attempt to discredit the concept altogether by attacking standard ways in which pre-theoretical intuitions about experience are marshalled in support of the hypothesis of qualia.[16] In shifting the debate, these attacks have exposed some important assumptions shared by arguments for visual qualia. The force of Dennett's attack stems from the way he employs the verificationist principle of natural–scientific inquiry against arguments which attempt to make sense of such notions as *raw feels, phenomenal properties* and a *subjective dimension of experience*. What this criticism exposes is the connection between the idea of qualia and the sense that our experience has a character that cannot be expressed, or expressed directly, in observable (i.e., verifiable) behaviour. The importance of this connection is indicated by the dilemma that Dennett's argument causes for defenders of qualia. For if they reject the verificationist criticisms, they are being anti-scientific. On the other hand, if they accept the criticisms while attempting to defend qualia, they are forced to reformulate their view of qualia to make them verifiable. But even thinkers who go so far as to hold that phenomenal properties are not specifiable independently of representational properties still want to maintain that there is something called *phenomenal consciousness*, which makes up the character of our experience, as opposed to what our experience is *of*.[17] But if this is all that one can say about qualia, one might well question whether that is enough to make the matter theoretically significant.[18]

In calling attention to Dennett's attack, what I mean to suggest is that the vulnerability of the notion of qualia to verificationist criticisms reveals the sense in which the intuitions driving philosophical accounts of them are connected to an intuition about the ineffability of experience. After all, ineffability is anathema to verificationism, since it suggests something beyond words, beyond behaviour, and so beyond what is observable. Hence, if Dennett can appeal to the verificationist sensibilities of qualia's defenders, it seems to me that he has won the debate. While arguing in this chapter against qualia as a philosophical concept, however, I will also be arguing against Dennett's attempt to quine them away. This brings us to my second point about ineffability. In the first chapter, I was interested in a way of understanding the relationship between our visual experience and expressions of it, more specifically, about how ascriptions of visual experiences are connected to expressions as criteria for ascribing those experiences. This approach, following Wittgenstein, involved a grammatical investigation of ordinary criteria for employing our concepts of *see* and *description of what is seen*. However, the idea that visual experience is ineffable involves a repudiation of our ordinary criteria for describing what is seen, of what it means to see, of what can be communicated about what I see, and of what is to count as an accurate or complete description of my visual experience. Ineffability suggests, in one intuitive leap, that these criteria fail to convey what these concepts really refer to. The experience of ineffability suggests that when we speak of what we see ordinarily, we do not mean what we in fact really mean, or what we ought to mean if we were speaking in accordance with the truer sense of the terms. On this view, to accept Wittgenstein's analysis seems to imply that we cannot experience anything that we cannot describe (linguistic idealism), or that perception can be reduced to expressive behaviour (linguistic behaviourism), or even that we have no experiences. It follows that, in making a plausible case for a Wittgensteinian approach to philosophical questions, the intuitions about ineffability must be defused and redirected.

Logical privacy (Daniel Dennett)

The concept of logical privacy offers a way of understanding the possibility that visual experience, or its phenomenal or qualitative properties – qualia – are incommunicable. This is not so much an argument for qualia as logically-private entities, but an exploration of the logical link between the concept of a quale and the concept of logical privacy.

In what sense is my visual experience something that only I can understand? It is of course possible to fail to know what someone else is seeing. It is also possible to see things that no one has seen. Nor is there anything unusual about finding oneself at a loss for words as to how to describe a visual impression, for example, of what one sees standing on the south rim of the Grand Canyon. In each of these cases, there is a gap between one's experience and one's capacities for expressing that experience. In each case, that gap can ordinarily be bridged. If I do not know what someone has seen, I can ask her; and we all experience new visual impressions almost every day – impressions that are different in subtle ways from anything else we've seen, that we can describe for others. Even in the case of unusual moments where we find ourselves speechless, our behaviour can betray what we are experiencing in imponderable ways. Logical privacy is distinguished from ordinary senses of privacy by its being essentially irreducible or unbridgeable.[19] This kind of privacy is what is entertained in the suggestion that even in the most ordinary of visual perceptions, I am at a loss for words; that in the strict sense of the word *see*, I cannot communicate what I am seeing. If visual experience is logically private in this sense, a picture is worth far more than a thousand words; no amount of blabbering will do.

The classic inverted-spectrum question originally formulated by Locke is a way of sharpening the idea of logical privacy.[20] The perception of colour is notoriously sensitive to context, such that two samples of the same colour can appear to be samples of different colours depending on circumstances. Given this relational character of colour, the question naturally arises whether we can know whether two people are experiencing the same colour impression. The fact that two people are both looking at the same physical object, for example, an ordinary red stop sign, does nothing to resolve the question as to whether they are seeing the same thing. It is the similarity of their visual impressions of the sign that is at stake, their 'subjective experience', and this cannot be ascertained simply by pointing to the sign and saying '*That* is the colour that I am seeing'. If visual qualia inversion is possible, we might pass our whole life going on red and stopping on green, and never come to know that what I mean by *red* is what you mean by *green*.[21]

Now if one attributes logical privacy to visual experience, one is in essence led to repudiate what conventionally counts as knowing what someone else can see, or how she is seeing it. Consider, for example, what ordinarily counts as having the same thought. We would say that everyone had the same thought when the second plane hit the towers; namely, that the first crash was no accident. Now if we ask why we are justified in making that ascription, we can point to various aspects of the circumstances. Of central significance is the fact that the first plane crash raised the question as to whether or not the crash was accidental, while commonsense probability precluded the realistic possibility of a second accident. What is important to note is that it is not part of our justification for that ascription that we had access to the inner workings of other people's minds. Of course, we did not, and given the circumstances, such access would in any case be irrelevant. In this sense, identity conditions for thoughts are not logically private, since they are bound up with the background circumstances of ascriptions. But if undetectable spectrum inversion is possible, then visual impressions must be individuated in ways that are logically independent of the publicly available criteria underlying our employment of perceptual concepts.

If visual experience is logically private, or has logically private properties, then what makes one visual impression similar to or different from another must turn on properties intrinsic to that impression. As logically private, an experience must have the raw feel or phenomenal qualities it has in a way that is logically independent of the things, relations and events perceived. For example, if my impression of the colour red is logically private, then I cannot express it by simply pointing to a colour sample. On the other hand, logically private experiences must have identity conditions determined independently of the ways we are inclined to respond to our experience, for example, by describing what we see in words, or picturing it in paint, or sighing in pleasure. Both directions of logical independence have intuitive support in ordinary ways of thinking about visual experience. On the one hand, we tend to think of our experience of red as something other than the colour red. On the other, we tend to think of our experience as something other than our ways of reacting to that experience, for example, by judging or describing it.[22]

This brings us to the concept of a quale. If visual experiences have the character they do in a logically private manner, they do so by virtue of the properties constituting this character. Such properties would not only be what I am referring to when I try to talk about what my experience is like, they would also be what I alone have access to. That is, they would make sense of the epistemic asymmetry between first- and third-person perceptual ascriptions; ordinary facts such as that I always know what I am seeing, while you often have to ask me, or that if I ask you what you saw, you can deceive me. On the view I am developing here, the concept of qualia is just what answers to this explanatory need. Qualia explain why experience is logically-private in the sense that they explain why the phenomenal feel of the experience can be separated from the facts about the background circumstances that ordinarily play a role in justifying an ascription. When we abstract the perception from those background circumstances, we end up with its qualia. Of course, this implies that if there are no qualia, then that abstraction process will leave us empty-handed. The latter is precisely what Dennett and Wittgenstein argue, although as we shall see, they do so for very different reasons. The difference illustrates two ways to overcome Cartesian dualism.

On this interpretation of qualia, the ontological and phenomenological issues that have been the focus of debate about qualia are secondary problems arising from a prior acceptance of the explanatory need to posit qualia. One of the chief virtues of Dennett's criticism is that he has managed to shift debate back to this deeper assumption. In 'Quining Qualia', Dennett's tactic is to argue that attempts to fashion versions of the inverted spectrum experiment amenable to verification fail for verificationist reasons. Thus, he considers versions of the 'intra-personal inverted spectrum' example, which is supposed to offer an empirically-verifiable version of the original Lockean version by containing the qualia inversion changes within a single mind. One version involves surgically produced visual colour qualia inversion, so that after surgery, the patient sees red grass and green fire. Since such changes in qualia could be correlated to localizable neurophysiological changes, whether two people were having the same or different experiences could be verified. But as Dennett argues, the empirical facts involved in the neurosurgical prank are not enough to determine whether the qualia themselves have changed, as opposed to the patient's *reactions* to them.[23] For example, if instead of the 'early qualia-producing channels' in the optic nerve, 'memory access links' are changed, then a qualitative difference in experience will still be noticed, but without a genuine change in the qualia. One will simply remember one's prior experiences differently from how they were, and so one's present qualia which have not in fact changed will appear to have changed. So the question is how it is to be decided which of these two ways of affecting qualia inversion has been affected. The verificationist criticism is that there is in fact no way of deciding this.

> Since *ex hypothesi* the two different surgical invasions can produce exactly the same introspective effects while only one operation inverts the qualia, nothing in the subject's experience can favor one of the hypotheses over the other. So unless he seeks outside help, the state of his own qualia must be as unknowable to him as the state of anyone else's qualia.[24]

Dennett goes on to expand this criticism, which he refers to as an 'intensification of the "verificationist" arguments against qualia',[25] by considering other ways in which qualia inversion may be hypothetically detected. The outcome of these criticisms is to undercut the possibility of logical privacy, and so the qualia posited to explain it, by showing that there is no reason for thinking that victims of so-called qualia inversion would be any better at detecting such changes than third-party neuroscientists. If there are ways of deciding when qualia themselves have inverted, as opposed to inversions in how we compare present with past qualia, then the very success of such thought-experiments undermines the presumed epistemic authority of the person who claims to know, in a way that no one else can, the qualitative character of her visual experience.

Consider 'Intuition pump #7', in which Dennett imagines two professional coffee tasters, Chase and Sanborn, whose job it is to ensure that the taste of Maxwell House coffee remains the same.[26] After six years, both admit that while they loved the taste of Maxwell House coffee when they first came to work for the company, they no longer like it. However, their respective explanations of just what has changed to make them dislike the taste differ. Chase says that the coffee tastes exactly the same to him now as it did six years ago, but that his coffee standards have evolved so that he no longer likes the taste of Maxwell House coffee.

> ... the coffee tastes just the same today as it tasted when I arrived. But, you know, I no longer like it! My tastes have changed. I've become a more sophisticated drinker. I no longer like *that taste* at all.[27]

In contrast, Sanborn claims that he no longer likes it because the taste itself has changed, while his standards have remained the same.

> But *my* tastes haven't changed; my ... tasters have changed. That is, I think something has gone wrong with my taste buds or some other part of my taste-analysing perceptual machinery. Maxwell House coffee doesn't taste to me the way it used to taste; if only it did, I'd still love it, for I still think *that* taste is the best in coffee.

On the traditional Cartesian view of qualia, both tasters have authority over these judgements, and cannot be mistaken about what has actually changed. But if there is no introspectively detectable difference between changes in qualia versus changes in how we remember past qualia, then neither taster has any privileged, first-person knowledge which would allow him to decide why he no longer likes coffee.[28]

This leaves a difficulty for the defender of logical privacy if he accepts that Chase could be wrong about which change has taken place. There are of course more extreme cases in which further considerations would decide the matter. What we know about physics and chemistry makes it certain that if someone claimed to have a real-life portrait of Dorian Gray, he would be mistaken. In more subtle cases, one might decide that neurophysiology could help to decide the question. For example, one might attempt to empirically confirm Chase's report by discovering whether and where neurophysiological changes had occurred; whether what had effected the experience was 'a change near the brute perceptual processing end of the spectrum or a change near the ultimate reactive judgment end of the spectrum'.[29] But any such tests leave a lacuna. Such tests must work by discovering correlations between neurophysiological events and behavioural outputs. The experience itself, the qualia, cannot be directly reached, while any linguistic report will always be ambiguous, making the correlation indeterminate.

> Qualia are supposed to affect our action or behavior only via the intermediary of our judgments about them, so any behavioral test, such as a discrimination or memory test, since it takes acts based on judgments as its primary data, can give us direct evidence only about the *resultant* of our two factors.[30]

The conclusion Dennett reaches is that insofar as the notion of qualitative properties of subjective experience makes sense, there is no reason for believing that individuals have any privileged access to their character, and that in general, their judgements will have the status of the vague hunches of a naive subject. Judgements about what has changed qualitatively in one's experience versus how one's reactive attitudes to one's experience have changed will, thus, be on a par with judgements about constancies in one's body temperature, or lighting intensity of a room.[31] On this analysis, the traditional property of logical privacy collapses from the pressure of verificationist assumptions, and along with it, the conception of subjects as having special access to their experiences. Correlated to the conception of qualia reconstructed for purposes of productive experimental psychology, there is the reconstructed conception of the individual as a primitive *autopsychologist* with respect to her experience, and with the hypothesis of private qualitative features of that experience having the status of a faulty hypothesis. Our pre-theoretical intuitions here are shown to be incoherent: ergo, qualia do not exist.

Now while Wittgenstein's analysis also aims at undercutting the possibility of logical privacy, and so the conception of qualia connected to that possibility, his diagnosis exposes a different kind of confusion. In turn, the exposure of that confusion leads to a different kind of insight. Rather than vindicating the verificationist assumptions of natural scientific enquiry against the incoherence of pre-theoretical intuition, the insights occasioned by Wittgenstein's approach have to do with how we understand language. Pre-theoretical intuitions are still culpable here, but the understanding they distort cannot be clarified by way of a more rigorous application of the verificationist principle, or a more scientifically-informed philosophy of mind. What is needed is not new information, but a new way of seeing familiar facts.[32] While Wittgenstein's approach does not count against Dennett's in that sense, it arguably captures what is philosophically compelling about ineffability, in a way that Dennett's does not.

On Wittgenstein's approach, the problem with private experience could be characterized as a problem about reference. While Dennett's attack takes its bearings from the counter-verificationist scent of the qualia hypothesis, Wittgenstein's approach is directed at the qualia defender's views on language, and specifically, the defender's sense that ordinary language is fundamentally inadequate for expressing her experience. The questions begin when one considers what sorts of intentional attitudes we should be able to take up with respect to our (logically private) experiences. Minimally, we should be able to refer to them, though not of course in any public language. If I tell the traffic police that the light was green and it wasn't, he can correct me, because I alone do not have privileged authority over when my use of the word *red* is justified. The practice of avoiding and receiving traffic violation tickets naturally depends upon such facts. In this sense, the identity conditions of my visual perceptions are bound up with criteria including, among other things, physical objects, for example, traffic lights, as well as the reactions of other people to those physical objects, for example, cops.

Rather, we should be able to inwardly or mentally point to them, specifically, point to a property of my experience that gives it the particular, subjective ineffable feel that slips through the seemingly coarse weave of public concepts. For present purposes, I shall use the term *quale* to refer to logically private aspects of a visual experience. Now if we can mentally point to a quale, then we should be able to name it; again, not using any word with a shared, public meaning, like *red* or *circular*, but a private symbol. Because its meaning is constituted by its designating the quale, no one else can understand what the name means. One might say that the term has thus been given a private semantics. To say that we should be able to take up these attitudes toward our qualia is to say that we should be able to do this if these qualia are indeed incommunicable. Interestingly, it does not follow from the claim that experiences are in fact communicable that we should be able to mentally point to them independently of their being instances of a public concept, since in that case there is no need to.

This picture offers another perspective on the phenomenon envisaged by the inverted spectrum. With the inverted spectrum, the differences and similarities between qualia are simply inverted in a way that does not disrupt practice because the inversion causes no behavioural modifications. In contrast, from a third-person perspective, the use of a symbol by the private linguist, where privacy is construed as necessary unintelligibility, can only appear as anarchic or unintelligible linguistic behaviour. Unlike the inverted spectrum, the linguistic practice of the linguist conflicts irremediably with the linguistic practices of third parties. While qualia inversion suggested differences in experience which were invisible or undetectable, private language suggests differences which are unintelligible. One might say that the private linguist gives the appearance of using the concept whenever she feels like it.

Now from an outside, third-person perspective, there are in fact three possibilities for interpreting the private linguist's unintelligible behaviour. She may in fact be interpreted as meaning some one thing by her use of the term, for instance, if the type of quale only occurs in her experience. Alternatively, she might be interpreted as *unsuccessfully* following a rule even though she intends to. Her mental descriptions of her experience are sometimes true, sometimes false, if the private term is applied in accordance with its meaning, but she does not realize when she is wrong.[33] It is also possible to interpret the private linguist as totally mistaken about the term's even having a consistent meaning, such that we cannot even speak about correct or incorrect uses. On this interpretation, she is not only mistaken that she always uses the term correctly, she is mistaken about the term's having a meaning in the first place. Here, the reason why us third-party linguists cannot catch on is just because there is no meaning to catch on to. Now the verificationist opts for the third interpretation by arguing that we have no good reasons for ascribing to the so-called private linguist rule-governed language employment (for accepting that his private symbols succeed in referring to distinct quale-types), just because we have no *evidence* of language.

On the interpretation of the private language arguments that I shall offer below, the interpretive problem is not one of lacking evidence, but of a conceptually confused notion of what the evidence is supposed to be evidence *for*. On that view, the interpretive options for understanding the behaviour of the private linguist above are only superficially distinguished; conceptual clarification reveals that those distinctions cannot be sustained. Showing this involves a dialectical struggle against the private language interlocutor who argues that we can make sense of the first possibility mentioned above; namely, that the person is actually employing his private symbol in a rule-governed manner, despite our inability to understand what that symbol means. Hence, the arguments against private language aim at showing that the idea of a use of a private symbol that is necessarily unintelligible to others is a conception of language use *which is itself unintelligible*. Since the distortions vitiating the picture of private language are effected by the condition of logical privacy underlying the account, the concept of logically-private semantics, *inter alia* logically-private experiences (qualia), is shown to be senseless. The positive result of the exercise concerns the light which the failure shines on the criteria constituting the concepts of meaning, visual sensation, following a rule, and ultimately, of speaking a language.[34]

The private language arguments

In order to find the real artichoke, we divested it of its leaves.[35]

It is a typical supposition that Wittgenstein's private language argument purports to show that private language is impossible because it fails to instantiate some particular adequacy condition that everything called *language* must fulfil.[36] On the interpretation I shall offer here, there is no one particular private language argument, but a series of such arguments, spread throughout the first part of *Philosophical Investigations*.[37] This view is related to my understanding of what is under attack in the discussion of private language and, importantly, of how the attack is to be effected. The object of criticism is not a developed position, for example, a particular theory of language, or a thesis about meaning. It is a set of intuitions about experience and what language has to be like, or would have to be like, in order to express our experience perfectly. As I shall argue, the private language arguments take the form of a dialectical struggle against the intuitions of a private language interlocutor, a private linguist who argues his case against what he takes to be the defects of ordinary language.

In speaking of that interlocutor, John McDowell characterizes the private linguist as attempting, in his appeals to private experience, a *lived refutation of idealism*.[38] That characterization applies nicely to my approach as well, where *idealism* stands for our ordinary ways of expressing our visual experience. The perceived defects of ordinary language that motivate the refutation have to do with its being too coarse to articulate the perceptual richness of what is immediately given. This failure is understood to result from the ways that natural language is constrained by the pragmatic requirements for effective communication. This failure of public language, which is supposed to illustrate the sense in which the perceptual *given* falls through the cracks of language, is developed by imagining the possibility of a phenomenologically perspicuous language: a private language is not structured by the needs of communication, and so is freed to capture in finer grain the logical multiplicity of visual reality. As I shall argue, the conceptual difficulties with private language that Wittgenstein's remarks are meant to expose have to do with an irremediable indeterminacy in the concept, like an artichoke whose leaves have been torn away in the search for the true artichoke. Methodologically, this involves an appeal to criteria: *that* the artichoke has been divested of its leaves is shown by comparing it to an artichoke whose leaves are intact.

Let's begin by considering two ways of understanding what the relevant sense of privacy for the arguments is. The first sense of privacy, which is at the heart of Saul Kripke's influential interpretation, concerns the solitariness of the private linguist; not that she cannot be understood, but that there is no one around to understand her.[39] The second sense, which I shall argue is the important one, concerns the *necessary unintelligibility to others* of the intentional states of the private linguist.[40]

On the first view, the important sense of privacy in the arguments against private language concerns the solitariness of the private linguist. On Kripke's interpretation, this picture takes the form of the thesis that the intentions of the private linguist to follow a given rule need not rely on any communal standards, constituted by agreement in judgements, in order to carry normative constraints on what is to count as conformity with a rule. The breakdown of this picture comes with seeing how any possible fact about the solitary linguist's intentions, insofar as those facts are construed individualistically, is not enough to impose normative constraints on the linguistic behaviour of the linguist. Here, we can construe *individualistic facts* to mean: facts about the rule follower which are non-causally independent of facts about that individual's physical and social environs.

On the second view of privacy, its relevance pertains to the inability of others to understand the meaning of the private symbol: they cannot learn how to apply it, and so, for example, the private linguist's use of the symbol can never be corrected by them. On this view, the possibility of private language represents the possibility of a rule establishing the meaning of a symbol which names or refers to a *quale* that cannot be accessed by third parties. The breakdown of this conception of privacy follows from the fact that no sense can be given to a semantics that is necessarily unintelligible to third parties. Unlike the first, the dissolution of the second conception of privacy does not yield any insights into the alleged social nature of meaning and rule-following.[41] Rather, it returns us to our ordinary concepts of language and meaning, while disabusing us of the kind of dissatisfactions that the private linguist perceives natural language to have.

According to Kripke, the core of the private language argument derives from questions about what it means for someone's current and future use of a word to conform to what was meant by that word in past use.[42] Kripke's approach goes about answering this question by considering possible facts about the linguist which could decide what she previously meant, in such a way as to establish what would count as meaning the same thing in new cases. The general problem that arises in the course of his investigation is that no individualistic facts about the linguist, which is to say, facts about the linguist considered in isolation from her social environs, could constitute what she meant. Non-semantic facts, such as the intentional conditions of states of consciousness, facts about past use, or dispositions to apply a private symbol 'S' in a certain way, all fail to maintain normativity since they can be variously interpreted. Any mental representation or image, the grasping of which might be held to constitute one's understanding of a given meaning S by 'S', could be variously interpreted, thereby specifying various and potentially conflicting uses as according with its meaning. Moreover, any instructions one might specify for interpreting a mental representation would themselves be subject to competing interpretations, leading to a regress. The possibility of bent rules undercuts appeals to facts about how 'S' was used in the past.[43] On the other hand, if one appeals to a disposition to apply 'S' in accordance with its meaning *S*, then one has at most offered a descriptive account of following a rule, not an explanation of the *normativity* a rule imposes on possible uses. That is, a disposition can explain only how I do, or will, apply 'S', not how I *ought* to apply it, if I am to use it to mean *S*.[44] Finally, appeal to immediate intuition, or to a *sui generis* meaning state, does not solve the problem either. The voice of intuition would still be open to different interpretations,[45] while a *sui generis* meaning-state would offer no explanation of the difference between what the linguist is inclined to do and what he ought to do.[46] This leads to the paradox, at *Philosophical Investigations* (201–202), which Kripke takes to be the conclusion of the private language argument and the central point of the *Investigations* as a whole.[47]

> This was our paradox: no course of action could be determined by a rule, because every course of action can be made out to accord with a rule. The answer was: if everything can be made out to accord with a rule, then it can also be made out to conflict with it. And so there would be neither accord nor conflict.[48]

On Kripke's reading, this paradox constitutes a sceptical conclusion which arises from any attempt to construe facts about what someone means by a symbol individualistically. In turn, the sceptical thesis gives rise to a thesis about the objectivity of semantic discourse. Individualistically-conceived attempts to do so cannot account for the normativity of meaning, and since facts of that sort are the only facts available, there are no facts *as such* about what someone means.[49] According to Kripke, the paradox, and the conceptual nihilism it seems to imply, can only be resolved if one relinquishes the idea that someone's meaning *S* by 'S' is constituted by facts about that individual considered in isolation from a larger community of language users.[50] On Kripke's version of the 'community view', only agreement with how a given community of language users is inclined to go on in its use of a symbol can offer the needed distinction between what counts as a correct use and what an individual is inclined to take as a correct use.[51]

The difficulty with Kripke's interpretation, relevant to my interest in qualia, concerns his notion of privacy. It was noted above that Wittgenstein explicitly states that the conception of privacy he is concerned with has to do with the necessary unintelligibility of the private linguist's language to third parties. On Kripke's view, privacy concerns simply solitary existence. On the latter view, the possibility is left open that we might observe from afar a Robinson Crusoe-type character, say, as hidden anthropologists, taking his linguistic behaviour to be expressive of genuine rule-governed use, and yet not be justified in attributing genuinely normative meaning-intentions to him. This is because, as long as we consider him merely to be following his inclinations, there can be no distinction between his being correct and his merely thinking that he is correct. Hence, Crusoe cannot have any intentions to mean something by his use of a symbol,[52] any more than we could take his sweating to have an intended meaning.

Now Kripke also argues that this does not mean per se that a solitary individual cannot be said to follow rules, but that an individual 'considered in isolation' cannot.[53] What he means is that, insofar as we do conceive of him as following a rule, we are 'taking him into our community and applying our criteria for rule-following to him'.[54] But this move sounds suspiciously like saying: we can only consider Crusoe to be following a rule if we consider him to be following a rule. Baker and Hacker question this move when they ask:

> What is it supposed to mean? Does it mean that in saying that he is following a rule we are applying our criteria for rule-following to him? Well – are there other criteria? This, presumably, is what 'rule-following' *means*.[55]

If there are no other criteria for rule-following, then Kripke's claims against private language collapse into the grammatical remark that if someone is to count as speaking a language, he must fulfil our (ordinary) criteria for speaking a language and that, if we cannot apply those criteria to him, then he cannot be said to be speaking a language. Put in this way, the conclusion amounts to either a grammatical remark, which is trivially or conceptually true, or an empirical proposition which is nonsensical. On Kripke's reading, it constitutes a sceptical thesis about rule-following, since he assumes that the justification of ordinary semantic ascriptions awaits a proof by reduction to a deeper level of objectivity. But the apparent vacuity of the statement suggests that the assumption is perhaps suspect.

The problem is connected to Kripke's understanding of privacy. Warren Goldfarb has called attention to the divergence between Kripke's sense of privacy and the sense Wittgenstein explicitly states to be the important one (*Investigations*, 243). However, he downplays its relevance for evaluating the cogency of Kripke's interpretation, suggesting that Kripke's version offers a more radical argument which, if cogent, supports Wittgenstein's version.

> What Kripke imagines is . . . a language the constitution of which depends on properties of each speaker taken in isolation. There is no notion of private

object, and no mention of necessary unintelligibility to others. Hence I shall call Kripke's notion that of a solitary language. Evidently, it is a more general notion than Wittgenstein's; so the impossibility of a solitary language would yield *a fortiori* that of a private language in Wittgenstein's per se.[56]

But Kripke's view of private language is not in fact more general or more radical than that of Wittgenstein. This is clear from *Investigations*, section 207, where Wittgenstein imagines a situation in which what appears to be a language spoken in an unknown country proves to be untranslatable, and remarks that however else it may be categorized, it cannot be called language.

> Let us imagine that the people in that country carried on the usual human activities and in the course of them employed, apparently, an articulate language. If we watch their behaviour we find it intelligible, it seems 'logical'. But when we try to learn their language we find it impossible to do so. For there is no regular connection between what they say, the sounds they make, and their actions; but still these sounds are not superfluous, for if we gag one of the people, it has the same consequences as with us; without the sounds their actions fall into confusion – as I feel like putting it. Are we to say that these people have a language: orders, reports, and the rest?

There is not enough regularity for us to call it 'language'.[57] What is relevant about the example is that while meeting Kripke's criterion of being social, in the sense of being non-solitary, Wittgenstein denies that their behaviour can be construed as a form of language, or rule-governed linguistic behaviour. While agreeing in some sense in their (unintelligible to us) vocalizations, they fail to make sense. The puzzle about this example is how we are to understand an 'apparently articulate language'. On Kripke's interpretation, it is taken for granted that a language is being spoken, that rules are being followed. On this picture, it would be possible, presumably, for a solitary individual to manifest all our ordinary criteria for employing a language and still not be meaning anything in his use of a symbol. This suggests the sense in which, for Kripke, those criteria stand in need of a justification, and one that ultimately cannot be given; hence, Kripke's sceptical solution. It turns out, on this view, that the most obvious solutions, which happen to be individualistic accounts of meaning, are no good, and this offers us an insight into the inherently social nature of meaning. But in *Investigations*, 207, the solitariness or sociality of the private linguist is irrelevant. It is possible *ex hypothesi* for there to be a society which nevertheless fails to fulfil the criteria for employing a language.

On the other hand, if a solitary individual's vocal behaviour did suggest the employment of a language and did prove to be intelligible to us, then his solitariness would also be beside the point. There would be something about his behaviour that suggested normativity; which counted as language. But what is the point at which behaviour not suggesting normativity becomes suggestive of normativity, even constitutive of what we mean by normativity? I suggest that this question is what Wittgenstein's investigation into privacy seems to be addressing. It is, in part, a question about what our criteria for applying the concepts of meaning, understanding and language are, not a question about what justifies those criteria. But the question of just what these criteria are never arises for Kripke, and so the question gets shifted away from *what* is being imagined to how what is imagined is *possible*. I think that this shift distorts Wittgenstein's interest in private language.

An apparently articulate language is not one that manifests all publicly available criteria for being a genuine language. The fact that it cannot be learned, that its symbols cannot be understood, is the salient feature of what is being imagined, and it is the most obvious way that this 'private language' differs from what ordinarily counts as language. As a limit case, the concept of private language is not merely the absence of language, since in ways it *appears* to be language: third parties try and fail to understand it. On the edge of what ordinarily counts as being language, the vocal behaviour called private language suggests, and at the same time repudiates, the idea that language is being employed. As such, it serves as a way to elucidate our criteria for what counts as genuine rule-following behaviour. Thus, for example, Wittgenstein's reason why the vocal behaviour described in section 207 does not count as language – because there is not enough 'regularity' in the behaviour – cannot be taken as a verificationist criticism of the possibility, on the grounds that nothing can confirm whether or not a language is being spoken by the tribe. There is something about the behaviour itself that precludes its counting as language; 'there is no regular connection between what they say, the sounds they make, and their actions; but still these sounds are not superfluous, for if we gag one of the people, it has the same consequences as with us; without the sounds their actions fall into confusion – as I feel like putting it.'[58] As Wittgenstein argues, in section 207, from the perspective of a third party, there is simply no basis for speaking of the inexplicable vocal behaviour of a person, or even a tribe, as language use. This is because the regularity manifested by language use is absent, specifically, regular connections between what someone says and how she behaves. It is not simply that we lack evidential grounds for the hypothesis that the private linguist is actually speaking a language. Having stripped away all of the ordinary criteria for ascribing language use to a person, there is nothing left that could count as behaviour-manifesting rule-following activity. *Ex hypothesi*, we cannot catch on to what someone means by seeing how their use agrees with how they explain what they mean. Nor can we grasp their meaning in terms of the role that uses of a given concept play in their actions. These are just some typical ways that we determine whether and what someone means by a concept. When these criteria are abrogated, as in section 207, the logical connections that those criteria have to the concept of language use are revealed. What determines whether someone is following a rule or not is no fact behind, and logically independent of, someone's behaviour. Nor is rule-following identical with that behaviour; *that* behaviour can in general only be identified as behaviour expressive *of* language use. Rather, rule-following activity is manifested, or expressed in and through behaviour, in regularly observable connections between vocal utterances and physical movement.

This is only one strand of the argument against private language, however. On one standard interpretation, private language is shown to be impossible because all description of experience is shown to be public, while a private object cannot be described; hence, there is no such thing as a private description of a private object. But, while in a sense true, this reading overlooks the fact that the interlocutor is moved by various intuitions to repudiate our ordinary criteria for describing and expressing experience. That is why the arguments against the possibility must be seen as being directed against the intuitions of the interlocutor; as designed to point out the unacknowledged consequences of repudiating those criteria. If the difficulty with the concept of private language does not stem from the fact that meaning is a social phenomenon, but rather with the ways it distorts the criteria for semantic ascriptions, an argument against it can only serve to point out these distortions and the phenomena suggesting them. This is why the private language arguments must be construed as dialectical responses to a private language interlocutor.

On the interpretation I am defending, the distortions in question are understood in terms of ways that the advocate of private language attempts to offset perceived defects in ordinary language by imagining a refined system of representation. The irony of the concept of private language is that the very reasons that suggest it as a refinement of ordinary (public) language are the same reasons that undercut its claim to being genuine language. As a refinement or idealization, the concept of private language represents a solution to a perceived defect of ordinary language. That perceived defect has to do with the idea that the expressive possibilities of language are constrained by the public uses language is put to, i.e. communication. It is precisely this intuition, which repudiates appeals to the social character of language as a means of communication, that needs to be addressed.

Consider an easy way with the sceptic. One response to the sceptic who worries about the possibility of undetectable inverted colour qualia is to point to the ways in which the conditions for effective communication involve the employment of criteria for the meanings of concepts which are public. If language is shaped by the need to communicate, and communication requires shared meanings, private language is a contradiction in terms: 'If language is to be a means of communication there must be agreement not only in

definitions but also (queer as this may sound) in judgements.'[59] Unless the
meaning of a word is constituted by shared criteria, what someone else means
by that word can always be misunderstood, despite how he acts or what he says
about what he means. That is why the terms of ordinary public language must
be 'one size fits all'. Someone who doesn't understand why the colour of stop
lights is called *red*, doesn't know what the term 'red' means, regardless of what
is going on in his visual cortex or brain when looking at one. He does not count
as understanding what 'red' means, in the sense that being able to see why *that*
is called red is a criterion for understanding what 'red' means.[60]

But to the private language interlocutor, this *one size fits all* suggests a gap.
Agreement in judgement does not guarantee agreement in definition, since it
might be the case that, despite our calling the same things 'red', we mean different things by that symbol because we have different colour qualia.[61] The
fact that the English word does have a shared meaning rooted in public practices, such as stopping at traffic lights, does not mean that there are no dimen-
sions to our visual experience ignored by the demands of those practices.

In keeping with this line of thought, one might respond that while ordinary
English is based on criteria that are not logically-private, that fact itself does
not speak against the possibility of logically-private entities but, to the contrary, the phenomenological defectiveness of natural language.[62] If I am not
constrained to make myself understood, or to understand others, then the idea
is that I could devise a phenomenologically perspicuous language which could
describe the inherent properties (qualia) of my visual experience.[63] Instead of
the various public purposes to which we put language, and the requirements
for accurate communication such practices impose on the way the meanings of
the word are constituted, the meanings of the terms of the private language
would be fixed wholly by the various kinds of visual impressions I experience.
Having given myself private, ostensive definitions of the words in my private
language, by assigning each term to a corresponding visual quale type, it
would be the inherent, logically-private properties of an impression-type that
would fix the meaning of each term. And this means that those properties
determine for me when to apply the terms of my language. In speaking the
language to myself, I am guided by the nature of the qualia themselves; as if
the qualia spoke for themselves, and in a way that no one else can understand.
So constructed, the ideal of a semantics which fits perfectly the inherent qualia
of my experience is suggested. Such a language would lack the perceived epistemological difficulties with knowing what someone else means in using a
word, for example, to describe what she sees. Since I *know* what I mean to
refer to, there is no possibility of a failure between how a word is used and
what it is used to mean.

This sort of refinement of language by the private language interlocutor can
be shown, however, to be a regressive dissolution of the concept of language.

Unlike natural language, private language is not supposed to be governed by publicly available behavioural criteria for meaning-ascriptions. That is just the reason why it cannot be understood. Now, if the private linguist cannot be justified in his claim to be following a rule via reference to his behaviour or to any public criteria, the possibility might be defended by showing that he is at least justified before himself. That is, the linguist must defend the possibility of private language by showing that his use is governed by a criterion. But as we shall see, this defence is just what cannot be given. The failure can be seen as the result of a dialectical strain, which the private linguist saddles himself with in asserting the possibility of private language and which ultimately proves impossible to resolve. On the one hand, in claiming that he is genuinely following a rule, he is forced to posit a criterion constituting the correct use of the term. On the other hand, he is constrained to characterize this criterion, in justifying his use to himself, in such a way that the meaning of the concept used is not, and cannot be, manifested in his behaviour. This engenders logical dilemmas of various sorts.

Consider the concept of being justified in one's use of a word. I cannot be mistaken about whether what I am seeing is in fact red, unless I do not understand, or misunderstand, what the word 'red' means.[64] On the other hand, while I often can know whether someone else sees red, for example, by asking him if he sees red, there is room on occasion for doubting his avowals. Now if I ask him to explain what he means by 'red', or to justify his calling something 'red', he might respond by pointing to a sample, for example, a stop sign, saying 'I mean *that* colour'. If I further ask him why he is justified in calling that 'red', he is justified in responding that that is just what the English word means. Here, justification comes to an end by reaching a connection that is purely conventional, and as such arbitrary. In this case, the sample serves as a criterion for applying the term, while someone's use of the sample, in explaining what he means, serves as a criterion for my ascribing rule-governed use of the term to him.

Now consider a private linguist's term for a private colour. One might think that such a term would lack some of the problems that ordinary colour terms exhibit. For example, if the person who is mentioned above points to a sample to explain what he means, I might misunderstand what he means.[65] This might suggest that, while no one else can understand him, he can understand himself perfectly, in the sense that he doesn't have to guess or catch on to any meaning. But now if I ask the private linguist what he means by his private term, he cannot point to anything, since nothing public can display what he means. The purported criterion he uses to 'justify' his use of his private term to himself is, thus, importantly different from a public colour sample (i.e. a stop sign) that can be appealed to in ostensively explaining the meanings of ordinary colour terms. Unlike the latter, the former is not independent of the private linguist's inclinations. If the public colour swatch, as a paradigm of a criterion for applying a concept, is analogous to a train schedule that someone consults to determine whether his knowledge of the train's departure is correct, then the private criterion appealed to by the private linguist is like an imagined train schedule which cannot itself be tested for its correctness. This analogy shows that in appealing to a private criterion, the linguist has not, as such, succeeded in giving sense to such a possibility.[66]

The problem of how a private criterion could serve to justify the use of a private symbol is connected to the problem of how the meaning of a private symbol could be established in the first place. In learning an ordinary word for a sensation, for example, pain, children are trained to use the word in accordance with certain conventions. Their grasp of the rule for applying the term is typically brought about by an interactive training process, whereby the adult prompts the child to use the word under the appropriate circumstances, corrects his mistaken uses, offers explanations of what the term means, etc., until the child catches on. Crucial to this process is the fact that the term being learned is connected to behavioural criteria; to natural expressions of the sensation. If there were no natural expressions of pain, adults could not prompt the child to use the word, nor could they correct his use.[67] That is to say, there are criteria independent of the child's inclination to call some sensation 'pain' which play an essential role in the child's learning to use it to mean *pain*. In the case of a private-sensation language, there cannot be any natural expression of a given quale-type, since *ex hypothesi* there cannot be any behavioural manifestations of what the private linguist means. This raises the question as to what kind of criteria can serve to determine what uses are to count as according with the meaning of the private-sensation symbol. To say that a private criterion is established by giving myself a private, ostensive definition, by impressing on myself a connection between the symbol and the quale-type it names, is thus vacuous. It is vacuous because, having stripped the concept of a criterion independent of the linguist's inclination, nothing has been left in the picture of private language to support the idea that a criterion plays a role in determining what accords with the meaning of the symbol.

> 'I impress it on myself' can only mean: this process brings it about that I remember the connection *right* in the future. But in the present case I have no criterion of correctness. One would like to say: whatever is going to seem right to me is right. And that only means that here we can't talk about 'right'.[68]

Unlike someone who is asked to explain what he means by 'red', the private linguist cannot point to anything other than the quale supposedly picked out by his private symbol.

A similar point is reached at 201–2, where Wittgenstein considers an interpretational view of linguistic understanding as an answer to the question of how the expression of a rule can show me how to follow the rule. This more general discussion of how rules for the use of words can logically determine what is in accord with their meaning dovetails with problems surrounding the possibility of a private-sensation language. In giving himself a private, ostensive explanation of the meaning of a term 'S', the private linguist must establish a connection between the quale pointed to 'mentally' and the symbol. Having established the meaning, the linguist can then go on to say '*This* is S', when he experiences a quale of that type, such that there is a fact of the matter whether his assertion is true or false. More, however, is involved with naming a quale than simply (inwardly) attending to a quale and saying to oneself 'S'. If I am pointing at a colour and say 'how nice', I have not thereby named that colour 'how nice'.[69] When someone explains to me what a colour term means, for example, by pointing to something and saying 'That's "burnt umber"', my understanding the explanation requires that I understand that what is being defined is a colour, and not, for example, a shape or texture, nor colour in general, but a particular colour. Moreover, I must understand that something is being named, rather than described or expressed. Understanding that a term is a name for something involves understanding how it is to be used. If one strips away the context and background set-up within which ostensive explanations are conventionally understood, then one ends up with a bare pointing that could be *interpreted* to mean just about anything.[70] Furthermore, just how the ostensive definition must be supplemented, and so what counts as an *adequate* definition, is determined by the circumstances surrounding the definition.[71] When we turn to the case of a private, ostensive definition of a quale-type, this creates a dilemma. If the meaning is supposed to be fixed by an inner act of mental pointing, this bare act leaves the *use* of the term up in the air. For example, it leaves it indeterminate whether 'S' is a name, and if it is, what kind of name it is, and what purposes one would have for employing it. So here is the rub: if the success of the private linguist's ostensive definition presupposes these ordinary grammatical distinctions, then his claim to necessary unintelligibility is compromised. It is no longer a private language.

> What reason have we for calling 'S' the sign for a *sensation*? For 'sensation' is a word of our common language, not one intelligible to me alone. So the use of this word stands in need of a justification which everyone understands.[72]

On the other hand, if we assume that these grammatical distinctions from natural language cannot apply to a private language, then we no longer have any conception of how a private, ostensive definition could serve to determine the correct use of a private symbol. On Kripke's reading, stripping away the familiar setting, against which ostensive definitions function, leads to a sceptical paradox: the ostensive definition could mean *anything*, and therefore that there is no sense in which the private linguist's use could accord or conflict with its meaning. Kripke takes this paradox seriously, as offering a metaphysical insight into the conditions for meaning and language. Given such circumstances, there is no fact of the matter about what the word means.

Now the problem with this conclusion is that it rests on the assumption that we can make sense of the concept of private language in the first place. If the interpretive problem is with the private language envisioned in the thought experiment, that does not imply that any such problem infects ordinary language. In the case of ordinary usage, it is obvious that the interpretive problem cannot arise, since there are criteria other than the individualistic facts addressed by Kripke to fix what someone means. More specifically, there are facts about how a word is used on occasions that serve to anchor its meaning what it does. And if the meaning of a term just *is* constituted by how it is used, then the problem of how a use can accord with a rule is misconstrued: 'if the meaning is the *use* we make of a word, it makes no sense to speak of such "fitting".'[73] This is another way that the artichoke is divested of its leaves, as the private linguist tries to find the 'pure artichoke' hidden within the public one.

Whereas in the use of ordinary words like 'red' no inner mental criterion is employed, a private language is constrained to employ a private criterion. But this implies that a private linguist be able to make mistakes, where it makes no sense to say that he could be wrong. This result flies in the face of the traditional (Cartesian) intuition about the incorrigible character of first-person mental ascriptions. That is, pointing out problems with how a private criterion could determine what accords with it ignores the sense in which I cannot be mistaken about what I mean, *inter alia* about my visual qualia, in the way that another person can be mistaken about what I mean or see.[74] The partial truth of the Cartesian intuition, that only I can know what I mean, is just the fact that it makes no sense for me to doubt whether I am having a particular sensation, like feeling pain or having a visual impression of red. Others can be wrong just because their criteria, for ascribing to me a kind of visual impression, are how I act, and in particular, what I say when asked to explain what I see or what I mean. Since criteria are defeasible (for example, I might be lying), appearances can be deceiving. Now when we consider my lack of doubt about my own experiences, one might think that this lack of doubt stems from the fact that I have cognitive access to something (my qualia or my intentional states) that no one else can have access to. That much is implied when one moves from saying that we do not know sometimes what someone means, to saying that we can never know what she really means.[75] A private language is one stripped of all public criteria, such that we are not only uncertain as to what someone means, but it is also impossible for us to catch on to what they could have in mind.

Now one way of filling out this picture is to say that my ability to use ordinary words like 'red' to describe what I see rests on an underlying act of recognizing an inner mental object which no one else has access to. Recognition involves my grasping that *that*, the occurrent quale, is of the kind that is called 'red'. Because a conventional connection has been established in the past between qualia of that type and the term 'red', I am justified in calling this quale the same, namely 'red'. On the other hand, since others can only relate my judgements to my behaviour, they do not, and cannot, know whether I am really justified in calling that quale the same. The difficulty with this as a model of the semantics of the ordinary word 'red', however, stems from the introduction of a private criterion. If my first-person judgements of my visual sensations are made true by fitting qualia of the appropriate type, this implies the possibility of my being wrong about what that type is. I would be wrong if I incorrectly identified the quale type, and so, for example, mistakenly took it to be of the type that is called 'red' when, in fact it was of the type called 'green'. But if I understand what 'red' means, then it makes no sense for me to doubt whether my impression really *is* red or not.[76] We can of course be mistaken in our judgements about what colours we are seeing, when as young children, we have not yet mastered colour terms. But in that learning process, it only makes sense to speak of young children as making mistakes because there are obvious criteria for their understanding or misunderstanding the meaning of a word.[77] But on the model discussed above, it has to be possible that someone could understand what 'red' means and yet doubt whether he was correct in calling a given quale 'red'.[78] This does not make sense.

Another way to make this point is to say that the Cartesian model implies a phenomenologically inaccurate picture of sensory experiences in the following sense. To the extent that the model involves a distinction between recognizing a quale of a particular type and remembering that *that* type is called 'red', the model supposes we can identify qualia which are called 'red' (or 'pain', or 'tingling sensation', etc.) without identifying them *as* red qualia. But that possibility does not seem to be true at all of experiences of red or pain. There are cases in which we can recognize things independently of knowing what they are called. For example, we can easily think of recognizing a particular kind of bird, and then grasping that *that* bird is called a sparrow. In this sense, it can be said that my employment of 'sparrow' does not rest on my identifying an inner or private object and subsequently using that object as a criterion.[79] But it makes no sense to speak of identifying something as red by first identifying it as some other type of entity which I am then justified in calling 'red' because of a rule connecting the two. Moreover, even if I could be said to identify red things by way of a prior identification in terms of another property, the first identification would simply generate a regress: why am I justified in identifying the first property as the property of a sensation which is called 'red'?[80]

Let's return to the concept of private language with these difficulties in mind. Unlike English words, logically-private sensation terms lack behavioural criteria such that the private linguist's having a certain sensation is not expressed in what he says or how he acts. Since there are no behavioural criteria for ascribing to him a given experience, there are also no ways that he could be seen to be correct or incorrect in his judgements about his sensations. But if there are no behavioural criteria for his being right about identifying a quale as of a certain type, this leads to a dilemma. Either the private linguist must be taken to employ a private criterion for the use of his private symbol, or he must be taken to lack a criterion altogether. If the former is the case, then this implies that it is possible for the linguist to be mistaken whether an occurrent sensation is called 'S' while fully understanding what 'S' means.[81] But if this is anything like understanding what 'red' means and yet being mistaken whether a given occurrent visual impression is red or not, this possibility is senseless.[82] On the other hand, if the private linguist's use is taken to lack a criterion, no sense has been given to the idea that he is using the symbol in a rule-governed manner to mean one thing rather than another.[83] It is important to note here that the lack of an inner criterion for the employment of a sensation term in the case of ordinary English terms like 'red' does not imply the same problem. This is because there are *other*, non-private criteria available: the very criteria that teachers and parents employ in training young children to use words in accordance with their conventional meanings. But when the private linguist interlocutor imagines a purer language divested of those seemingly 'extrinsic', or merely pragmatic, criteria, and instead built upon the inherent properties of his experience – his qualia – he is not imagining something impossible, but something devoid of all essential details. What he takes to be the real artichoke is in fact the empty carcass surrounded by extraneous leaves.

Sameness and the semantics of ineffability

What light do the results of Wittgenstein's arguments against private language shed on the ineffability intuition? Is Wittgenstein arguing that visual experience is *not* ineffable with respect to the characteristics of being logically-private or inarticulable? I hope that by now the answer to this is clearly negative, and that Wittgenstein is not simply remaining agnostic on the issue. Consider logical privacy. As I have interpreted the private language arguments, each of the ways that the private linguist took his private symbol to constitute a refined semantics, in comparison to ordinary English, can be shown to be a fatal impoverishment of the concept of a symbol and an experience that is purportedly picked out by that symbol. If these arguments are plausible, then they change one's understanding of the ineffability intuition.

From the third-person standpoint with which I approached the concept of private language, the gist of the argument was that ordinary criteria for ascribing language use to a person or community involve reference to a normative regularity in their behaviour, constituted by way of an agreement between what they utter (vocalize) and how they act. This suggested a connection that the ineffability intuition obliterated: namely, the connection between what someone means by a word and what role that word plays in his actions. If ineffability was supposed to indicate a subjective dimension of experience where the meanings of a person's (or community's) words are covertly constituted, then the intuition is of course misguided. But if we take it to bespeak the diverse criteria we employ in attributing normative regularity to a language user, the intuition is fecund. What someone means is not located somewhere in his cerebral cortex or visual system, or for that matter, in the intentions of an *ego cogitans*. Meaning is not *located* anywhere, although our ascriptions of meaningful language use are based on criteria, such as how someone behaves.

As we saw, Dennett's attack on qualia rested firmly on a verificationist principle. According to that view, a seemingly rule-governed vocalization which could not be translated would simply fail as evidence of language, since the hypothesis that the private linguist was following a rule would be unverifiable. This is in fact how he interprets the private language arguments.[84] But this view distorts the gist of the exercise. On the one hand, Dennett's remark overlooks the fact that a denial of private language would be as nonsensical, in light of Wittgenstein's investigations, as an affirmation. This is because the problem with private language is not that it is not possible because, for example, it cannot instantiate some *a priori* adequacy condition that anything which is to be called language must meet. Rather, it is because the notion cannot be made fully intelligible. This failure is not effected by comparing the interlocutor's suggestions to some criterion deduced from naturalistic research into language, but simply by comparing the interlocutor's use of concepts with their ordinary uses. This is not of course a knock-down, drag-out argument meant to attack faulty premises or faulty inferences, but one which aims to effect a change in how one sees the facts and their significance. I have argued that the private language arguments are best understood as being directed against a certain dissatisfaction with natural language. In leading the private linguist-interlocutor's uses of notions such as sensation, rule, criterion and language back to the circumstances of their ordinary employment, the arguments work to question the intelligibility of the conception of privacy forwarded by the interlocutor, not to deny the possibility of privacy.

Wittgenstein's point is that the fact of language employment is not something for which we need behavioural evidence. Rather, what we call language employment is something manifested *in* someone's behaviour. Whether or not that behaviour does in fact count as manifesting language use is something which is not decided by any individualistic facts about those linguists, but rather by the judgements of those who would know; namely, language users. None of this precludes the possibility of revolutionaries or geniuses whose discoveries, manifested in strange linguistic innovations, are not immediately intelligible to their tribe. But it does mean that the distinction between the nutcase who is speaking gibberish and the genius whose unintelligible utterances in fact pick out a new phenomenon, or a new way of seeing an old one, can only be given sense by a future revelation of the genius's authenticity.[85]

The concept of qualia is supposed to make sense of the idea of our visual experience having certain inherent properties (qualia) independently of the ways that experience is reacted to, judged or conceived. On Dennett's analysis, this idea succumbed to a verificationist argument which undercut the claim of the coffee tasters to incorrigible knowledge of what the Maxwell House coffee tastes like independently of their reactions or standards. His argument concluded with the suggestion that if a distinction between inherent taste and reaction could be maintained, then it would fall to an empirical neuropsychology to decide where a change in taste was to be located. The private language arguments also level a criticism against the distinction between experience and reaction so construed. Any inner quale which might serve as a criterion for applying a concept would carry with it the possibility of discord with the criterion, thus impugning the incorrigible status of avowals. On the other hand, if first-person ascriptions do not rest on a private criterion, then either the private linguist cannot be said to be following a rule, or his concept use must be taken to rest on public criteria, as in the case with ordinary English colour terms.

These considerations do not imply that a distinction cannot be drawn between my experience and how I react to it, but it does suggest that qualia are not needed to make sense of the distinction. Rather, like all conceptual distinctions, this one rests on criteria. This shows that Dennett's conclusion is misleading insofar as he takes the dissolution of the notion of avowals' incorrigibility to imply that the distinction between experience and reaction can only be clarified empirically. This is a misleading conclusion because it tacitly assumes, in the guise of an empirical discovery, a neural criterion for drawing the distinction. While that criterion may be perfectly justifiable, and even a necessary presupposition for neuropsychology, it overlooks all of the other ways the distinction might be drawn; *inter alia* it overlooks the other reasons we might have for drawing the distinction, and other needs which might subserve its significance.

As I have portrayed it, the ineffability intuition has to do with a sense of being confronted with the limits of natural language. We are led to the concept of qualia by trying to flesh out this picture of there being something that cannot be put into (public) words, that defies translation. The picture is one in which ordinary public language is too coarse, in part because the criteria for what is to count as similar to, or different from, are shaped by the pragmatic needs of communication.[86] A private language, by contrast, would have a semantics fixed by the inherent properties of my visual experience, that is, by my visual qualia. But as we saw, eliminating ordinary criteria for what is to count as the same as, or different from, a given experience, or property thereof, leads to a hopelessly indeterminate conception of a criterion.

This throws into a new light the private linguist's assumptions regarding the expressive limitations of natural language. If natural, public language is not defective in the ways the interlocutor imagines it to be, then his inabilities to convey the private contents of his experience have more to do with his own shortcomings as a particular speaker of ordinary language, or with his own unreasonable demands on what that language should allow him to do. What those shortcomings and unreasonable demands might be is not explicitly investigated by Wittgenstein. But it is plausible to speculate that they have to do with such things as the difficulty of mastering a language or the difficulty of becoming a good communicator. If my experience is articulate and meaningful as it stands, my inability to express what it contains can be attributed to the impersonal constraints posed by shared systems of representation, rather than my own lack of mastery of those systems. But that is like blaming a musical instrument for one's own lack of musical fingers and musical ears. There's a personal responsibility to find meaningful things to say that can be passed off on to language.

I have suggested that Wittgenstein's treatment of the concept of private experience offers an insight into the phenomenon of ineffability that Dennett's does not. The intuition about private experience is connected to the idea that my immediate experience presents me with a given reality which transcends all the limited conventions available for articulating discursively what I see. In this sense, ostensive references to what is understood as private experience represent a kind of lived refutation of the idea that what we see and how we see it are shaped by the categorical distinctions we bring to experience. Conceiving the possibility of such refutation involves establishing the possibility for a private language, where the meanings of the private symbols would be established by ostensively defining the inherent phenomenal kinds of one's experience, based on inherent quale-types. These qualia would then serve as paradigms guiding one's employment of the private symbols. They would serve this role just because what lies before my awareness carries with it its own significance; a meaning that it has independently of whatever purposes I might have for referring to it or naming it. This represents the characteristic logical *purity* that private language intends. Simply by attending to a quale, and, in fact, in virtue of doing so, I would understand what I am attending to in such a way that I would be able to recognize the same on future occasions. Hence, the similarities and differences reflected by my private language would be freed from the Procrustean understandings of sameness and difference in public, workaday language.

So, one lesson of the private language arguments is that disregarding those public criteria for sameness only results in an unjustifiable pretence that the activity resembling language is in fact rule-governed. One particular criterion of sameness, that is, a criterion of what is to count as the same as some quale that I ostensively defined for myself, cannot be had, just because without a practice of usage too many understandings of what would be 'the same as' *that* can follow. Things in themselves, in particular visual impressions, can offer no bedrock for determinate reference, just because it makes no sense to talk of intrinsic similarity.

> 'A thing is identical to itself.' There is no finer example of a useless proposition, which yet is connected with a certain play of the imagination. It is as if in imagination we put a thing into its own shape and saw that it fit.[87]

This throws the ineffability intuition into a new light. Consider the concept of an ideal description of what is seen; a description which would capture *exactly* what is seen. Ineffability suggests that there is such a description, but one which is too rich and too subtle for (human?) language. Such a description would be unlike ordinary descriptions which, employing criteria shaped by various instrumental needs, necessarily overlook certain features, emphasize others, and represent their content under a particular light.[88] The criterion for accuracy and completeness would thus have to be something like: correspondence with the experience itself, with the visual impressions or qualia themselves. Having abstracted the idea of a description from any use it may subserve, however, it is not clear what the description could be said to *convey*. For instance, an ideal description would be like an 'ideal clock', with hands that always point to the immediate moment 'now'.[89] In a sense, such a clock would not refer to anything beyond the 'immediate moment', since it would not refer to the present as one moment among others, as one time among others, and as having a *conventionally* defined duration. Such a clock, we might say, refers to time in a way that does not subserve any particular instrumental need. And that might suggest that it is therefore purer or more accurate. So then one might, in turn, imagine that we could use that ideal measurement of the present to determine the accuracy of various time-keeping devices, in a way analogous to how a private-qualia language might be thought to serve as a criterion for the validity of ordinary concepts or grammatical distinctions. But it is easy to see, of course, that that idea is absurd. A clock that pointed only to the immediate present moment, the 'now', would not merely be useless for *practical* purposes, it could not be said to be telling time at all. It would not be clear why we would want to call it a clock. Analogously, a private language which employed concepts only referring to my qualia could not be used to say anything, and so would not be a language. This shows why the attempt to refute idealism is misdirected. It is not that language gets in the way, or that qualia by their very nature cannot be referred to. It is that the ways that what we see can be described outstrip the way any given description represents them, and so the way a given description could be used to represent them. The sense in which visual experience is ineffable is the sense in which no description we can offer of what we see will ever guarantee that there are not other true things to say, or other ways to say them, regarding what is seen.

On Dennett's view, there is a sense in which experience is ineffable, but it is merely what he calls a 'practical ineffability'. It is not surprising that this sense is construed, insofar as it has any positive cognitive value, as a vague premonition of a truth that can only adequately be understood from within the framework of naturalistic, perceptual psychology. Consider 'Intuition pump #13: the osprey cry'. In this example, Dennett imagines identifying an osprey visually, and then hearing its cry; a cry which is described in Peterson's bird guidebook as 'a series of short, sharp, cheeping whistles, *cheep cheep*, or *chewk chewk*'.[90]

> So *that's* what it sounds like, I say to myself, ostending – it seems – a particular mental complex of intrinsic, ineffable qualia. I dub the complex 'S' (*pace* Wittgenstein), rehearse it in short-term memory, check it against the bird book descriptions, and see that while the verbal descriptions are true, accurate and even poetically evocative – I decide I could not do better with a thousand words – they still fall short of *capturing* the qualia-complex I have called S. In fact, that is why I need the neologism, 'S', to refer directly to the ineffable property I cannot pick out by description.[91]

Arguing explicitly against Kripke's interpretation of Wittgenstein, Dennett goes on to dismiss sceptical worries about a private, ostensive definition being irreducibly ambiguous by attributing the referential difficulties of linguistic description to the informational richness of the osprey call. According to Dennett, in ostending the qualia complex identified as an osprey call, I am tacitly identifying a property-detector in myself; one which, given suitable field-training, may serve me as a highly reliable way of identifying ospreys. The perceived ineffability of the cry is merely practical in the sense that the informational complexity of the call, and along with it, the informational sensitivity of my nervous system, belies any translation into ordinary discourse.

Like his diagnosis of the difficulty in distinguishing between changes in what is experienced and changes in reactions to what is experienced, Dennett's analysis also misleads by tacitly introducing a neuro-physiological criterion for deciding what is to count as the same.[92] His example of hearing an osprey call and identifying a property-detector is of course perfectly plausible, but it trivializes the results of the private language arguments. We can, of course, decide to adopt criteria for what we experience based on correlations we can draw between events in the world and events in the nervous system, but then that would be a *decision*, which would necessarily ignore other criteria we might want to adopt for various other reasons. Our experience will not decide this for us, and neither will better empirical knowledge of our perceptual faculties. There are too many ways that two different entities, for example, percepts, could be said to be the same; too many valid reasons we could have for calling two entities instances of the same.

Finally, Dennett chalks the interest in qualia up to an irrational fear of science and materialism on behalf of their defenders, as a 'last ditch defense of the inwardness and elusiveness of our minds, a bulwark against creeping mechanism'.[93] This might very well be true of the motives of some defenders of qualia. However, from the perspective of Wittgenstein's criticisms, Dennett's diagnosis can be turned on its head. Verificationist criticisms of the possibility of private experience might plausibly be seen as expressions of a characteristic psychological need that the natural scientist has to justify his methodological constraints. In denying private experience, the scientific philosopher can be seen as saying: nothing that is irrelevant to my methods exists; in effect offering a metaphysical justification for the relevance of those methods and the interests driving their adoption. When we turn to aesthetic perception in the final chapter, this result will be put to use.

4

Causality and visual form

... 'naive language', that is to say our naive, normal way of expressing ourselves, does not contain any theory of seeing – does not show you a theory but only a concept of seeing.[1]

Between naturalism and visuality

What does it mean to understand perception naturalistically? How much of the meaning of vision is socially constituted? How does Wittgensteinian analysis negotiate the distinction between nature and culture in the study of perception?

Much debate and ongoing controversy surrounds the issue of just how scientific and humanistic accounts of perception should be understood to relate to each other. Generally, the issue is an example of the 'two cultures' problem, diagnosed originally by C. P. Snow and still lingering within the academy. More specifically, the issue pertains to the relative epistemological virtues and liabilities of naturalistic vision science on the one hand, and on the other, the humanistic study of visuality one finds in the burgeoning field of visual culture studies. A Wittgensteinian way to see the connections involved is to examine how each epistemological context relates specifically to the ordinary grammar of sight, while at the same time paying attention to the meta-theoretical confusions one is liable to fall into in grasping that relation correctly.

When our view of the mind's relationship to the body and the world was still broadly Cartesian, there was a straightforward way to understand the relationship between science and the humanities. Science studies bodies, or matter, and the causal order of the natural world, while the humanities study minds, or the incorporeal, free, rational being which, in human beings, resides mysteriously in an ontologically distinct body. Cartesianism is, however, in ill repute in both contexts, even though both are still working to free themselves from the conceptual vestiges of that framework. Now, conceptual change means fluctuations in criteria; just the kind of issue that Wittgenstein's grammatical investigations are meant to shed light on. As I shall argue in what follows, grammatical analysis sheds light on the questions raised above by showing how both naturalistic and humanistic accounts of sight piggyback epistemologically on ordinary grammar, contributing to its scope, but neither justifying nor repudiating its validity. On occasion, scientific discoveries do cause us to revise our conceptual use, but then the use has changed because now how we act has changed. This is because, as Wittgenstein's enquiries suggest, meaning is constituted by practice or use. A concept of seeing is valid in the same sense that a way of life is valid. Analogously, a concept of seeing is best understood as a complex web of convention and nature, too intricate and vast in its ramifications to generalize about, but available for clarification in light of specific philosophical questions.

Naturalism in the study of perception

In vision science, the post-Cartesian view of the embodied mind focuses the enquiry on understanding how perception and cognition fit into the causal order of physical nature. The root of the problem with the Cartesian view of perception, on this view is that, since perception is an activity of an immaterial mind, it is difficult to understand how perceptual experiences could relate causally to the world, or to the body, since the mind qua incorporeal cannot enter into causal relations with physical nature. For instance, it seems that if perception gives us knowledge of the world, it must do so on the basis of some sort of causal relationship with the object of perception: if perception is not causally effected by its object, it is difficult to see how it could be cognitively receptive to it. An even deeper problem with Cartesianism is that it violates the more fundamental scientific principle of the Conservation of Momentum or the Causal Closure of Nature,[2] by entailing that one can have effects without causes. Naturalism in perceptual theorizing can, therefore, be defined rather straightforwardly in terms of how one understands the relationship between explanation and causality when it comes to analysing the meaning of psychological or mentalistic concepts. Richard Rorty's definition will thus serve my present purposes. He says that naturalists of the philosophy of mind are those who 'believe that all explanation is causal explanation of the actual, and that there is no such thing as a noncausal condition of possibility'.[3] It should be noted that this formulation straddles the distinction sometimes drawn between naturalism understood as an explanatory framework (methodological naturalism), and naturalism as an ontological thesis (metaphysical naturalism).

Methodological naturalism stems from thinkers such as Hume and Hartley, and concerns the attempt to provide psychological phenomena with the kind of explanations given in natural sciences such as physics, optics and astronomy. It involves the important aspect of giving an epistemically-neutral account of perception and belief-formation. In contrast, metaphysical naturalism, which originates with thinkers such as Hobbes and La Mettrie, is an ontological thesis in which *to be* is equated with material existence, where matter is defined in terms of its causal properties.[4] The theories of early vision that I examined in the second chapter help to illustrate these features; for example, the idea that visual form is meaningful in virtue of its syntax, which can be specified in terms of local, physical, hence causal, properties of signals and their relations. There I tried to show how grammatical analysis stood epistemically in relation to those theories. So this raises the question: Is Wittgenstein a naturalist? Is his approach to perceptual psychology naturalistic?

On one reading, he is clearly not an epistemological naturalist. If naturalism involves causal explanation, and so the analysis of perception in terms of causal mechanisms, then he would seem to be an idealist. Consider again Wittgenstein's discussion of aspect-seeing where he begins by laying down a distinction between conceptual and causal analysis. Speaking of the phenomenon of noticing an aspect he says: 'Its *causes* are of interest to psychologists. We are interested in the concept and its place among the concepts of experience.'[5] Remarks like this support the view of Wittgenstein's philosophy as a kind of de-transcendentalized Kantianism, in which a radical discontinuity is assumed between the normative and the natural. For instance, Richard Rorty interprets Wittgenstein as drawing that very distinction as part of a last-ditch effort to maintain the autonomy of philosophy, against natural science, by cordoning off a special philosophical subject-matter (depth grammar) that requires a special philosophical method (grammatical investigation).[6] This reading is often cut from the same cloth as the idea that Wittgenstein is an ordinary-language philosopher who dogmatically elevates colloquial discourse into a canon for ascertaining meaningful language use; this as a way of attacking philosophical *theorizing* about mind and language, in much the same way that the logical positivists used verificationism to attack traditional metaphysics.

In another sense, however, Wittgenstein is clearly not an idealist. Epistemological naturalism is generally associated with the rejection of the distinction between *a priori* and *a posteriori* knowledge, and so a rejection of the idea that there is a kind of knowledge that cannot be corrected in light of future evidence. On the critical realist theory of knowledge, often associated with naturalism, beliefs which cannot be corrected cannot be disconfirmed and so lack any genuine cognitive content. In defending the autonomy of ordinary conceptual grammar, is Wittgenstein assuming some kind of knowledge that cannot be corrected by future experience? Yes and no. Consider the analogy to Kant that is often drawn by naturalist critics of Wittgenstein. In Kant's rejection of naturalism as an epistemological doctrine, he was content to draw a methodological and apparently metaphysical distinction between the natural and the normative. While research in the domain of nature involves enquiry into the causal conditions for a given phenomenon, the domain of normativity is construed in terms of a taxonomy of transcendental conditions for the possibility of the phenomenon as studied naturalistically in science.[7] These conditions involve not only the principles of logic, but conditions for 'experience' itself. According to Kant's theory, the peculiar status of the subject-matter of transcendental philosophy, the analysis of normativity, did not serve as a basis for undercutting the possibility of an empirical science of mentality, but only certain ways in which such a science might be interpreted.[8]

Like Kant, Wittgenstein works with a distinction between empirical and conceptual (or grammatical) ways in which a statement or a concept can be taken. But the analogy with Kant applies less to the idea of a distinctive subject-matter (depth grammar or logical syntax) and more to the idea of being able to adopt different explanatory perspectives on psychological phenomena. In the case of Wittgenstein, there is no appeal to transcendental *a priori* structure. On his view, the attempt to offer an explanation of the 'objective validity' of our concepts is to misunderstand how the semantics of such concepts are fixed; specifically, the role criteria play in our use of systems of representation and communication. That is why Kant's attempt to offer such an argument leads into 'metaphysics' in Wittgenstein's pejorative sense of the term as an enquiry resting on a confusion of the conceptual and the empirical. Unlike Kant, Wittgenstein does not criticize the introduction of causal criteria into conceptual analysis *per se*, but only insofar as causal criteria are taken to explain ordinary conceptual practices. He even illustrates how a new conceptual criterion might be introduced when he discusses the Necker cube:

> Imagine a physiological explanation [for why noticing an aspect seeing of the Necker cube is a genuine case of seeing]. Let it be this: When we look at the figure, our eyes scan it repeatedly, always following a particular path. The path corresponds to a particular pattern of oscillation of the eyeballs in the act of looking. It is possible to jump from one such pattern to another and for the two to alternate ... Let this be the explanation. – 'yes, that shows it is a kind of *seeing*.' – You now have introduced a new, a physiological [causal] criterion for seeing.[9]

In this sense, one might call Wittgenstein a naturalist, since he does not believe that our concepts are timeless. On his view, however, rather than explaining ordinary use, causal analyses *contribute* to the grammar of psychological terms by introducing new criteria. As I argued above, this does not mean that seeing cannot be explained, but only that what is explained by an empirical, psychological theory of visual perception is never all, or even most of, what we ordinarily mean by 'see'. Our understanding of what it means to see, as embodied in the ordinary use of perceptual expressions, is *not* subject to correction in light of future evidence, in the same way that the rules of chess are not subject to correction in light of future evidence. That does not mean that the game of chess may *never* change in the future, as it undoubtedly has in the past. But if the rules of chess do change in the future, it will not be because we have discovered what the 'true' rules are, or what the (until now) hidden essence of the game is. It will be for some other reason, for example, because changing or adding a rule makes the game more interesting or more fun to play.

In the case of psychological concepts, grammatical changes can occur because of changes in our beliefs about the world, or changes in the world itself, which upset the natural background conditions upon which we employ language. These are the kinds of changes that epistemological naturalism emphasizes. Take the example of the shame that medieval monks once felt in wearing eyeglasses. It was once believed that poor eyesight was expressive of moral weakness. No doubt a connection was once believed to exist between the inability to see right from wrong and the inability to see, for example, who is at the door. One can imagine how the ways people spoke of and understood cases of physiologically-impaired vision *changed* when genuine scientific discoveries in the physiology of vision disproved this connection. This does not imply, however, that there are no connections between ethical and ocular blindness. Surely there are many ways that our ethical beliefs and dispositions and social institutions affect our perceptual habits and epistemological agendas. It is just that now it no longer *makes sense* to blame certain kinds of blindness on someone's ethical shortcomings. There are surely other kinds of blindness that can be so blamed. Much injustice turns on the sometimes deliberate, but often pre-conscious, choice of individuals to not see certain political realities.

So, epistemological naturalism is a useful theory of knowledge if understood in the above sense. Where it goes wrong is by insisting that naturalistic explanations of sight are the only genuine explanations of sight; or correlatively, that naturalistic understanding is the only genuine form of understanding of mental concepts. But if meaning is determined by use, understanding is embedded in practice, and explanation is related to the teaching of the practice. Then ordinary explanations of 'see' which, for example, ostensively define seeing in terms of conventional criteria qua rules for the correct (i.e. grammatical) use of the word, are genuinely explanatory. They are explanatory in the sense that they lead to understanding: understanding as knowing how to go on. Such explanations are akin to explanations of how a particular chess piece functions in the game, for example, 'the pawn starts *here* and can move this way and cannot do this', etc. To insist that epistemological naturalism precludes non-naturalistic explanatory forms is, therefore, to set up natural science as an ethical authority, as the ultimate arbiter, not simply of theoretical knowledge, but of practical knowledge as well. That is called scientism, although as I've argued above, I don't think that naturalism entails scientism.

While conceptual grammar is epistemologically autonomous in the relevant Wittgensteinian sense, homespun *theories* of perception surely are not, and usually are corrected, or simply repudiated, by developments in naturalistic knowledge of mind. Take the now long-since refuted extromission theory of seeing. According to this theory, perception is the result of a reaction between particles projected from the eyes, and particles emitted from perceivables. One can imagine why someone might have thought that seeing involves the physical extending of the eye out into the world. As Rudolf Arnheim describes it, seeing can often feel as if it is a kind of touching, almost like an invisible hand. The experience suggests a certain hypothesis.

> In looking at an object we reach out for it. With an invisible finger we move through the space around us, go out to distant places where things are found, touch them, catch them, trace their borders, explore their texture ... Impressed by this experience, early thinkers described the physical process of vision accordingly.[10]

The theory is false, but a less untruthful model of sight was not available until the beginning of the modern scientific revolution in the sixteenth century when thinkers such as Descartes, Kepler, Snell and da Vinci began to understand light, and specifically the laws governing the propagation of light waves. Minimally, if understanding sight scientifically involves understanding what light is, then one needs to understand James Clerk Maxwell's laws of electromagnetic radiation. On top of that, mind science is many years away from understanding even the most basic features of mentality, and the issue of consciousness has not yet been downgraded from a complete mystery to a legitimate scientific problem. Naturalistically conceived, we are barely justified in claiming to understand what it means to see.

The difficulty stems largely from the difficulty of understanding the complex causal mechanisms and relations involved with perception and cognition. The extromission theory illustrates the problem well: how does sight serve to connect the mind to the world without seeming to make contact with it? It is easy to grasp here that what is at issue is the understanding of seeing as a causal process. It is this particular epistemic interest that naturalism as a metaphysical doctrine articulates.

As an ontological thesis, metaphysical naturalism has to do with our conceptual criteria for ascribing reality to a thing: to be real is to have causal properties. As such, the thesis implies, against idealisms of various sorts, that there is nothing about the mind that cannot be explained in terms of causal relations. This rules out, for example, Descartes' notion of an *ego cogitans*, as the spatially-unextended, immaterial substance of the mind; Kant's transcendental ego as the unity of the noncausal conditions of experience; Heidegger's

analysis of human nature in terms of *Dasein* as an existential–ontological structure; and of course, the Judeo–Christian notion of the soul, as an unchanging,
eternal and spiritual structure. Is Wittgenstein a naturalist in this metaphysical sense? Again, I'll have to say that the answer is yes and no. The ambiguity
of the answer turns on just how one understands the metaphysical claims of
naturalism. In order to understand where Wittgenstein's analysis leads here,
I'll focus first on the question of the extent to which causality enters into the
conceptual analysis of perception as a psychological state, by examining Paul
Grice's version of the causal theory of perception. Then I shall move on
to examine the doctrine of minimal physicalism in the philosophy of mind,
to see how causal criteria are used to define the content of perceptual states.
Here I'll make use of Jaegwon Kim's account of the thesis of psychophysical supervenience to show how Wittgenstein's understanding of metaphysical
naturalism diverges from the way it is usually understood in the philosophy
of mind.

The causal theory of perception (Paul Grice)

> Of course, if water boils in a pot, steam comes out of the pot and also pic-
> tured steam comes out of the pictured pot. But what if one insisted on
> saying that there must also be something boiling in the picture of the pot?[11]

Isn't the very idea of explanation rooted in the idea of causality? To explain
what something is seems to mean, essentially, to explain the causes of its being
what it is. If a metaphysical naturalist sees causal explanations as the only genuine explanations, then it seems obvious that we cannot call Wittgenstein a
naturalist. As I interpreted his analysis of psychological concepts, explanation
is connected more to understanding than to causality, while understanding is
connected to conceptual practice, not to theoretical comprehension. Does this
make Wittgenstein an idealist of sorts? An examination of the causal theory of
perception, construed as an analysis of the concept of *seeing*, helps to shed light
on this question and, therefore, on what is epistemologically cogent about the
doctrine of metaphysical naturalism.

The epistemological relevance of the causal theory of perception might
seem to have passed away with the issue of external world scepticism.[12] Independent of the sceptical problematic, however, the causal theory of perception
offers a model for understanding how causal terms can be understood to enter
into the analysis of visual perception. Grice's version helps to locate points of
intersection between the semantic studies of concepts, offered by Wittgenstein, and the ontological and methodological implications of naturalism for
the study of psychological phenomena. On Paul Grice's model of the causal

theory of perception, the idea of a causal connection enters into the logical analysis of the concept of seeing.[13] As he argues, it is a literal contradiction to say that some perceiver S is seeing an object p and to deny that p is causally responsible for S's visual experience of p. The problem with this move, or what I shall refer to as its restricted validity as an interpretation of the concept of seeing, is that for many uses of the term, 'see' is not only *not* analysable in terms of a causal relation, it is not analysable in terms of a relation at all. What kind of state is to count as *a perceptual state*, for example, a state of seeing, as opposed to one of imagining, an apple, and what counts as a perceptual state with a particular content p, are matters fixed by criteria for employing the concept of seeing. As I shall put it, the phenomena playing these criterial roles in the ordinary use of the English word 'see' are not *necessarily* amenable to characterization in terms of a relation between an observer and a perceivable, let alone a causal-nomological relation. This is not to deny the responsiveness of seeing to what is seen, but only to question the way that the causal theory of perception insists that it be understood.

The basic structure of the causal theory of perception is simple and follows from the logical structure of the relation between cause and effect. More specifically, it follows from a nomological conception of causality which takes cause and effect to be, minimally, logically-distinct, independently specifiable entities. Having adopted the causal schema, Grice's argument consists in showing that (i) there is something that plays the role of the percept-effect (i.e. a sense-datum), and (ii) that it is a causal relation of sorts that the percept must stand in with the perceptual object in order for it to be true that S sees p. I shall focus on the second part.[14] The logical independence of cause and effect is, on the view of causality operative in the theory, generally connected to the further assumption that entities defined as elements of a causal sequence fall under a covering law, which describes a nomological relation between the two entities. The nomological relation posited between cause and effect is related to the idea of the informativeness of the senses, where what is informative about some thing, for example, an optic array, stands in a relation of nomic dependence to how things are in the world.

Grice begins with a statement of the necessary and sufficient conditions for seeing, borrowed from H. H. Price: 'It is a necessary and sufficient condition for its being the case that X perceives m that X's sense-impression should be causally dependent on some state of affairs involving m.'[15] According to Grice, the causal connection to m is shown to be a necessary condition for seeing since it is logically contradictory to say that X sees m, if m isn't causally related to X's sense-impression of m.[16] As he makes the point, if 'X sees a clock on the table' is true, then the clock on the table must be *causally responsible* for X's having the experience of seeing the clock. Grice means by this that it is not enough that the clock be present, on the table. For example, it may be the case that X has an experience of a clock on the table even though the clock on the table is not causally responsible for X's seeing it. There may be a complicated optical illusion set up, using mirrors of various sorts, which conceals the clock from view while at the same time giving X the impression that he is visually perceiving the clock. Analogously, we might imagine the proverbial brain scientist of the future who manages to stimulate the proper neurons in such a way that X experiences (what he takes to be) a percept of a clock. Suppose that the scientist stimulates X's brain in such a way that he experiences a percept of the clock exactly as it would appear if X were seeing the actual clock; the only difference being that the actual clock would not be causally responsible for X's perception. According to Grice's argument, it is incorrect to say that, in the case of the optical trick, X is seeing the clock. Grice argues that it is precisely the clock's not being causally responsible for X's percept that explains *why* it is incorrect.[17]

Now one might be puzzled for at least one of two reasons by Grice's explanation of why the person who is receiving a visual experience of the clock via the brain scientist, and not the clock itself, is not justified in speaking of 'seeing the clock'. For one, we can certainly imagine situations, for example, in a brain research laboratory, where X would speak *informatively* of seeing a clock on the table when asked by the scientist to report what he was experiencing. Imagine the scientist poking and prodding at various clusters of neurons in X's striate cortex and asking him to report his subjective experience. The scientist hits one set and X responds, 'now I am seeing a clock on the table'. Wouldn't the scientist understand what X was saying? Is X wrong in speaking of seeing the clock in this case? Is he incorrect or not justified in this use of the words 'I see a clock on the table'? The first thing to note here is that it is implausible to deny that he is justified in speaking of *seeing* the clock simply because the causes of his impression differ from ordinary cases in which we would speak of seeing a clock on the table. In imagining the above context, we are imagining a certain way of understanding what 'X sees *m*' means; a use of the concept of seeing in which talking of seeing a clock, while in the office of our brain scientist, would be in accordance with the meaning of the concept. If one accepts this as a possible understanding of 'see', then Grice's so-called analysis turns out to be a stipulation that the only proper understandings are ones based on causal criteria. One might understand this as an arbitrary decision on Grice's behalf.

Simply because there are apparent differences in the two uses of 'see' here does not of itself entail that one of them is illicit. An analogous mistake is made when one insists that it is wrong to speak of seeing, for example, Elvis on television; that in the strict sense of 'see', one sees an image or representation of Elvis on the television screen. The naturalness of speaking of seeing Elvis on television reflects a criterial similarity in the use of the concept, hence a continuity of meaning. For instance, in having a visual impression of Elvis on the television screen, we find ourselves confronted with his image, unless of course we turn off the television, or go into the other room. Seeing Elvis on television is, in this sense, very different from imagining that Elvis is on television. But even if one grants Grice's assertion that it is the ordinary case in which the clock itself is causally responsible for X's visual experience of the clock that illustrates the proper sense of the concept, one might raise an analogous objection. In response to Grice's question as to why the ordinary, and not the causally-deviant, case of seeing the clock is in accordance with its true meaning, one might be inclined to answer that that is just what we mean in speaking of seeing a clock. In turn, the reason we are not justified in speaking of seeing the clock, in the case of the manipulative brain scientist or the optical trick, is just that we *are not* seeing the clock; that that situation does not count as seeing a clock. Rather, what counts as being seen are, respectively, a brain image and a mirror image. This shows that what is at stake here is, at least at one level, the justification for how we use the word.

Now this answer to Grice's question as to what justifies us in speaking of seeing in the causally-normal case, and not in the causally-deviant one, does not really seem to be an answer at all. After all, to say that X is right to speak of seeing the clock in the first case, just because that is what 'seeing' means, doesn't explain or justify X's use of the concept. The question just gets transferred: why are we justified in counting *that* as a case of seeing? What is it about the meaning of the concept of seeing that makes the first use true and the second false? If what Grice was originally after was an analysis of the concept of seeing in terms of necessary and sufficient truth-conditions, then this kind of explanation offers no help. But this is just what needs to be questioned: what it means to explain the meaning of a concept like *see*. Is this result naturalistic?

If one has already assumed that all explanation is causal-nomological explanation, then clarifying the meaning of sight by pointing to the relevant behaviour in context does not elucidate a criterion for applying the concept, but simply indicates an associated behavioural manifestation of seeing: seeing-behaviour. It is significant that Grice's example of a use of 'see' is abstract, in the sense that it makes no mention of any behaviour or background circumstances we would ordinarily associate with seeing. That there is no mention of behaviour suggests that we need not imagine any behaviour or context in order to illustrate what 'see' means. (In fact, we did have to imagine what such behaviour would look like – for example, how we would ordinarily know that someone was seeing, or could see the clock – in order to understand why the example was an example of seeing.) This is already to suppose an answer of a particular kind to the question as to how we are to give an account of the meaning. If the meaning of the concept is determined by its referring, or attributing, a perceptual state to someone, the example need not say anything about the behaviour of the perceiver.

Why does Grice assume that the concept of sight bears no logical connections to behaviour? For one, it would seem to be a plausible assumption, even a truism, that one cannot see, on some accounts a strict sense of 'see', Xena's seeing of the clock. We can only infer, on the basis of what we can see, her physical movements and noises, and of what we already know about the situation, for example, that she needs to be at work by nine, that she is seeing, or has seen, the clock.[18] But why draw the distinction here between what can be seen, in a sense narrower than how 'see' is usually employed, and what is inferred on the basis of what is seen? That a narrower sense of 'see' would have to be employed here is shown by the fact that we typically speak more broadly of seeing, for example, how someone is feeling, or that she is thinking about what to wear, or that she has just figured out the solution to a puzzle. We often do not draw a distinction between physical behaviour which can be seen, and some internal state which cannot be seen but is inferred from what is seen. That is, there are various reasons for thinking that behaviour is not logically distinct from psychological ascriptions.

Let's consider the example of seeing the clock on the table again, but this time add some flesh to the bones. Xena walks into the room, looks at her arm to find no watch, and is about to ask me something, when she spies a clock on the table. 'I'm late!', she shouts, rushing out of the room. I look at the clock which reads 9:07, and I also know that she is supposed to be at work by 9. Now take the question: what makes it true that Xena has seen the clock? The answer suggested above was: *that* is just what 'see' means. If asked to explain why the example illustrated the meaning of 'see', one could point to various aspects of her behaviour and various aspects of the context. For example, one is the fact that Xena realized that she was late for work, and that only the clock could inform her of the time; in order to be informed by the clock, she had to have seen it. One might also point to her facial expression, the expression of noticing the clock: her eyes fixing on the clock's face, the moment of pause in her bodily motion, her subsequent utterance 'I'm late'. In this situation, it is also important that her prior behaviour suggested that she did not know what time it was, and that the clock answered her question, and that the clock was the only thing that could answer her. When I refer to these various aspects of the context of the ascription to Xena, I am offering reasons – justifications – for using the concept of seeing in this way.

To clarify, this Wittgensteinian criticism of Grice's causal theory of perception surely does not mean that the theory per se is false as an analysis of the concept of seeing. Such a claim would assume that there is one analysis of the concept of seeing that captures all of its grammatical articulation. But that is just the assumption that I criticized in Chapter One as the 'Socratic model' of semantic analysis. Rather, my point is that Grice's analysis is true of *some* uses of 'see', or not true of all uses. As such, this criticism illustrates a central principle of Wittgenstein's approach to conceptual analysis.

> ... one has to say that in many cases where the question arises 'Is this an appropriate description or not?' The answer is: 'Yes, it is appropriate, but only for this narrowly circumscribed region, not for the whole of what you were claiming to describe.'[19]

Take an ancient version of the causal theory of perception that I mentioned earlier, the extromission theory of perception. That theory, like empirical theories of perception generally, attempts to give an account of the causal relationships involved with perceptual states, and it is incorrect. As it turns out, the eye does not emit microscopic particles but only takes in light waves via the transduction of photonic energy into neurochemical energy in retinal cells. But that doesn't mean that it is simply wrong that the eye does send out looks. People give each other looks all the time, cast off glances, and touch things with their eyes. When I speak of someone casting a glance at something, I am not usually referring to a causal process taking place between her visual system and an object. More likely is that I am referring to her behaviour and how it has been affected by something about that object. Reference to a causal-nomological connection does not enter into the meaning of the use.

This does not mean that I am referring to her behaviour qua behaviour, as logical behaviourists would tend to say, nor that I am inferring on the basis of her behaviour that she is seeing. The first thought evokes the thesis of logical behaviourism, the second, some form of mentalism, and the same criticism which applies to the causal theory of perception generally also bears on these doctrines. Logical behaviourism is just the view that statements which appear to be about mental or psychological states are actually about, in the sense of being logically equivalent to statements about, behaviour or dispositions to behave in various ways. But this is to collapse the distinction between seeing-behaviour that is accompanied by seeing and seeing-behaviour that isn't – for example, a blind person who is inscrutably adept at navigating the edge of the sidewalk.[20] On the other hand, mentalist views of psychological ascriptions interpret such statements as referring to internal physical states of a perceiver. For example, according to a functionalist analysis of seeing, to speak of Xena as seeing the clock is to attribute to her a particular internal state with certain causal powers that, as part of a background proto-theory of human behaviour, account for the observable evidence (current and prior behaviour), and yield predictions of future behaviour. Now as analyses of specific uses of the concept of seeing, there is nothing problematic about these theories of mental ascriptions. But if construed as models valid for every use of the concept of seeing, then they are clearly inadequate.

For instance, both theories distort the expressive connection between behaviour and seeing which obtains in many ordinary senses of seeing. There is an analogy to be drawn here between the sense in which we speak of seeing someone's face in a portrait or drawing, and do not limit the application of 'see' to the material composition, for example, the ink and paper, of the drawing as the true object of vision. That is, we do not speak of inferring from the physical marks on a piece of paper that a drawing is of a face, unless the drawing portrays the face in, say, an abstract or mannerist style. In such cases, we may need to learn to see how the drawing can be seen as a drawing of a face. That is, we may need to learn how to *see* the drawing, period. In cases where no such difficulties present themselves, however, it is more common to speak of the material composition of a drawing as visually *expressing* a human form, in the same way that a certain emotion is expressed by an audible melody. Analogously, we speak of someone's physical behaviour as expressive of their mood. Unless their behaviour is difficult to read, for example, if we cannot tell whether someone is pretentious or simply insecure, we do not speak of the state they are in as something behind, or hidden behind, her behaviour. Now if Xena's behaviour is just expressive of her seeing the clock in this sense, then it is an arbitrary and misleading stipulation to say that her seeing the clock cannot itself be seen, or directly perceived. Her seeing is just there to be seen.

By speaking of the expressive aspect of behaviour, I mean to refer to the way in which behaviour typically associated with psychological states is *about* what it typifies visually. There is something at once more arbitrary, and at the same time, closer conceptually, about the 'relation' between the sense in which someone is sad, and the way that his face shows his sadness, than the way that one proposition entails another analytically. A sad facial expression is more than simply a particular muscular configuration. Sadness is expressed *in* the face, it is not (typically) *inferred* from the face's appearance. In that sense, the sadness is not something entailed by the physical shape of the face. The connection is closer conceptually than entailment, in the sense that each term of the relation contributes to the semantics of the other. This is most obvious in the case of behaviour which cannot be identified independently of its being identified as behaviour *of*, for example, someone who sees, or is hesitant, or is extremely nervous. There are many ordinary examples, and many more easily imagined, in which the behaviour cannot even be specified in any other than a vague, inarticulate gesture. At the same time, it is not as if sadness could not have been expressed differently, or that given different circumstances, the same physical shape could not have been the expression of a different emotional state, say, one of recognition, or intense joy. The connection is more arbitrary than entailment in the sense that we can imagine different behavioural expressions as being expressions of the same psychological state in different circumstances. The logical behaviourist goes wrong in identifying the relation as one of entailment because he takes statements about mental states to be *about* behaviour. But when given behaviour is pointed to as a criterion for a psychological state, for example, that of seeing, the behaviour is pointed to as being *of* seeing. The seeing is not the behaviour itself, it is what the behaviour is about. As Wittgenstein asks: 'What do psychologists record? – What do they observe? Isn't it the behaviour of human beings, in particular their utterances? But *these* are not about behaviour.'[21]

So where does this leave us with the question of naturalism? Broadly construed, an ontological rejection of naturalism could be understood as the thesis that regularities in visual experience which fail to be explicable in causal-nomological terms reveal the distinctive ontological character of the mind. Now if Wittgenstein is saying that, in many senses of the concept, seeing cannot be explained in causal-nomological terms, is he committed to an anti-naturalistic metaphysical thesis? I don't think so. For present purposes, let's define idealism as such a thesis about the distinctive ontological status of mind. Now the first point to make is simply to register a similarity between idealism in that sense and metaphysical naturalism. On the idealist conception of the limits of naturalistic philosophy of mind, and contrary to Wittgenstein, the methodological inapplicability of causal analysis has nothing to do with logico-grammatical connections between psychological ascriptions and behavioural criteria or with the contexts within which such ascriptions are made and to which their semantics are sensitive. In this sense, the idealist view has this much in common with the naturalist view, that they both deny any such connections. As such, they both deny what I referred to as the expressiveness of behaviour, and so the expressivist functions of psychological expressions. In this sense, Wittgenstein's analysis is neither naturalistic, nor idealistic. Rather, it purports to show that the distinction itself rests on a false premise that they both share. They both drastically underestimate the logical complexity of the concept of seeing, and by extension, the concept of mind.

Psychophysical supervenience (Jaegwon Kim)

The prejudice in favor of psychophysical parallelism is a fruit of primitive interpretations of our concepts. For if one allows a causality between psychological phenomena which is not mediated physiologically, one thinks one is professing belief in a gaseous mental entity.[22]

The same dialectical position can be reached by a different route if, instead of thinking about how perception as a process or state is explained, we focus on how perceptual content is measured. A naturalistic understanding of the content of perceptual experience tends to assert that what one sees is always something the structure of which can be completely described in terms of causal-nomological regularities. Call such a view of reality *minimal physicalism*, which we can define, following Jaegwon Kim, as the metaphysical thesis that: 'Only causally-relevant or efficacious properties should count as individuating properties.'[23] Ever since the mind–body problem was reintroduced into mainstream philosophical debate in the late 1950s, with the thesis of mind–brain identity or type physicalism, the primary aim of serious philosophers of mind has been to reconcile mind with minimal physicalism. On Kim's accounting, the solution to this problem is the thesis of psychophysical supervenience, which arose out of criticisms of type physicalism, specifically Hilary Putnam's argument for multiple realizability, and Donald Davidson's argument for anomalous monism.[24] According to the psychophysical supervenience thesis,

> Mental properties *supervene* on physical properties, in that necessarily, for any mental property M, if anything has M at time t, there exists a physical base (or subvenient) property P such that it has P at t, and necessarily anything that has P at a time has M at that time.[25]

Now this thesis has an important consequence for how we think about the actual content of our experience, where by 'actual' content I mean naturalistically permissible content. According to the supervenience theory, every internal psychological state of an organism is supervenient on its synchronous internal physical state in the above sense. Now Kim grants the semantic externalist's point that psychological states are typically individuated in terms of, in the sense of being described using, concepts with references external to a person's internal states. As we saw with the private language arguments, what I mean by a particular symbol depends in part on facts about what I have used it to mean in the past, while third-person ascriptions are tied to behavioural criteria and are context-sensitive. Now according to minimal physicalism, perceptual states are individuated by their causal properties. Given a nomological concept of causality, this means that only internal properties of a mental state can individuate that state, since causality so construed is a local relation requiring physical proximity. Essentially, only syntactical properties count as individuating properties, and so the supervenience thesis requires a distinction between the real, causally-efficacious content, and the virtual, causally-inert content, of a perceptual state. In defending the supervenience thesis, Kim thus utilizes the distinction between narrow and broad content, or between internal and noninternal states, where only the former is taken to be the scientifically proper reference of psychological concepts, or the reference of physicalistically conceived concepts.

Within each noninternal psychological state that enters into the explanation of some action or behavior we can locate an 'internal core state' which
can assume the explanatory role of the noninternal state . . .[26]

To take a now familiar example, this means that one's visual experience of the
duck-rabbit as a duck, is not a real, individuating feature of what one is actually experiencing. This is because, as involving the concept of a duck, the
experience is noncausally dependent on facts about one's past and future relationships with ducks; surely facts which are not supervenient on *synchronous
internal* properties.[27] While from the standpoint of ordinary perceptual ascriptions, my experience is individuated by the concept of a rabbit, as when I say,
'Now I'm seeing a rabbit', minimal physicalism precludes semantic relations
as individuating properties of an experience. So this raises a question. Given
this distinction, between the noninternal state specified by the expression, and
the internal explanatory state that the supervenience thesis requires us to
posit, how does minimal physicalism require us to interpret the status of the
former, i.e. noninternal, state? If the (externalist) semantics of the noninternal
state are what preclude its having genuine causal connections to events in the
world, then we must conclude that such states either have no causal properties
at all, or that they have *nonphysical* causal properties. But both options are
inadmissible to minimal physicalism. If one argues that such states, or aspects
of them, lack causal properties altogether, then one must deny the objective
validity or truth, of any such ascriptions, making them epiphenomenal. That
would mean that, when I claim to see a duck, my statement does not describe
objectively my perceptual state: where a true description of my experience
would refer only to internal, i.e. syntactic properties of the state. On the
other hand, if one takes psychological states to have non-physical causal properties, the principle of the causal closure of nature is violated by adopting some
form of interactionist dualism.

So, does minimal physicalism reveal that Wittgensteinian claims about the
arbitrariness or autonomy of grammar entail ontological dualism or idealism
in the philosophy of mind? I don't think so. The underlying motive of physicalist theories of mind is to reconcile our understanding of psychological concepts with what we know about the nature of reality from our base science,
which is physics. Given its epistemological interests, physics requires descriptions of experience which are constrained by its specific metaphysical and
nomological requirements as a science. Other interests require different ways
of describing how things are, or in the terms of the immediate context, they
require different ways of measuring the content of perception, different mea-
sures of sameness and connectedness and relevance. The dilemma above,
which would have us choose between accepting noninternal states as either
unreal or as ideal, only faces us if we have already presupposed a certain

conception of causality; what I have been referring to as a nomological conception. The nomological view of causality requires us to think of causal statements as resting on a proto-theoretical knowledge of causal laws that underlies the perceived phenomena. This reflects the epistemological interests of natural scientists looking for law-governed regularities in experience, but does it reflect every other interest we might have when we ask someone what she can see? Is it plausible to say that this is the relevant measure of sight in the everyday context of colloquial discourse?

Now if, following Wittgenstein, we accept the epistemological autonomy of our ordinary understanding of what our perceptual experiences are of, are we committed to some form of weird Cartesian non-physical causality? No, we are not. Where the supervenience theory goes wrong is by assuming that the only genuine form of causality is nomological causality. For that notion, which is proprietary for physics but not, say, aesthetics or ordinary discourse, distorts the ways in which perceptual states are individuated in terms of their causes. The distortion arises from the mistaken idea, based on over-generalizing the epistemological interests of natural science, that all genuine causal relations are nomological relations. Now, if there are good reasons for thinking that the highly ramified concept of seeing cannot be analysed as a statement describing truth conditions, or a naturalistic model describing causal mechanisms, then there are reasons for believing the same about the concept of causality.

In her criticism of the long-standing idea that causality involves a necessary connection between two events,[28] G. E. M. Anscombe writes of Hume that

> The discovery was thought to be great. But as touching the equation of causality with necessitation, Hume's thinking did nothing against this but curiously reinforced it. For he himself assumed that NECESSARY CONNECTION is an essential part of the idea of the relation of cause and effect, and he sought for its nature.[29]

Against this conception, Anscombe argues that it is often the case that we are justified in speaking of knowing the cause of an event without supposing at the same time that there is some exceptionless generalization which that causal connection instantiates. Instead, she suggests that if we wish to find a less distorting characterization of the notion of causality, we should replace the idea of necessary connection with the idea of the 'derivativeness of an effect from its causes'.[30] This would serve to indicate the sense in which what we think of as a special concept with a specific logical content is, in fact, a concept abstracted from a large number of ordinary causal concepts; before someone can master use of the concept of causality, they must master the use of causal concepts like burn, scrape, bend, squeeze, massage, etc. Take Wittgenstein's example of being punched. Here, there is no question of doubting our knowledge of the relation of cause to effect.

> Don't we recognize immediately that the pain is produced by the blow we have received? Isn't this the cause and can there be any doubt about it? – But isn't it quite possible to suppose that in certain cases we are deceived about this? And later recognize the deception? ... Certainly there is in such cases an experience that can be called 'experience of the cause'. But not because it infallibly shows us the cause; rather because *one* root of the cause-effect language-game is to be found here, in our looking out for the cause.[31]

If there is no room for doubt here, in the sense that the use of the concept of causality here leaves no logical space for questioning the application, then there is no reason for assuming that what we *really* mean, in speaking of the causal connection between fist and face, is that some general law concerning the necessity of B-type events following from A-type events is being instantiated. But that is just what, according to Anscombe, the standard view of causality requires us to assume.[32]

If there are reasons for doubting that our employment of the concept of seeing rests on a theory about its meaning, or that a single analysis could articulate its logical ramifications, then there are reasons for thinking the same regarding the concept of causality. The nomological conception assumed by the supervenience thesis is based on the paradigm of experimental science, but a grammatical investigation of the concept reveals other paradigms. These different paradigms can be distinguished in part by the ways in which knowledge of the cause of an effect is determined. Norman Malcolm, for example, discusses the examples of fixing a lock and of someone's making an eccentric move in a game of chess to confuse his opponent. In the first case, he imagines someone examining a dead-bolt lock that will not move. Upon finding a piece of metal inside the lock and fitting it back into the mechanism, the key turns. According to Malcolm, if someone were to object that 'You did not actually *prove* that the cause of the lock's not working was the separation of that loose piece from the rest of the lock', the objection would be felt to be academic or empty.[33] In the second example of the eccentric chess move, the cause is discovered by asking: 'When the game is finished someone asks B, "What caused you to make that strange move?" B answers: "I wanted to disconcert my opponent".'[34] If the semantics of the concept of a causal relation are fixed in part by logical connections to behavioural criteria, including the contexts within which the concept is learned and used, then for many ordinary uses of the concept, calling something the cause of an event, for example, a visual impression, is actually a way of reacting to what is seen: '*We react to the cause.* Calling something "the cause" is like pointing and saying: "*He's* to blame!"'[35]

Things that we see affect us in many different ways. Our visual experiences affect us in many different ways. Images, for example, can affect us by shocking us, by making us speechless, by arousing or confusing or misleading us, or by enlightening us. These are all objective forms of causality, of one thing affecting another. It might seem that to be realistic in one's thinking about these relations one has to prune down what counts as genuinely experienceable content by limiting it to what one knows with certainty from the standpoint of physics. But minimal physicalism is arguably a form of antirealism, which attempts to rule out of epistemological court any perceptual content not certified by forms of knowledge employed by physics. Donald Davidson helpfully describes antirealism as a 'manifestation of the irrepressible urge in Western philosophy to ensure that whatever is real can be known'.[36]

> Most reductive isms should count as forms of antirealism: idealism, pragmatism, empiricism, materialism, behaviourism, verificationism. Each tries to trim reality down to fit within its epistemology ... We are allowed the terminology of our old ontology as long as we agree to accept only what can be cobbled together out of entities or experiences we can for certain know.

If there are different senses in speaking of causality, then there is not one correct way in which something, for example, a perception or a concept, can be responsive to the world. If this line of thought is cogent, then the noninternal perceptual states that trouble the minimal physicalist are not unresponsive to the world; they are merely responsive to the world in a different way from that of internal states. In this sense, one can reject metaphysical naturalism without thereby accepting Cartesian dualism or transcendental idealism. All one would then be rejecting would be the assumption that physics speaks to all of the diverse interests we can have in explaining what we mean when we say that we see how things are.

Visuality and postmodern social theory

In what sense and to what degree is our visual experience a social construction?

If our experiences are often individuated by concepts which we share with other language-users in our society or tribe, then there is no question that participating in a certain social practice is a condition for having certain experiences. Different societies and different historical epochs are distinguished by their different ethical, political and cultural priorities and being able to participate in them requires that individuals learn to internalize those priorities by developing the perceptual and cognitive habits that participation requires. It follows that a comprehensive understanding of the grammar of sight would need to include, in addition to naturalistic theories of the visual system, enquiries into the forms of visual understanding embodied in human culture. Call these forms practices of looking. What is the epistemology of visual practice?

I want to approach this question by looking at a still-developing field of broadly humanistic study of perception, called visual culture studies or visual studies. The emergence of visual studies as an interdisciplinary approach to visual meaning (involving such disciplines as media studies, art history, queer theory, anthropology, design and architectural theory, nonempirical sociology, literary theory, urban planning, women's studies, post-colonial studies, iconography and semiotics) is a useful context in which to address questions about the social nature of meaning in vision. What is exciting about visual studies as an emerging interdiscipline is that the criteria establishing both the relevant subject matter as well as the appropriate methodology are still greatly in flux. As a teacher of aesthetics and epistemology, and a visual artist, I have myself been exploring ways of studying and teaching visual culture and perception and I found Wittgenstein helpful in sorting through the debate. Visual studies is very much in the epistemological spirit of Wittgenstein's *Investigations*. Recall that one of the main lessons of the whole discussion of aspect perception was that we can fail to appreciate the grammatical complexity of perception by assuming too narrow a view of what it means to understand perception, or of which form of explanation offers genuine knowledge of the ability to see. Further, explanation of the concepts expressed in natural languages is generally tied to practice and the ability to go on. This means that one is liable to run into confusion by assuming that the practical perceptual skills of, say, a landscape painter or an ecologist, can be explained as a theoretical or proto-theoretical kind of knowledge. If the epistemological justifications for claims to perceptual knowledge are internal to practices of seeing, internal to the grammar of the concepts employed in those practices, then the clarification of that grammar, together with forms of organic and historical human life with which that grammar is entwined, identifies a specific yet vast domain of inquiry into perception qua practices of seeing. Call this a Wittgensteinian angle on visual studies.

This attention to the role of criteria in practices of seeing, together with a sense of their heterogeneity and multiplicity, points to just the kind of epistemological open-mindedness that one finds in the ongoing debate about how and what visual studies should be studying. Consider a small sampling of some of the questions that are now part of the movement's philosophical eros. There are questions having to do with how perception is shaped by social conditions generally: *How is the visual field shaped as a social construction?* There are questions about how perception as a process is understood in different societies and historical epochs: *How did ordinary people understand what it means to see in fif-teenth-century Florence?* Or how the perceptions of specific subgroups of a society are shaped for political reasons: *Who is privileged within a scopic regime?* There are questions about images generally: *What do images want?* Or about their social uses: *Whose fantasies of what are fed by which visual images?* Or about how a certain subgroup is represented in a particular medium: *How are people of colour repre-sented in film?* Or questions about the social and psychological effects of a parti-cular medium: *How does television affect your sense of community?* There are questions about how a certain subjective position or spectatorship is con-structed: *What is the male gaze?* And there are questions about acts of seeing: *What is the difference between glancing and looking?* And so on.

Now, while the general ontological and epistemological open-mindedness of visual studies bears affinities with the spirit of Wittgenstein's philosophy, there are also ways in which his philosophy can be used to reveal conceptual confusions within the field. Like the critique of metaphysical naturalism, a Wittgensteinian critique of certain ways of thinking about visual studies turns on understanding the limits of specific epistemological contexts. If nat-uralists sometimes misconstrue just what epistemological sacrifices their onto-logical and methodological principles demand of them, researchers engaged in the humanistic study of sight as a social construct sometimes exaggerate the autonomy of the meaning-constituting practices they study as elements of social structure. Like physicists, or thinkers enamoured epistemologically with physics and the hard sciences, sociologists and cultural theorists can exaggerate the principles demarking the domain of enquiry. One such confu-sion, which I shall examine below, has do to with the false assumption that all questions about visual form or visual meaning are in fact questions about social meaning, in the relevant sense of meaning. I shall refer to this assump-tion as constitutive of postmodernist visual studies, or what amounts to the same, visual studies as a form of postmodernism. As I shall argue, what Witt-genstein helps us to see is that postmodernist visual studies, which is defined largely as a philosophical revolt against Descartes, ironically reveals a tacit Cartesianism in how it thinks about the relation of images to reality, and of meaning to truth.

While there are various approaches to visual studies which are not accu-rately characterized as postmodernist, there is clearly an historical and meth-odological connection between the respective frameworks that still influences the epistemology expressed in the debate. As Margaret Dikovitskaya argues, visual studies grows out of the cultural turn in the humanities, as is defined by its critical position against art history.

The cultural turn brought to the study of images a reflection on the complex interrelationships between power and knowledge. Representation began to be studied as a structure and process of ideology that produces subject positions ... The scholarship that rejects the primary of art in relation to other discursive practices and yet focuses on the sensuous and semiotic peculiarity of the visual can no longer be called art history – it deserves the name of visual studies.[37]

This genealogy makes visual studies doubly adverse to anything we might learn about perception from naturalistic enquiry. On the one hand, cultural studies goes back to the inverted Hegelianism of one of the founders of sociology, Karl Marx, with his notion of human culture as superstructure. If one approaches the study of visual meaning from a broadly Marxist perspective, then the epistemological interest lies in unmasking what appears to be natural meaning, as in truth *phantasmagoria*, or oppressive ideological instruments of the hegemonic economic interests of society. Insofar as natural science enters into this picture at all, it tends to be seen as itself a socially constructed system of meaning. On the other hand, as emerging out of cultural studies, postmodern visual studies approaches the study of visual meaning on the basis of the concept of meaning employed by structuralist linguistics. The arbitrariness of meaning, which poststructuralists understand to follow from structuralist linguistics, is taken to have decisive significance for our concepts of truth, objectivity and meaning. In an epistemological elaboration of this line of thinking in Jean-François Lyotard's account of postmodernism, the principles of objective truth and ethical progress for human society both fall into a form of nihilistic idealism. Ferdinand de Saussure's understanding of the arbitrary connection between signifier and signified undermines the idea that a system of representation like natural language works atomistically by attaching symbols to independently identifiable entities in the world. Rather, a symbol-language is employed such that the referential connections between a sign and an object are determined by the overall functioning of the system. As Anthony Woodiwiss describes the relevance of this for visual studies,

> The move from regarding what is seen as a product of simple vision to seeing it as a product of visuality or a system of visualization is the other side of the coin represented by the shift from regarding language as a collection of pictures to seeing it as a system of picturing.[38]

What are the implications of this view of meaning for the epistemology of visual studies? The view implies certain conditions on what we can say that images mean and on how we understand their representational connection to the world.

Take the concept of *visuality*. The term is meant to denote the specific object of visual studies, which is distinguished from *vision*, or the sense of sight construed naturalistically. Visuality refers to everything about vision that is socially constructed. Epistemological difficulties arise from the distinction, however, insofar as the distinction itself is understood to be socially constructed. According to Hal Foster,

> Although vision suggests sight as a physical operation, and visuality sight as a social fact, the two are not opposed as nature to culture: vision is social and historical too, and visuality involves the body and the psyche. Yet neither are they identical: the difference between the terms signals a difference within the visual – between the mechanism of sight and its historical techniques, between the datum of vision and its discursive determinations – a difference, many differences, among how we see, how we are able, allowed or made to see, and how we see this seeing or the unseen therein.[39]

The autonomy of visuality, which includes the autonomy of the ways in which visuality portrays its relation to the natural – to vision – means that, like the Cartesian ego which cannot in a sense be wrong about its own inner first-person experiences of the visual world, visual culture practices are self-validating in that they cannot be criticized or understood in terms of criteria external to the practice. They can only be acknowledged, and attempts to conceal visuality – the socially-constructed aspects of the experience of sight – can be unmasked. Ruled out methodologically, and even ontologically, are considerations of how the social processes of visual meaning construction may be shaped, conditioned, or even altered, by the visual system as naturalistically conceived and appreciated within the larger context of the evolutionary biology and political ecology of human culture. Thus no thought is given to so much as having a theory of perception, or to a naturalistic theory of knowledge for that matter. What are the epistemological liabilities of this framework?

I argued above that naturalism in the philosophy of mind could be misconstrued as undermining the truth of ordinary perceptual ascriptions, for example, by construing the employment of psychological concepts as resting on a folk-psychological theory about the mind. The same criticism can be levelled against the claim, made by some sociologists of visuality, that individuals in certain epochs or cultures have an understanding of sight dominated by a form of false consciousness, or in a quasi-Marxist sense, by a 'scopic regime'. The term is used by thinkers with broadly postmodernist sensibilities to refer to visuality as a form of ideology to be unmasked. As forms of ideology, scopic regimes exert their influence by conditioning what individuals ruled by them think of as ordinary commonsense beliefs about what they see and about the nature of perception itself. As Foster puts it,

> With its own rhetoric and representations, each scopic regime seeks to close out these differences: to make of its many social visualities one essential

vision, or to order them in a natural hierarchy of sight. It is important, then, to slip these superimpositions out of focus, to disturb the given array of visual facts . . .[40]

For instance, in Jonathan Crary's analysis of the visuality of modernity, he identifies Cartesian perspectivism, the mercantile-empiricism of Dutch painting, and the Baroque interest in perceptual obscurity and ocular ambiguity. The purpose of the exercise is not to evaluate the epistemological merits of the regimes, since that would be to violate the very idea of visuality as a form of culture, but merely to expose them *as* social constructs, rather than views of some natural reality. Cartesian perspectivism, for example, is characterized as a scopic regime in which the image of the *camera obscura* is deployed as a socially constructed artifact disguised as a scientific model of vision: 'As a complex technique of power, it was a means of legislating for an observer what constituted perceptual "truth", and it delineated a fixed set of relations to which an observer was made subject.'[41]

Because the idea that nature might condition visual meaning, or that images might be about some super-cultural, or trans-cultural form, can only be theorized as social structure masquerading as natural structure, postmodernist visual studies basically rejects the idea that an image could ever represent reality, or that artists could ever truly be interested in reality, in something beyond the solipsism of their place and time. For example, in distinguishing visual studies from art history, Martin Jay argues that visual studies rejects the assumptions that images have some objective meaning to be analysed, that criteria for interpreting images are not historically relative, and that images can reveal more than the ethical and political commitments of their creators. This epistemological and ontological solipsism naturally also applies to the visual culture studies itself: the methodological assumptions of visual culture theorists are themselves culture-bound.

> We may learn to wean ourselves from the fiction of a 'true' vision and revel instead in the possibilities opened up by the scopic regimes we have already invented and the ones, now so hard to envision, that are doubtless to come.[42]

Now the great irony of this approach to the study of visual meaning is that, while defining itself largely as a rejection of Cartesian metaphysics and epistemology, the framework ends up reaffirming the same problematical assumptions it is trying to escape. For example, like Cartesian epistemology, postmodernist visual studies disregards the epistemological orientation of ordinary language and its semantic autonomy in ordinary life. Only by doing so can the idea of unmasking sight as dominated by scopic regimes make any sense.

... what allows the notion of scopic regimes is the recognition that vision is not a spontaneous power in the way that commonsense supposes when it tells us that 'seeing is believing' and when it generally exalts sight over all the other senses. Rather, it is constructed power as many doubters of sight's trustworthiness have suspected for as long as common sense has exalted it. This constructedness is what is registered by the use of the term visuality instead of vision.[43]

But if the meaning of perceptual concepts, as those concepts are employed instrumentally within forms of life and practices of seeing, gain their meaning within those interpretive practices, then there is nothing to reveal. The meaning of sight is not available to be unmasked as a scopic regime because meaning does not rest on a quasi-theoretical, or folk-psychological, stance towards experience, as both the scientific reductionist and the postmodernist assert. It is constituted by the practice within which it comes to matter that a distinction is drawn between seeing and interpretation. The open-ended character of these practices is illustrated by the point that the normativity of rules cannot be formalized as being opposed to the embodied ability to participate in that practice. The projection of a rule into future contexts can, in some cases, require unpredictable, and not always socially-acknowledged, innovations or even ruptures in what the rule has been understood to require in the past. Whether the new usage is in fact a new meaning, or just a natural articulation of an existing concept, is a distinction that, like other kinds of grammatical distinctions, turns on what that distinction might be used to say within a practice, and whether and how it could matter to say it. All of these epistemological concepts are, however, too fine grained for postmodernism's distinction between vision and visuality.

Consider the issue of perceptual relativity which is implied by postmodernist visual studies. Perceptual relativity is the doctrine that what you see and how you see it are socially-determined and that there is no way to see how things truly are because there is no such thing as a perspective on nature which is not a socially-constructed perspective. Now from a Wittgensteinian perspective, perceptual relativity is either trivially true or it is false. It is true in the uninteresting sense that when a being can be said to perceive something, it does so from something that can be called a perspective. No one could argue against this, and surely Plato, the great arch-nemesis of postmodernists, was aware of the problems that perspective and power pose for thinking clearly.[44] But perceptual relativity, as driven by the conceptual relativity that postmodernists infer from linguistics, critically oversimplifies and underestimates the epistemological richness of perspectives. This is because, in order to emphasize the autonomy of perspective, a practice of seeing needs to be formalized in order to establish the line that cannot be crossed into the forbidden space of trans-cultural, or trans-historical, truth. They want to limit what can be called true, or what we can understand by the meaning of an image or a visual experience to a particular tradition. But as Paul Feyerabend characterizes it,

> The trouble here is that traditions not only have no well-defined boundaries, but contain ambiguities and methods of change which enable their members to think and act as if no boundaries existed: potentially every tradition is all traditions. Relativizing existence to a single 'conceptual system' that is then closed off from the rest and presented in unambiguous detail mutilates real traditions and creates a chimera. Paradoxically this is done by people who pride themselves of their tolerance toward all ways of life.[45]

The statement expresses Feyerabend's epistemological anarchism which is motivated by the recognition of the abundance of being or the infinite informational and semantic richness of the world. Because the world is so endlessly informative, at any and every level of perception, every explanation is necessarily, and helpfully, an oversimplification. Almost every explanation, or analysis or interpretation, has some epistemological virtues, and some liabilities. Even dead-wrong theories are valuable for the contrasts they reveal. Now if there are innumerable ways to count differences between cultures, there are also innumerable ways to count similarities, and that shows you why postmodernism is making a tacit metaphysical assertion in claiming that difference is more ontologically basic than similarity. Those potential similarities that we might discover across cultures are all those aspects of their ways of life which are understandable universally. The postmodernist idea that visuality is purely a social construct discounts universality, in part, by denying that any valid naturalistic accounts can be given of the connections between vision and visuality. For example, postmodernism in visual studies does not seem to draw any conclusions from theoretical work on the neurobiology, evolutionary psychology or even the political ecology of vision, as strategies for generating hypotheses about features of visual perception which are common to either the human species as a whole, or to mammals or even living creatures as a whole. Like many strands of twentieth-century sociology, postmodernist visual studies tends to think of the human body and mind as a social construction and, hence, end up asserting the same empiricist positivism that they start out railing against.

From a Wittgensteinian perspective, postmodernism lapses into metaphysics in his pejorative sense, as a confusion between the conceptual and the empirical. This is because it overlooks the actual operation of meaning at the level of ordinary, natural language. Its scepticism about the possibility of nonsocially constructed meaning or knowledge rests on its tacit assumption that such knowledge would depend upon some special objective criterion, an Archimedean point which transcends every particular practice, and so every particular criterion of meaning which is actually employed for purposes of genuine communication. As the argument goes, because we cannot make sense of a trans-cultural Archimedean point, we cannot ever compare our thoughts or pictures to the world in order to see if they are correct. What Wittgenstein's analysis reveals is that, as Hilary Putnam puts it, there is no metaphysically innocent way of saying what thought or language cannot do.

> . . . if we agree that it is *unintelligible* to say 'We sometimes succeed in comparing our language and thought with reality as it is in itself,' then we should realize that it is unintelligible to say, 'It is *impossible* to stand outside and compare our thought and language with the world.'[46]

Not being able to find an Archimedean point, postmodernism's Cartesianism caves in on itself and sees nothing but metatheoretical chaos. Like the private linguist from Chapter Two who ignores all of ordinary criteria involved with assigning meaning to utterances or ascriptions or pictures and ends up with nothing, the postmodernist overlooks the ways that normativity is established within practices, disparaging such pre-theoretical contexts as the domain of ideologically-structured commonsense, in order to ground their truth in some imagined foundation.

Postmodernism is also tacitly Cartesian when it comes to the issue of value. Postmodernism's positivist upholding of the fact/value distinction expresses in a different way its repudiation of so-called 'metanarratives' about truth and ethical progress in human society. Because values are theorized as fundamentally unnatural or socially-constructed, it is a naturalistic fallacy to think that a particular ethical outlook or concept of freedom could be objectively more or less true or justified than another set of values. The subterranean link with Cartesianism is that nature is not a source of value or meaning, but is a machine to be put to work, technologically and semantically, to serve human purposes, while culture is the domain of arbitrary, irrational tradition masquerading as naive realism.

The irony of this Wittgensteinian critique of postmodernist visual studies is that postmodernism has drawn inspiration, via Thomas Kuhn's historical approach to the philosophy of science, from Wittgenstein himself. But Wittgenstein does not draw the same metaphysical conclusions about meaning and truth that postmodernists do. There are interpretations of Wittgenstein which do read him as offering, for example, a social theory of meaning. Saul Kripke's influential sociological reading interprets the conclusion of the private language arguments to be that agreement with a community of language speakers is a necessary condition for there to be any semantic facts at all about anything. While I argued that the private language arguments imply no such conditions on language-use, the upshot seems to be that much of what we articulate about our experience is structured by the interests of interpersonal communication, rather than intrapersonal representation. Insofar as Wittgenstein's approach construes meaning as use, in terms of conceptual practice, meaning has irreducibly externalist, and so publicly-available conditions. But Wittgenstein's view does not support any thesis that all meaning is socially constructed; in fact, it gives us conceptual resources for grasping what is false about such an idea. The epistemological mistake lies in their assumption that the indeterminacy of meaning, stemming from the arbitrary relation between symbols and things, implies antirealism. But semantic indeterminacy, for example, in the case of the context-sensitivity of perceptual ascriptions, only implies the antirealism of those semantic properties if one has made other ontological assumptions, such as materialism.

It might sound strange that epistemological postmodernists are also obliged to be materialists when it comes to their philosophy of mind, but only if you think that they have freed themselves dialectically from their struggle against Descartes. In order to assert the independence of visuality from vision, and so the socially-constructed character of the very distinction between vision and visuality, they must presuppose some picture of what naturalistic theories of perception can explain about perception, cognition, language and even social structure. This is so that they can be sure that what they are interested in clarifying or unmasking, such as meaning, is something that naturalistic enquiry surely has nothing to say about. So they need a conception of natural scientific explanation as offering a picture of the world as essentially (a) devoid of subjectivity and, therefore, (b) a world devoid of meaning and value. But the mechanistic view of nature, described and argued for by Descartes, fits this description perfectly. As the architect and complexity theorist Christopher Alexander puts it,

> The picture of the world as a machine doesn't have an 'I' in it. The 'I', what it means to be a person, the inner experience of being a person, just isn't part of this picture. Of course, it is still there in our experience. But it isn't part of the picture we have of how things are.[47]

The paradox of this for postmodernism is that, as a critical theory of knowledge, which seems to emphasize art over science and imagination over induction, it is actually, in terms of its metaphysics and its epistemology, a repudiation of the artist and the scientist both. Alexander argues this from the standpoint of a practising architect. The mechanistic picture of the world is contradicted by the fact that some buildings are beautiful and wonderful places to live, while others are ugly, dehumanizing and horrible places to live. But according to the mechanistic view, beauty and ugliness, the feeling of wholeness and the feeling of fragmentation, are feelings and values, and as such, not real properties of things in the world. Therefore, statements about them lack objective truth value, and there is no such thing as rational discussion about them. In his long meditation on the nature of form, as a theory of architecture, he makes the case, by close examination of hundreds of examples, as well as his own long experience with the design and construction of buildings, that the mechanistic picture has been disastrous for artists.

> The process of trying to be an artist in a world which has no sensible notion of 'I' and no natural way that the personal inner life can be a part of our picture of things – leaves the art of building in a vacuum. You just cannot make sense of it ... The mechanistic idea tells us very little about the deep order we feel intuitively to be in the world. Yet it is just this deep order which is our concern.[48]

And of course, it is just this deep order, and the possibility of having an interest in it, that postmodernism denies, and in ways which are surprisingly dogmatic given everything postmodernism also claims about freedom and the unmasking of epistemological regimes.

While Wittgenstein argues for the autonomy of the semantics of natural language, and so the epistemological well-groundedness of ordinary ungrounded discourse, he also observes that concepts change because practices change. Conceptual practices can sometimes be revealed to rest on what we understand about how things are in the world, as I illustrated earlier with the case of the medieval monks who thought that ocular blindness was caused by moral blindness, hence something to feel ashamed about. Thus, natural science often introduces new concepts, or new uses of older concepts, making criteria fluctuate. Given new facts about nature that emerge from scientific inquiry, the way we use certain concepts can start to lack sense, and new uses can suddenly become meaningful. Although Wittgenstein could not see it yet, the global ecological collapse that industrial modernism has wrought reveals that our modern concept of freedom is untenable because it is inconsistent with the laws of ecology, specifically, ecological limits to economic growth. From the standpoint of this ecological revelation, the Parisian *flâneur*, whom both Charles Baudelaire and Walter Benjamin identify as a postmodernist hero, who delights in the multifarious visual cultures of industrial capitalism, is as naive politically as a recreational shopper dreamily floating through the air-conditioned arcades of an American shopping mall.

5

Aesthetic experience

A work of art forces us − as one might say − to see it in the right perspective but, in the absence of art, the object is just a fragment of nature like any other; we may exalt it through our enthusiasm but that does not give anyone else the right to confront us with it. (I keep thinking of one of those insipid snapshots of a piece of scenery which is of interest for the man who took it because he was there himself and experienced something; but someone else will quite justifiably look at it coldly, in so far as it is ever justifiable to look at something coldly.) [1]

Neurology, pictorial realism and the innocent eye

What is aesthetic experience?

Given his philosophical sensibilities, it is not surprising that Wittgenstein's philosophy should appeal to artists, writers, and other creative personalities. His philosophy is about seeing things clearly, and seeing how we see, not about constructing theories which explain why. In this final chapter, I shall continue my dialectical exploration of Wittgenstein's philosophy of perception by considering how this framework treats some basic questions about aesthetic perception. While illustrating the same epistemological lessons we've canvassed in earlier chapters, our current discussion will bring out another aspect of Wittgenstein's peculiar interest in perception: the sense in which philosophy and art are less different than they are taken to be; that is, where philosophy is not essentially about explanation, nor art about self-expression, but where both explanations and self-expressions are vehicles for seeing more deeply and purely. In the first part, I shall address the question of pictorial realism in painting and photography in order to explore, in Wittgensteinian fashion, criteria for counting something as a realistic portrayal of something. My aim here is to further develop my point that Wittgenstein's instrumental view of images leads away from the poststructuralist denial of reality to a robust realism about meaning. I shall use the issue of realism to show how one might understand what is epistemologically distinctive about an aesthetic interest in seeing. In the second part, I continue this discussion within the context of a neurological theory of the nature of art. Here I offer a qualified Wittgensteinian critique of Semir Zeki's 'neuroesthetics'. Examining the ways in which neurology can and cannot be said to inform aesthetic judgements, I develop a reversal to the classical Baumgarten conception of aesthetics in which artistic interests in perception can be understood as epistemologically autonomous from the claims of natural science. As in the prior chapters, using Wittgenstein dialectically avoids the construction of theories that are anathema to his interests, while also avoiding the empty and boring claim that seeing is just what we ordinarily take it to mean.

Photography and criteria for pictorial realism

Isn't it obvious that if I take a photograph of what I am looking at – of what I can see – that that photograph is a more realistic, more accurate representation of my visual experience than if I draw or paint it?

I've heard this question raised many times, especially by artists, and there's a particular aptness in the way it is posed. There's something very natural about expressing one's visual perplexity in just these terms. As I shall argue, the Wittgensteinian answer is that photography is not per se more realistic than painting, or any more traditional artistic medium. The concept of realism, like any other, is a tool whose appropriate employment turns on what our interests are. Where poststructuralist semiotics tends to understand the instrumental character of language to imply antirealism, Wittgenstein draws the opposite conclusion; namely, that the world contains an endless abundance of reality which is available to us through our different systems of representation. The confusion about realism arises from thinking that there must be only one best way, one criterion of realism, for getting at how things really look to be. The question about photography betrays this same confusion by implying that all of our interests in visual reality can be collapsed into one that truly concerns the world.

As we saw in the case of aspectual seeing, Wittgenstein's method in the *Investigations* is to reveal conceptual criteria to counter the Socratic intuition that concepts necessarily have a focal or univocal meaning. What are our criteria for counting an image as a realistic portrayal of an object? Consider the example of Vincent van Gogh as he sits painting sunflowers. Now imagine two images of his visual experience: the first, a painting by van Gogh of what he sees, something like his painting *Two Cut Flowers*, which he painted in Paris in August 1887; the second, a photograph taken from the same position at the same time. Since nothing pertinent turns on historical accuracy, we can imagine a very high-quality photograph, e.g. an image produced by a high-grade digital camera. Which image is a more accurate expression of van Gogh's visual experience, and why? What criteria do we have for measuring the realism of an image?

I choose van Gogh here because he is known for his emphatic stylization, which sometimes provokes questions like: was it madness that caused him to paint like *that?* Or was it a problem with his eyes or his brain? Or did he consciously *stylize* what he saw? These questions are interesting because they presuppose an affirmative answer to the question whether a photograph *as such* is more realistic than a painting, as a report of visual experience. No one asks of the photographer, for instance, whether she really experiences the world as frozen slices of time. Why assume that photography is more realistic than, say, impressionist painting? For Fox Talbot, who invented photography in the 1830s, the immediate appeal of the new medium lay in its ability to do something that could not be done without considerable draftsmanship. Not being able to draw, he called photography 'nature's pencil'.[2] Photography was seen, and can still be seen, as the mechanical perfection of a representational and aesthetic task long assigned to the craft of painting. The usual story is that as photography led to the perfection of the long-standing Renaissance ideal of pictorial transparency in painting – the attempt to capture the purely visual aspects of experience – painting could only continue by giving up on transparency, by consciously distorting the image, by becoming more 'subjective'.

There's some truth to this story, but everything turns on how one understands the idea of transparency. One way to unpack the idea of transparency is to draw a distinction between the content of an image, or what it represents, and the style or design of the representation, or how it represents. Transparency then amounts to the condition whereby an image represents a content without employing a style, or mode of representation, which distorts or comments upon the content. Now the idea of a mode of representation has, minimally, a technical as well as a psychological interpretation. Speaking of the technical sense of style, Marshall McLuhan remarks that photography has no syntax, unlike drawing which receives its syntax from the human hand.[3] Unlike the complicated task of translating three-dimensional objects in space via rules of linear perspective to a two-dimensional surface, no grammatical rules are followed or need to be followed when 'writing light' – the literal meaning of photography – to a photo-sensitive surface. In this sense, the distorting feature of style, from the Latin *stylus*, has to do with the marks left by the device used to create the image; marks which have no semantic meaning (don't refer to anything), and so get in the way of *transparency*. The technical sense of style is related to the psychological sense. Style can also be defined in terms of the user of the medium. In contrast to the content of an image, which tells us something about the world, style has to do with the perceiver's (artist's) *attitude* towards what she is perceiving. Hence, we get a sense of the obsessive character of van Gogh's interest in the night sky from the way his brush insistently encircles the stars in *Starry Night*. We might say that the style of the painting tells us more about van Gogh than it does about the sky. To use Mallarmé's distinction, style registers the *effect* of what is seen on the artist, and not simply *what is seen*. Consider Daniel Dennett's remark that the importance of the camera for science is that cameras are 'stupid'.

> In order to 'capture' the data represented in its products, it does not have to understand its subject in the way a human artist or illustrator must. It thus passes along an unedited, uncontaminated, unbiased but still re-represented version of reality to the faculties that are equipped to analyse, and ultimately understand the phenomena.[4]

This view of the greater objectivity of the photograph, over the illustration or painting, fits nicely into the dominant naturalistic interpretation of seeing as an information-processing process which has been adaptively shaped by evolutionary forces. While the purpose of seeing is fundamentally biological survival, the content of perception is defined in terms of picking-up information relevant to that aim: naturally, not an aim we've chosen but which has been chosen for us by Mother Nature, so to speak. On this view, photographs are more realistic, and more accurate reports of what we see because they carry higher-grade information about the environment. They are causally responsive to the environment in ways that paintings are not.

Is this a metaphysical claim, that photography is more realistic than painting? Yes, it is. By claiming that a photograph always counts as more realistic, one is simply stipulating that there is only one appropriate measure of realism. Of course, there is some truth in saying that photography is more realistic, and we can see this partial truth if we construe the concept of being realistic, *à la* Wittgenstein, as a tool for a particular purpose, rather than a logical picture of a fact. Are there things about visual experience that photography can capture better than painting? Surely. Photography for the first time made accessible to human examination certain complicated temporal phenomena that could not even be perceived, let alone painted. For example, photography is what allowed Eadweard Muybridge to confirm Leland Stanford's contention, which was controversial at the time, that there are moments at full gallop when all of a horse's feet are completely off the ground.[5] The fact that photography could be used in this way to show that a long-standing pictorial convention, which had painters always leaving a foot or two on the ground, illustrates a sense in which photography *is* more accurate or realistic than painting. Likewise, the transparent character of photography is often illustrated with reference to the instantaneous character of 'taking' a photograph. Because painting is a temporally-extended activity, taking hours and even weeks or months, it cannot capture the 'moment' of perception in the way that photography can. While a moment in time can be painted, it can't be painted in a moment. This gives photographs, and not paintings, a unique reference to the moment in time when they were snapped.

However, it is easy to get the wrong idea here about what the higher informational quality of photography implies for how we evaluate the truth or content of visual representations. Like any medium, photography involves informational biases that emphasize certain aspects of what is perceived and ignore others. These biases are evident in the fact that there is no question of confusing a photographic reproduction with visual experience itself. Despite its relatively high-definition information, a photograph of a sunflower is easily distinguished from our visual experience of the sunflower.

The biases of photography have long been noted. For one, a photograph does not offer an exact *transcription* of the information encoded in the varying light intensities constituting a visual field, but rather a *translation* of one scale of intensities onto another. The fidelity of the photograph lies in the way it preserves the ratios between the lightest and darkest points in the visual field, not on whether the darkest point in your visual field has the same light intensity, chromatic character, tone, etc., as the darkest point in the photograph.[6] Photographs also have a crisp edge where they *end*, making them unlike your visual field which has no crisp edge, no edge at all really. Wittgenstein comments on this.

> It is a remarkable fact that we are hardly ever conscious of the unclarity of the periphery of the visual field. If people, e.g. talk about the visual field, they mostly do *not* think of that; and when one speaks of a representation of the visual impression by means of a picture, one sees no difficulty in this.[7]

And of course, a camera also has to be *pointed*, and decisions have to be made about the distance, angle, lighting, timing, lens, etc, that can result in endless variations concerning which aspects of the object or scene are emphasized and which are thrust into the background. As for the issue of time, the instantaneous character of photography is as much a bias as it is an informational enhancement. A photograph doesn't just catch a moment in time, it redefines what counts as 'the moment'. One tends to represent visual experiences that are amenable to the available means of expression. For example, holding a camera can cause one to notice momentary visual compositions, like a shadow cast on a sidewalk, that one would never think to notice if one was looking for something to draw. There is an important sense in which the instantaneous character of photography makes the medium less realistic, and more abstract, than say a drawing in pencil or ink. James Elkins makes this point in talking about why people usually do not like to see pictures of themselves. True, vanity plays a part in our disappointment, but there's a reason connected to the medium itself.

Photographs clip out instants in time, and since we see in overlapping moments and usually base our sense of a person on a fluid sequence of moments and motions, a single photograph can often seem wrong. (Painters blend moments, so that few oil portraits have the weirdness of snapshots.)[8]

A photograph captures how things look at an instantaneous point in time, but a painter can represent how a person looks over the course of an hour, or how a town centre looks between one o'clock and five o'clock in the afternoon. If time were merely a sequence of disconnected moments, then the momentariness of photography wouldn't have this bias and would not distort the 'information' in this way. Perhaps we would prefer photographs of ourselves more, but then we would have an altogether different kind of identity and existence.

These biases, however, are only part of the reason why the objectivity of photography is not guaranteed by the medium itself. It is sometimes said that photographs do not lie. The problem with this statement is that pictorial truth depends not solely on the structure of an image, but on what that structure is *used* to show. That is, speaking of the accuracy of a visual image presupposes a method of projection which specifies what the image is *about*. Now, the statement that photographs do not lie is not wrong per se, since we can think of occasions when it would make sense to say so. Think of the ways that a private detective might use an incriminating photograph as evidence of adultery; here the lies of the adulterer are contrasted with the truth of the photographs. But the same picture, say, of a man and woman having sex, can only be called veridical *if* it is understood what the photograph is *about*; in this case, evidence of adultery. The photograph is not *essentially* a photograph *of* an adulterous act. If the photograph is interpreted as an image portraying the lovers at some point in the past, before they had even met, then it might very well turn out to be false. And of course, the same photograph could be used to represent a variety of different ideas, for example, the fact that human beings have sex, or how they have it, or the kind of bed they like or dislike to use. In this sense, pictures neither lie nor tell the truth; only particular *uses* of pictures do so. That pictures require interpretation is often overlooked just because often it is *understood* how a picture is meant to be taken. A photograph of a flower could be seen as a photograph of a particular flower on a particular day, or just of a particular flower, or of a sunflower, or of flowers in general, or of a plant or of plants in general, or of living things, or yellow things or things that attract bees, etc., etc. Like all images, photographs have no intrinsic intentionality, no essential aboutness. Meaning is use.

The point here can be understood as a comment on the original question about the greater realism of photography. For the question asks about the realism of photography *as such*, not, for example, a particular photograph with reference to a particular question of fact. But if images have to be interpreted, then you can't ask about how a given medium shapes a message without looking at how the medium is *used*. That is, you cannot determine what a particular medium will allow you to express about a visual experience until you look to see how it is used, or can be used, to express an experience.

By emphasizing the need for interpretation, I do not mean to be arguing against the possibility of realistic portrayal. For instance, some tend to have the following intuition about the question of pictorial realism: realism strictly speaking is impossible because neither photography nor painting, nor any known medium, can be said to be a 'truly' realistic report of perceptual experience. For isn't it true that anything I could give as an expression of my experience leaves something out, or could be misconstrued? We explored this intuition concerning the ineffability of visual experience in Chapter Three as a misguided dissatisfaction with natural language. There, I argued that ineffability expressed the semantic over-determination of experience, rather than the existence of pre-linguistic, logically-private qualia of consciousness. A similar confusion can be diagnosed in the context of judgements about pictorial realism. To say that every visual expression of my experience as such fails at perfect realism presupposes a *criterion* for what is to count as being realistic. The criterion underlying the judgement is this: an image is a realistic portrayal of an experience if the image is *indiscernible* from the experience itself. Since any ordinary image we can point to can be distinguished easily from the experience it is meant to report, they can all be said to fail in achieving complete veracity. But there are confusions involved with this criterion for realism. It is helpful to observe that if we were to insist on this criterion, we would have to discount most of the things that conventionally count as – that we are ordinarily justified in calling – 'accurate representations'. That's a bit like defining 'shoe' with reference to something only worn by an obscure clan of Buddhist monks in Tibet, such that nothing we would ordinarily call 'shoe' counts as one. In fact, a photograph, as well as a painting, can be – can count as – an accurate representation of something without perfectly resembling what it is of. To say of a beautiful line drawing that it is a remarkable likeness of someone does not mean that the person in reality looks to be made of lines or pencil marks. Think of occasions when, looking at a beautifully crafted portrait drawing you have the thought, 'That looks just like her'. If you define visual accuracy in terms of indistinguishability then such remarks are certainly wrong. But there's some truth in saying that a drawn portrait *looks exactly* like the person herself. The point is that accuracy or realism is relative to our informational needs or interests. As Ernst Gombrich points out, in his discussion of stereotypes from *Art and Illusion*,

> To say of a drawing that it is a correct view of Tivoli does not mean, of course, that Tivoli is bounded by wiry lines. It means that those who

understand the notation will derive no false information from the drawing – whether it gives the contour in a few lines or picks out 'every blade
of grass' . . .[9]

This might sound a bit trite. After all, there's nothing particularly controversial anymore about the relativity of pictorial accuracy. But the commonsense
idea that photographs are more 'objective' than drawings rests upon a failure
to acknowledge just this kind of relativity.

Informational interests and visual form

There are other assumptions in play that undercut reflections on informational relativity and motivate the judgement that photographs capture more
accurately, or objectively, our perceptual experience. Despite the fact that
pictures do need to be interpreted, and that interpretation is shaped by one's
informational interests, one might still hold onto the idea, following Dennett,
that a photograph is more accurate than a drawing or painting because it is
richer informationally. Thus, instead of defining an accurate picture as one
which is indiscernible from the visual experience itself, one could define it in
terms of how many informational interests it potentially serves. Gombrich
considers this criterion: 'The complete portrait might be the one which gives
as much correct information about the spot as we would obtain if we looked at
it from the very spot where the artist stood.'[10] For example, we might say that
a photograph of a sunflower is more accurate than a van Gogh painting of one
because it can be put to more informational uses than the painting. There are
two basic problems with this, however. The first is connected with the idea of a
perfectly informative representation, approximation to which would serve as
a measure of its accuracy. It is not clear at all what could be meant by a representation that could address any possible epistemological hunger we might
bring to it. The idea of a god's-eye picture suffers the same conceptual difficulties of a map that, because it includes every conceivable detail of the terrain it
represents, ends up being the same size as the terrain, and so, useless as a map.
The second problem has to do with the fact mentioned above, that all media,
hence all representations produced by a medium, involve informational trade-
offs. It is implausible to assume that one might be able to derive from a photograph of a sunflower the particular kind of 'information' that van Gogh was
interested in portraying in his paintings. Without seeing his paintings, we
would have no idea which visual properties of sunflowers had peaked van
Gogh's interests. A photograph may be more help to a botanist than a painting, because it gives, for example, details about the flowers that van Gogh was

either not interested in or simply failed to see. But neither can the information contained in van Gogh's painting be extracted from a photograph.

At this point, one might raise the objection that one cannot speak of a van Gogh painting containing 'information' about certain visual properties of sunflowers, since information is relative to epistemic need, and paintings don't seem to satisfy any epistemic needs, at least any we could specify in an interesting sense. As the objection might go, if we can speak of paintings as expressing certain informational interests, these interests are *subjective*, and concern the *effect* of the visual appearance of the flowers on van Gogh, and not anything objective about the flowers themselves. But what can 'objective' mean here? It cannot mean that the photographic medium introduces no biases, or that it more closely approximates indiscernability to the experience itself, or that it is per se more informationally relevant than the painting. If the argument is that the information contained in the photograph is more objective because it is not filtered through van Gogh's mind and his arms and his particular interests in sunflowers, then the response is that 'more objective' is relative to informational interests which are not met by information which is filtered in that way. Conversely, it makes equal sense to say that the way in which the visual appearance of the sunflower is filtered through the camera is informationally irrelevant to van Gogh's particular interests, hence 'less objective' than his painting of sunflowers.

So what might van Gogh's interests in sunflowers have been such that his painting serves to capture the 'information' relevant to them? As the art critic Robert Hughes argues, the romanticism of van Gogh's stormy life, especially his madness, tends to distort our appreciation of the sanity of his paintings. Far from being a projection of his psychosis onto the objects he saw, van Gogh's style is rightly seen as a systematic device for capturing the forms that caught his visual imagination.

> The notion that [van Gogh's] paintings were 'mad' is the most idiotic of all impediments to understanding them. It was van Gogh's madness that prevented him from working ... As a draughtsman, van Gogh was obsessively interested in stylistic coherence. Just as one can see the very movements of his brush imitating the microforms of nature – the crawling striations of a gnarled olive trunk, the 'Chinese' contortions of weathered limestone – so the drawings break down the pattern of landscape and reestablish it in terms of a varied, but still codified system of marks: dots, dash, stroke, slash.[11]

It is rather empty to characterize his interest here as an interest in the visual properties of the flower that give him the particular aesthetic experience he has while looking at them. There is no more direct characterization of what van Gogh was interested in than his painting itself. The painting, we could say, is a logical criterion, which determines the kind of experience we can attribute to him.[12] If we want to say what van Gogh's interests were, which is to say, what kinds or aspects of visual truth he wanted to render, we point to the painting and say, '*That's* what he was interested in'. In this sense, there is no more *direct* or accurate expression of what van Gogh saw than his paintings. A photograph would be less realistic.

The idea that the purpose of seeing is to gather information about the environment in ways which have proved adaptively advantageous in the evolutionary past is of a piece with the general evolutionary-psychological view of the human mind as an adaptation, or series of modular adaptations. But the relevance of that concept of seeing for perceptual psychology or the philosophy of mind does not entail the relevance of that concept *for every interest* we can adopt towards our visual experience. If not the information-processing definition of perception, then how should we conceive of van Gogh's artistic interest? To say that his interest is in the *aesthetics* of visual form is not so much wrong as it is unhelpful, because it is circular. This is where I think Paul Valery's definition of seeing as forgetting the name of the thing seen helps to indicate a limitation on the information-processing concept of seeing. This definition better captures the kind of interest that many artists would relate to: the idea that seeing is not something that we do automatically, but rather a state which needs to be achieved.[13] It is the idea that we are, for the most part, *blind* to our visual environs precisely because we are so well adapted to them, and that because we *know* what we are seeing, we do not have to *look* at it, and hence, do not see it.

In this sense, visual truth is not what is necessarily captured in a photograph (although it might very well be so captured). It is an image which represents the *form* that served as the impetus to create the painting in the first place. Visual form is not information that Mother Nature has designed our visual system to pick up from the world; it is what emerges into our visual awareness on those often rare moments when we suddenly feel like we are seeing something about the world after having been blind to it. The accuracy of an image, in this sense, turns on the power of the image to engage the viewer in the same ways that the artist herself was engaged when she saw the form. This notion connects with two common sayings about successful works of art. The first is the idea that successful works are ones that have the power to create that sense of seeing as an achievement. As Hughes describes it, 'It is a characteristic of great painting that no matter how many times it has been cloned, reproduced and postcarded, it can restore itself as an immediate utterance with the force of strangeness when seen in the original'.[14] The second idea is that great paintings end up shaping our very experience of the original subject matter, as when we think of how van Gogh saw sunflowers when we ourselves see sunflowers. Call this an aspect of the concept of aesthetic experience.

Neuroesthetics and the grammar of beauty (Semir Zeki)

> People nowadays think that scientists exist to instruct them, poets, musi-
> cians, etc. to give them pleasure. The idea *that these have something to teach*
> *them* – that does not occur to them.[15]

In the previous section, I wanted to show the sense in which the question concerning the greater realism of photography points to a conceptual difference in
the *interest* that visual artists have with perception.[16] My idea here is that a
Wittgensteinian approach to the question of pictorial realism offers a way to
appreciate aesthetic experience as a kind of perception with a distinctive epistemology. Put differently, the claim is that we might very well misunderstand
how artists are interested in perception, and so what they have to teach us
about sight, if we assume that the information-processing conception of
seeing adequately characterizes their interests. In the remainder of the chapter, I shall pursue this line of thought by looking at an attempt to ground aesthetics in neurology.

Although recent years have seen a growing interest in the relation between
art and cognition, towards the broader goal of 'naturalizing' aesthetics, the
topic is by no means a new one. To talk about naturalizing aesthetics is even
redundant in a sense, if you consider that Alexander Baumgarten's original
use of the word 'aesthetic' referred to a general science of perception, with a
focus on perception in the fine arts. In recent years, the cognitive revolution
in perceptual theory, involving the new synthesis of evolutionary biology,
computational psychology and neuroscience, has given new impetus to this
approach to the study of art and aesthetic experience. A model for this kind
of thinking is offered by the neurologist Semir Zeki, who has proposed that
our understanding of the purpose of art must be grounded in the neurobiology
of the brain. While I do not wish to claim that a biological aesthetics will
shed no light on art or aesthetic experience, the idea that aesthetics must be
based on neurobiology is clearly a form of scientism. My basic argument
against Zeki's project is that his attempt to ground aesthetics in neuropsychology goes astray conceptually in a variety of ways by collapsing together psychological–theoretic and aesthetic–artistic interests in visual perception.
My broader point, which connects to the issue of naturalizing aesthetics, is
that perceptual and aesthetic concepts are enriched by these new scientific
projects, in the sense that they cannot and, therefore, ought not to be replaced
by, or reduced to, them. If there are things to learn by assimilating art into
science, there are things to learn by going in the opposite direction, using artistic conceptions of perception to enrich scientific interpretations of visual
experience. Think of Wittgenstein's approach to aesthetic experience as a
reversal of Baumgarten.

Semir Zeki's *Inner Vision: An Exploration of Art and the Brain* develops a constructivist approach to the neurological study of art which aims to show that the function and nature of art can be understood as an extension of the nature and function of the visual mind/brain. It must be emphasized that Zeki's account is meant only to 'lay the foundations of a neurology of aesthetics' and offers really only a sketch of a 'neuro-esthetics'.[17] Nevertheless, the assumptions framing his discussion reflect the standard conceptual framework employed in mainstream cognitive science. The basic picture is simple.

> All visual art is expressed through the brain and must therefore obey the laws of the brain, whether in conception, execution or appreciation and no theory of aesthetics that is not substantially based on the activity of the brain is ever likely to be complete, let alone profound.[18]

In turn, specifying the relevant laws of the brain requires that we specify the function of vision since, as Aristotle observed, the question of *how* a mechanism functions is secondary logically to the question as to what a mechanism *does*, that is, its proper function. What is the function of seeing? 'We see in order to be able to acquire knowledge about this world.'[19] But what kind of knowledge? Knowledge is relative to purpose, so we must define the purpose of seeing. What is the purpose of sight? As a neurologist, Zeki is interested in the neurophysiological mechanisms that allow the visual system to acquire the kinds of knowledge about the world which proved adaptive to our visual system's ancestors. If the function of art is an extension of the function of the visual system in the brain, then the function of art is: an extension of the task of giving knowledge about the world, in the form of constancies of perceptual experience. How might that function be extended? If art follows the same rules as the visual system, then visual art-making is about representing constancies that capture knowledge about objects, events, relations, etc. in the world.

Now one might already want to question where this is going if one has reservations about the traditional mimetic theory of art which holds that art imitates nature, and that art is successful *qua art* if it imitates nature *faithfully*. After all, to talk about the function of art as that of representing perceptual constancies sounds like mimesis, and there are all kinds of problems with the mimetic theory. Picasso disparaged it when he pasted the label from an actual bottle of Suze into a painting rather than going through the trouble of painting it. Aside from the problem that the mimetic theory doesn't offer a way to distinguish between imitations of nature which are, and ones which are not, works of art, the mimetic theory leaves our interest in art mysterious. As Arthur Danto puts it, 'Who needs, and what can be the point and purpose of having, duplicates of a reality we already have before us?'[20]

To be fair, the neuroesthetic model is more complicated, although not in a way that avoids the limitations of the mimetic theory. For one, Zeki adopts a more Aristotelian than Platonic view of mimesis: not that art tries to resemble nature visually, but that art copies nature in the manner of doing or growing. Art imitates not nature's visual appearances but nature's creative processes. Consequently, pictorial representation need not stop at optical fidelity the way a camera does, but can push ahead into more stable perceptual constancies; not how an object appears at a unique moment in space/time, and from a specific and so, accidental, perspective, but the thing itself, the Platonic *eidos* of the object. For example, cubism can be interpreted as a mimetic enterprise which tries to capture the object through time and simultaneously from different perspectives, thus overcoming Plato's objection in the *Republic* that art can only grasp appearances, while noetic intuition captures the unchanging universal form that makes the thing what it is. On the other hand, Zeki adds a Kantian twist to his mimetic view of art. Our ability to recognize objects by perceiving perceptual constancies is not explained by saying, along with Plato and Aristotle, that we passively 'grasp' the form of a thing, the way a wax tablet captures the form of a mould pressed into it. As all modern neurologists of vision argue, visual perception is an inherently active process of deciphering constant features of objects from the flux of their temporal, changing, perspectival appearances. The form that helps us to capture those invariant features of objects is not something out there in the world which our mind passively receives; it is a mental representation which our brain constructs as part of its proper function in acquiring knowledge of the world. As Zeki puts it, referring to Plato's example of a painting of a couch, the Platonic Idea in neurological terms is 'the brain's stored representation of the essential features of all couches that it has seen and from which, in its search for constancies, it has already selected those features that are common to all couches'.[21]

Now one of the surprising implications of Zeki's theory of art is that *artists are actually neurologists*. This conclusion follows from Zeki's basic constructivist assumptions about the function of vision and of art as an extension of that function, and it answers the question, what do artists have knowledge of. As Zeki puts it, what artists study is the brain and its organization, albeit in a rather indirect and uncomprehending manner. When an artist is captivated by an image and is moved to represent it in her medium of choice, what is actually compelling her is 'something about the organization of the visual brain'. Like neurologists proper, artists

> ... [experiment] by working and re-working a painting until it achieves a
> desirable effect, until it pleases them, which is the same thing as saying until
> it pleases their brains. If, in the process, it pleases others as well – or pleases
> other brains as well – they have understood something general about the
> neural organization of the visual pathways that evoke pleasure, without

knowing anything about the details of that neural organization or indeed *knowing that such pathways exist at all.*[22]

This answer is also supposed to explain the concept of aesthetic experience or aesthetic pleasure. The beauty that an artwork expresses is a kind of pleasure that is the result of the brain's inherent problem-solving, constancy-discerning activity being turned on itself.

Now there might very well be things to discover when you construe a painting as data for neurological inquiries. One of the most interesting cases that Zeki discusses concerns the connection between Piet Mondrian's idea that all visual form can be broken down into straight lines in rectangular opposition, and the hypothesis that the basic neurological building blocks of visual form in the brain are cells that respond in very selective fashion to lines of specific orientation. Here, it might very well make sense to speak of Mondrian as having quasi-neurological interests in perception.[23] However, to assume that visual artworks *must* be so construed is scientism: the false assumption that science supplies the conceptual measuring stick for judging the epistemological credentials of diverse forms of perceptual exploration. In Zeki's case, scientism pertains to the assumption that visual form – what visual artworks are *about* – must be cashed out in evolutionary-neurological terms. It is this assumption that leads Zeki, for example, to discount what artists have to say about their own work. This makes all conceptual art, for example, unintelligible.

It is one of the aims of perceptual neurophysiology to give an account of how the visual field is constructed in the brain. It is a conceptual stipulation of this approach that visual form is defined functionally in terms of biologically-relevant information about the world, and mechanistically, in terms of the activities of cells within the larger modular organization of the brain. But just because we might be able to account hypothetically for certain features of perceptual experience, or of our reaction to a visual image, does not imply that there are not other accounts of what we see, or of what we see something *as*, that are equally valid or equally true. In fact, it is precisely this externalist dimension to perceptual content – the idea that factors external to our individual psychology play a role in determining the visual meaning of what we see – that has been a theme of twentieth-century avant-garde aesthetics. The idea that art *transfigures*, as opposed to transforming, an object, so that the physical object/stimulus remains physically the same while its 'meaning' changes, is one of the most exciting innovations of Marcel Duchamp and many of the conceptual artists who have taken up the suggestion. But neuroesthetics, like other kinds of aesthetic formalism, can't theorize that idea because it has already reduced down its concept of aesthetic experience to a size that will allow it to be naturalized.

Consider Zeki's conception of artistic satisfaction as neurological satisfaction of the artist's brain. That there's more at stake in the aesthetics than subjective preferences is not entirely obvious, and is completely obscured when the experience of beauty is interpreted in terms of subjective preferences or pleasure. This happens when, to the question, 'What do you mean by saying that the sunflower is beautiful?', you respond by saying 'I mean: I like it', or something to the effect that beauty is about your personal, subjective experience of displeasure at what you see. This detaches the experience of beauty from anything essentially to do with the *form* of the object and locates the meaning of the perception of beauty within the subject. Sometimes, this is precisely what we *do* mean when we speak about beauty, for example, when we are talking about personal preferences for certain colours, or shapes, or voices, or personalities. But if we try to fit all of beauty into the concept of pleasure, then we end up distorting the articulation of our experience; we obscure the phenomenology of the perception of beauty. In Wittgensteinian terms, we distort the conceptual phenomenology of beauty. This is not because the experience of beauty is not pleasurable. I think that it often is – although it can also be painful and even terrifying – but because the pleasure experienced is not the reason why we find something beautiful; it is the effect of the beauty, or part of the meaning of the beauty.

If Zeki goes astray, conceptually, by reducing beauty to pleasure, the opposite mistake has also been made. That pleasure might also make up part of the meaning of beauty has not always been acknowledged. There is of course a long tradition in aesthetics, going back at least as far as Immanuel Kant's *Critique of Judgment* (1790) that sharply distinguishes beauty and pleasure, and it is the root of all formalist views of art and aesthetics. The distinction is based on the idea that the perception of beauty is disinterested, in the sense that it is not connected to having practical or theoretical interests with the beautiful things. The distinction is helpful in some ways, but it can easily be over-exaggerated. Far from being disinterested by beauty, beauty makes us 'interested' in things in a holistic sense. True beauty arouses us epistemologically.

What the equation of beauty as a kind of pleasure leaves out is the sense in which the perception of beauty is pervasively connected to a more engaged relationship to the thing. A quite ordinary meaning of the perception of beauty is that it registers a kind of attitude towards whatever it is we find beautiful that we think to be important for some reason. Whatever else it is, beauty upsets indifference. To find something beautiful, as opposed to finding it merely attractive or pleasurable, is to become interested in it, to want to understand it, to desire to possess something about it, to become vigilant to the possibility announced through that perception. We don't want our children to take aesthetic pleasure in pulling off the legs of insects, and we would find it reprehensible if someone who was in a position, say, to stop a mugging were instead to take pleasure in the bodily movements or screams sounded in the struggle. This is why the idea that aesthetics is not immediately connected to ethics − the doctrine of *aestheticism* − is false. Much like love, the perception of beauty is an act of the will. To find something beautiful means that we find its existence to be something good, something to be reproduced. As Socrates pointed out, the most intuitive response we have to beauty is procreative: to draw it, or to photograph it or to tell someone about it.[24] If ethics makes any sense at all, it involves our willingness to bring more good into the world and less bad. There's an important sense in which we can be said to have obligations to see certain things as beautiful and certain things as ugly. Perhaps seeing something as beautiful is willingness to bring more of what it represents into the world.[25] When it comes to the perception of environmental structures like ecosystems, villages or constructed dwellings, the architect and complexity theorist Christopher Alexander has argued compellingly that the perception of beauty is the perception of the deep geometrical structure of wholeness. Because we are so habituated into thinking of beauty as a subjective impression that the world makes upon us, we can have a hard time taking seriously the idea that beauty, as the sense of wholeness, is actually a cognitive insight into the nature of living form and even the underlying process which unfolded that form.[26]

Evolutionary and neuro-psychology is a fascinating framework for generating empirical hypotheses about the causes of human behaviour and offers a compelling answer to the difficult question of how the human mind fits into the causal order of physical nature. But our concepts, specifically, our psychological concepts, because of their practically endless complexity, can and need to be analysed in many different ways, depending on our epistemic interests. Obviously, having a brain is a necessary condition for being able to make or appreciate art. Not many people these days would want to argue otherwise. But it does not follow, as Zeki supposes, that art must therefore obey the laws of the brain. It is true, as Zeki points out, that no painters have made ultra-violet images, just because, unlike bees, we are not equipped to perceive ultraviolet radiation. Chess players must obey the laws of physics, but if you want to know why or how people play chess, physics isn't going to be much help. Qua biological entities, artists can be construed as having epistemic interests in perception defined in terms of their biological needs. But there are no compelling reasons, other than perhaps for purposes of neurological enquiry, to assume that the interest an artist has in what she sees can be defined in biological terms. Just because evolutionary psychology seems to be able to explain some aspects of human behaviour does not mean that it therefore must be able to explain everything about human behaviour.

The conceptual possibility of pure seeing

Don't think, but look![27]

To conclude my discussion of aesthetic experience, I shall illustrate the point made above by looking at Zeki's neurological critique of what he calls the 'myth of the seeing eye'. The idea of the seeing eye is an aesthetic, and we should add epistemological, ideal of seeing without understanding, or perceiving without judging, in which the phenomena experienced is met on its own visual terms. A similar ideal is found in Zen Buddhism.

> Zen is about just seeing. If we know how to just see without adding any thought or calculation to what's seen, we'll not have any problem. When a Zen teacher tests someone, they're checking out their ability to just see ... Just seeing can be demonstrated in numberless ways. None of them, however, involves knowing, finding, or looking for the right answer.[28]

Now from a neuropsychological perspective, this is of course impossible and even nonsensical. As Zeki argues, the very idea of a seeing eye is incoherent, and is based on certain pre-scientific assumptions about the psychological process of seeing that are empirically false. For instance, to speak of a seeing eye is to assume tacitly the hypothesis that vision is a two-part process, involving the formation or registration of an image (seeing) and then the interpretation of that image (understanding) by the brain. Accordingly, to speak about impressionism as an attempt to see purely with the eyes and not the brain is to hypothesize a process of deinterpretation of our experience; a phenomenological reduction to a cognitively-uninterpreted, unpenetrated image. On Zeki's analysis, this hypothesis is false, since there is no firm distinction between seeing and understanding. In fact, there is no retinal image at the back of the eye, but a photosensitive layer of cells which can detect changes in light intensity and wavelength by transducing the energy contained within particles of light (photons) into electro-chemical pulses. Hence, to say that Monet painted with his eye 'is of course nonsense: Monet, like all other artists, painted with his brain, the eye acting as a conduit for transmitting visual signals to the brain'.[29] So does this mean that Zen Buddhists don't know what they are talking about, even when they claim that they have straightforward ways of determining whether a Zen student is really seeing only with her eyes? That can't be right.

According to Zeki, the idea of a seeing eye is also false because it construes seeing as a passive process, as opposed to active understanding or judgement. This misconception is often attributed by modern perceptual psychologists to the so-called naive realism of the ordinary, pre-scientific individual. Because it doesn't seem like anything is going on in our heads when we see something, non-psychologists form the idea that seeing is a purely passive process, in which the visual forms of entities in the world are impressed on our mind, like a foot impresses its shape in wet sand. But as the neuropsychology of perception reveals, seeing is an inherently active process of deriving knowledge, relative to our biological interests, from the coded light picked up by our eyes. The active process of information-processing begins not with the brain, but already in the retinal cells of the eye, which are tuned to fire only given, highly specific stimuli. Hence, again, artists have been misled by their own intuitive, but false, thinking about perception.

The upshot of these two points is that, contrary to Valery and all those who see art as attempting to capture something beyond what is understood, beyond what can be captured discursively, seeing cannot be distinguished from understanding. There are cases, Zeki concedes, when people can be said to see something without being able to name or recognize what the thing is, even though they have knowledge of that kind of object. But the phenomenon is a disorder, visual agnosia, not a paradigm of true sight, and the alleged separation of sight from understanding is only relative to a particular cognitive ability. Take the example of the agnostic patient who, while being able to draw a picture of St. Paul's Cathedral in London, was not able to recognize the cathedral in his own drawing. Zeki's point is that the agnosia here is only a 'selective imperception', or 'an inability to either see or understand a particular attribute or aspect of the visual world'.[30] For while the patient could not recognize the cathedral in his drawing, he could recognize the individual details within it, just as a patient suffering from prosopagnosia – the inability to recognize familiar faces – can nevertheless recognize the details of a face, i.e. the eyes, nose, mouth. According to Zeki, far from vindicating the possibility of distinguishing seeing from understanding, cases of visual agnosia support the neuropsychological conception of perception as a massively modular process, in which visual information is divided into innumerable subprocesses or modules, each of which takes on a specific cognitive task within the overall cognitive division of labour in the visual system.

Now Zeki is undoubtedly right in his criticisms of the seeing eye if the idea is taken to rest, as it undoubtedly does for some artists, on certain rudimentary hypotheses about perception and neuroanatomy. But why make the assumption that the idea necessarily implies such hypotheses? Why assume that artists are actually talking about neurology? In fact, for all of the empirical cogency of Zeki's criticisms, he begs the question, in the beginning, by tacitly introducing a neurological criterion for analysing the concept of seeing. Consider the first point about the retinal image. Zeki's assumption is that the difference in the meanings of the concepts of *see* and *understand* is constituted by neurological facts, to which the concepts in some sense refer. To see without understanding, strictly speaking, means: to experience an uninterpreted (retinal) image.

Ergo, because there is no such thing as an uninterpreted retinal image, there is no such thing as seeing without understanding. However, nothing about what it means to see forces upon us just this way of distinguishing seeing from understanding, for there are other logical criteria for distinguishing the concepts. As we saw in Chapter One, being able to see that something is the case, e.g. that the blueprints look sound, is much different from merely understanding that they are sound, and does not imply that no concepts are involved. Likewise, there are various things to be said in saying that someone sees an object without understanding what it is, or understands what it is without actually seeing what it looks like. The distinction between visual appearance and reality need not, and in fact generally is not, drawn in terms of the distinction between the eye and brain. Rather, it is drawn in terms of what can be immediately taken for granted, and what is inferred on the basis of what is taken for granted. It was a premise of the classical foundationalist empiricism that what is taken for granted could ultimately be identified with some immediate empirical content, uncontaminated by theoretical or linguistic mediation; but that idea is no longer tenable, thanks in part to Quine's demolition of the analytic–synthetic distinction.

Now, surely some artists can sometimes get the wrong idea and misconstrue what it means to see, or what their aesthetic interest implies about the visual system. Anyone who tries to draw from life inevitably realizes that knowledge of what the object is can often get in the way of drawing what one sees. For example, knowledge of the objective size of an object can interfere with perceiving the apparent size of an object relative to other objects in one's visual field. The observation can give rise to the idea that seeing, and understanding what one sees, are two completely different mental faculties, and that it must therefore be possible in principle to see in a conceptually-neutral manner, to see solely 'with the eye'. And if this is what Monet meant, then he was wrong and Zeki is right.

However, just because pure seeing cannot be identified with the awareness of an uninterpreted retinal image does not mean that the concept is therefore empirically wrong; it just means that that particular way of justifying the concept is untenable. Accordingly, to say that Monet painted with his eye rather than his brain need not be taken to be implying anything about neurology at all, but only that Monet, in some important sense, allowed us to see how things appear, rather than trying to represent what they are. Now if you ask what that specific sense is, the most direct answer is: look at the paintings. This is not a rejection of the question. It is just a rejection of the idea that there is some better epistemological vantage point where Monet's perceptual interest can be assessed or understood.

Neither does Zeki's neurological view of seeing disprove the passivity of sight. Aristotle, who was the main target of the classical empiricist understanding of perception, says that perception involves the mind's being impressed by the form of the thing seen, where the sensory organs mediate this process, and where things generally are construed ontologically as a composite of form and matter. Hence, perception is passive, less like a fist that twists what it grasps, and more like wet sand receiving the print of a foot. Aristotle's view is considered naive because it does not take into consideration the need to explain just how the sensory organ transmits the form, and this view is also blamed for giving rise to an equally naive view of truth – naive realism – which allegedly holds that things are exactly as they appear. But we need not take the passivity of seeing to mean that there are no causal mechanisms involved. Compared grammatically to imagining or willing, seeing is passive, or can be passive, in the sense that it is richly receptive to the world. To argue that seeing can also be conceived of as an active process does not refute the other view; it complements by contributing to the logical grammar of the concept of sight. Of course, it is true that those who are trying to theorize about the causal mechanisms underlying visual perception may be misled by certain ways of understanding the passivity of perception. It is also plausible that, as Rudolf Arnheim argues, the visual arts have been traditionally misunderstood as requiring less intelligence than the liberal arts and sciences because perceptual skills were taken to involve no cognitive activity.[31]

In any case, the idea that to see means to forget the name of the thing seen does not imply that seeing is passive. To the contrary, forgetting can be an active process, and many visual artists would agree that attempting to forget what the thing is that you are studying visually, in order to become aware of how it actually appears, is an extremely difficult, tedious and often exhilarating activity. This is because it is connected to the difficult task of self-knowledge, with all of its pitfalls and political obstructions. Consider Nietzsche's idea that all art and philosophy serve 'to remedy and aid the service of growing and struggling life'.[32] Now while romantic art responds to a hunger caused by an impoverishment of life, and seeks rest and tranquillity, Dionysian art expresses the suffering caused by an over-fullness of life, an 'overflowing energy that is pregnant with future'.[33] The distinction turns on the relation of the artist to herself, where the romantic has yet to fully embody her senses, or has yet to fully accept her embodiment with the field of becoming. Only the Dionysian artist has come to terms with her perspective, her solitude.

For the pious there is as yet no solitude; this invention was made only by us, the godless. I do not know of any more profound difference in the whole orientation of an artist than this, whether he looks at his work in progress (at 'himself') from the point of view of the witness, or whether he has 'forgotten the world', which is the essential feature of all monological [i.e. Dionysian] art; it is based *on forgetting*, it is the music of forgetting.[34]

Zeki's project to ground aesthetics in neuropsychology goes astray in a variety of ways by collapsing together psychological-theoretic and aesthetic-artistic interests in visual perception. Perceptual and aesthetic concepts are extended by new scientific projects, in the sense that they cannot and, therefore, ought not, to be replaced by, or reduced to, them. If there are things to learn by assimilating art into science, there are also things to learn by going in the opposite direction, using artistic conceptions of perception to enrich scientific interpretations of visual experience. That is the Wittgensteinian lesson here: If we are to make any progress in clarifying the hugely ramified meaning of beauty in our lives, aesthetics needs to be pursued with a much deeper appreciation for the complexity of the concept of seeing. Appreciating this complexity means here, minimally, not constraining how we understand aesthetic interest to what we can learn from neurology. The deep simplicity of the world that so much art attempts to reveal, and therefore to enhance, will only be lost to an epistemology that stipulates a neurological language to describe visual form and aesthetic eros.

Epilogue

Wittgenstein as an ecologist of meaning

Our civilization is characterized by the word 'progress'. Progress is its form rather than making progress being one of its features. Typically it constructs. It is occupied with building an ever more complicated structure. And even clarity is sought only as a means to that end. For me on the contrary clarity, perspicuity are valuable in themselves.[1]

Although I criticized, in the first chapter, what I called the 'Socratic model' of explaining the meaning of a word, there are some important senses in which Wittgenstein's philosophy is essentially Socratic in nature. Far from being an anti-philosopher clinging dogmatically to the inertia of custom, Wittgenstein shares with Socrates a similar philosophical eros for transcendence and a more meaningful life. One feels this in the passionate character of his writings; but it can be difficult to make sense of his ultimate intentions. In this epilogue, I shall conclude the study by arguing, first, that the aim of Wittgenstein's thought is the enhancement of human freedom, and second, that the difficulty in grasping this ethical orientation of his thought stems from the radical character of his understanding of freedom. Wittgenstein's holistic understanding of meaning and language implies, or is implied by, an ecological understanding of freedom. This is the fundamental ethical difference between his earlier and his later work. While the *Tractatus* describes a transcendental ego ontologically-distinct from a world to which it relates itself by representation, the *Investigations* describes an organic being whose 'interior' is semantically, and so metaphysically, interdependent with the 'external' natural and social world. On the latter view, the inner does not relate to the outer by representing it, but by *extending* and *enhancing* it. Accordingly, human freedom is not actualized by our powers of representation which allow us to epistemologically, and then technologically, dominate nature. Freedom is actualized by our awareness of the intricate reciprocal relations of determination and dependency, which link us together into a larger natural and social whole and give our life its meaning and direction.

It is not so easy to see that Wittgenstein is a philosopher of freedom, especially if one focuses on Wittgenstein's anti-philosophical voices in *Philosophical Investigations* sections 89–133. His remarks about philosophy – as a battle against the bewitchment of our intelligence by means of language (section 109); as having the 'depth' of a grammatical joke (111); as arising from bad analogies (112); and as uncovering nonsense (119) – all tend to suggest that philosophy itself is a disease to be cured of. In turn, the appearance that Wittgenstein gives of identifying philosophy as a pathology of reason can be taken, in spite of his often dazzling ability to raise intriguing questions, to be *a reductio ad absurdum* of the ultimate significance of his work. This view is given special impetus from Wittgenstein's remarks that philosophy 'leaves everything as it is',[2] and that we must '*accept* the everyday language'.[3] This is because the injunction to accept our modes of expression as they stand suggests a repudiation of both the classical ideal of the examined life, as well as the modern Enlightenment ideal of autonomous rationality. So construed, acceptance means submission to conventional wisdom: submission of logos to nomos in the former case, and in the latter, of science to history. For example, this interpretation is given a dramatic sociological spin by Ernest Gellner who interprets Wittgenstein's epistemology of ordinary language as a form of reactionary anti-cosmopolitanism.

> This is the real essence of Wittgenstein's development: the populist idea of the authority of each distinctive culture is applied to the problem of knowledge. In answer to (say) Hume's question, what justification is there for inductive inference, the answer would be: the peasants on our village green have always done it and we, as loyal sons of Ruritanian culture, will defend Ruritanian customs (including induction) to the death! Our cosmopolitan enemies, eager to dominate us and to assimilate us to the bloodless civilization of their metropolis, are trying to deprive us of our customary dances, music, and induction.[4]

Far from being submissive, however, Wittgenstein's notion of acceptance is properly understood as a name for a radical vision of human freedom. First of all, to 'accept the everyday language-game' cannot not simply mean: to *speak* the everyday language-game. Speaking everyday language games is something that everyone speaking a particular language does.[5] In contrast, acceptance, in Wittgenstein's sense, is something to be achieved. To tell someone that she must accept something only makes sense, and only has value, if she has already failed to accept it. It is effecting this acceptance which marks the empowering dimension in Wittgenstein's philosophy. We have seen the sense in which Wittgenstein's view of meaning as determined by use leads us to see descriptions as 'instruments for particular uses' rather than as pictures of facts. The particular purpose that Wittgenstein's own descriptions serve is, as he puts it, 'to make us recognize those workings [of our language]'.[6] By extension, this recognition must involve our coming to recognize that those descriptions in our ordinary language-games are also instruments for particular purposes. As instruments, they can be employed towards diverse ends.

   Now if it is possible to *fail* to recognize this instrumental character of description, that can only mean that we have failed to recognize the ways in which the meaning of a word or a sentence depends upon how it is used; moreover, that we have failed to recognize that words do not dictate the ends towards which they are to be used. In effect, we have tacitly granted to words powers which they do not have; powers to determine the ends they serve, and how they are to serve those ends. We have 'idolized' our words, in the traditional sense of attributing to mere human artifacts powers only wielded by rational agents. On this line of thought, to accept ordinary human speech is to acknowledge our part, our responsibility, in deciding what is being said in speaking them.[7] Correlatively, it means to accept that our thoughts are not necessarily our own, but depend on our community and the larger natural world.

The great irony here is that Wittgenstein is often read as a sceptical philosopher who questions how we can ultimately connect to the world. It is tempting, for example, to read Wittgenstein's point, that having a stereotype of (or concept of) a rabbit is a logical condition for being able to experience the duck-rabbit as a rabbit, as an argument for antirealism. According to Arthur Danto, Wittgenstein's examination of the duck-rabbit implies a kind of linguistic idealism, where 'we have no access to the world save through our representations of it', that 'we cannot even intelligibly draw the distinction between description and reality in order, for example, to say that the one fits the other', and that 'experience is indelibly linguistic'.[8] On this view, it is hard to see how acceptance of our conventional forms of expression could yield philosophical freedom, since the picture suggests a kind of irremediable confinement within our representational conventions and epistemic norms.

This picture can be turned on its head, however. In his well-known study of the problem of style in art history, E. H. Gombrich raises the question as to how to explain the rapid developments in Greek mimetic representation from the beginning of the sixth century and the end of the fifth century BCE.[9] According to Gombrich, an essential condition for the change has to do with the Greek discovery that pictures in themselves are neither true nor false, and that the possibility of using an image to represent reality depends upon a method of projection supplied by the artist (or the spectator). Only when a stereotype is grasped as a tool which is more and/or less useful for purposes of representing reality, and not a picture of a fact to be accepted as true or rejected as false, can it so much as occur to the artist to consider the ways in which that schema might be improved or corrected.

I know of a small girl who became worried and pensive when many Christmas cards began to arrive in her home. How could one tell which was the "correct" rendering of Holy Night? It is a natural question and one which even engaged the mind of Christian theologians in the East and the West. But where it is asked in all seriousness, illustration in our sense of the term cannot exist. It demands the *freedom* of the artist to picture to himself what it may have been like when the heavenly child lay in the manger and the shepherds came to adore it [emphasis mine].[10]

In this sense, accepting the everyday language-game does not mean resigning oneself to unameliorable modes of expression, but rather to assume responsibility for making those modes speak to how things are. The freedom in question concerns the awareness that the representational conventions do not themselves force upon us their interpretation, nor decide for us the representational task which they are to serve. Representational conventions themselves do not decide truth; truth is revealed or suppressed by how individuals and communities use those conventions. One might put the point in terms of the duck-rabbit: once you discover that what you thought was a picture of a duck can also be seen as a rabbit, there is a sense in which you are slightly less unfree than you were prior to the discovery. You now have a choice.

As a form of ethics, Wittgenstein's grammatical analysis of seeing concerns more than just individual choice. Elucidating the instrumental nature of language leads to a holistic view of meaning, where to understand a sentence is to understand a language, which in turn is to understand a form of life. This is essentially an ecological view of meaning in which the aim of the philosophical enquiry is to reveal the complex relationships of interdependency between systems of representation and contexts of life. While empirically-grounded, ecology is also a normative science in that the study of the interactions of elements and being within ecosystems is guided by concepts of what a healthy, flourishing ecosystem looks like. The ultimate aim of any project to illumine the meanings of concepts central to human life, like the concept of sight, can only be to understand what we ought to use these words to mean, in order for us to flourish as human beings, and biologically, as centres of unfolding wholeness.

Thinking of Wittgenstein as an ecologist of meaning is a helpful way to see the unity of some themes in this work. For instance, the externalist view of meaning that arises in Wittgenstein's criticisms of Cartesian dualism echoes an ecological reversal of the idea that freedom involves the autonomy of the subject as an individual. Ecology sees individuals as organisms, among other organisms located within ecosystems. Within this framework, the continuities are as evident as the boundaries of individuality. This is because ecosystems involve the continuous flow of energy and nutrients, through and among the living organisms and the abiotic, or non-living, materials that together make up the biosphere: the continuous, self-maintaining field of living activity that is as alive as any cat or cell or coral reef. Matter is not simply something we work with our hands or machines in order to pursue happiness, but something that is continually cycling through us in the forms of carbon, nitrogen, sulphur, phosphorus, oxygen and hydrogen. As Wittgenstein helps us to see, meaning flows through and among us as well. The theoretical distortion of this ecological character of meaning does not merely confuse the rational study of language; it engenders alienation by imposing a false sense of interiority and separateness on individuals. Alienation is bad. From this angle, it is easier to see that Wittgenstein is not an anti-philosopher per se; he is just against forms of thinking and models of explanation which undermine or conceal the true conditions for freedom. His antipathy towards constructionism in philosophy, and his ambivalence towards modernity and science in general, are often construed as forms of nostalgic romanticism. But Wittgenstein has no aversion to true progress, only to the ideology of progress.

This takes us back to the artichoke. Ecology describes not only the flows of energy and nutrients within the life world, but flows of information as well. Our conception of the natural and social world, as mediating the flow of information, is thus itself part of the system, and so changes in our views of the world literally change the world itself. This can be misconstrued as the negation of the possibility of objective knowledge, since it seems to deny the mind-independence of meaning. But the analogy to ecology pushes in the opposite direction. If freedom is understood not as the power to objectify, but the awareness of interdependency, then the ecological inseparability of thinking and being points towards, not nihilism, but thinking as a form of life. This is what is most conspicuous about Wittgenstein's thought in the *Investigations*: it is *alive*.

On this ecological view, freedom is *not* essentially opposed to nature. If, instead, nature is viewed ecologically, not as inert 'resources' to be represented and expropriated, but as increasingly complicated patterns of integration and wholeness within biodiversity, then freedom might plausibly be seen as a moment within the development of nature itself. From this perspective, to remove oneself from contact with (or awareness of) ecological constraints on how one lives is to remove oneself from the place which gives one's life meaning. Correlatively, to be free is not to master nature; it is to live in community with nature, where freedom is a shared project; where nature offers us sustenance and direction, and where we in turn offer nature our own uniquely human insights into how nature's ecological ends of wholeness and biodiversity can be furthered. If Wittgenstein did not spell out these larger ethical implications for his study of philosophical grammar, it is plausible to explain this by saying that he was too alienated, from his body and from membership in any real community, to be able to effect a connection. But he did leave us with the record of his burning pathos for such a living connection. There's a lot of love there.

Notes

Introduction   Towards a grammar of sight

1. Ludwig Wittgenstein, *Philosophical Investigations* 2nd edn, G. E. M. Anscombe, trans. (Oxford: Blackwell, 1998), section 129.
2. Unless otherwise noted, all references are to Wittgenstein's later thought in the *Investigations* and the associated manuscript material.
3. Specifically, Wittgenstein (1998). Corresponding manuscripts that I shall occasionally refer to include *Last Writings on the Philosophy of Psychology, Vol. 1* (1982), *Remarks on the Philosophy of Psychology, Vols 1 and 2* (1980) and *Zettel* (1970).
4. In speaking of semantic richness, I mean to refer to the diverse things that those concepts can be used to say, and to the diverse ways in which the possibilities for those uses are fixed by the larger contexts within which they are employed.
5. *Cf.* Wittgenstein (1998), section 43: 'For a *large* class of cases – though not for all – in which we employ the word "meaning" it can be defined thus: the meaning of a word is its use in the language.'
6. For example, William Lycan interprets Wittgenstein as offering a use theory of meaning. *Cf.* W. Lycan, *Philosophy of Language: A Contemporary Introduction* (New York: Routledge, 2000).
7. My approach to the study of visual meaning might seem to be ignoring the deeper issue in the philosophy of perception: the question as to whether *meaning* is a natural kind. In Fodor's review of Hilary Putnam's book *The Threefold Chord: Mind, Body and World, London Review of Books*, 22 (2000), he levels a criticism similar to the one mentioned above at Putnam's use of Wittgenstein to attack representational theories of perception. The present study bears some important similarities to Putnam's approach to the philosophy of perception in those lectures. However, whereas Putnam attacks the explanatory cogency of representational theories of perception, by attacking what he takes to be their unacceptable sceptical implications (i.e. we end up only *directly* perceiving mental representations rather than real physical objects), my approach supports no criticisms of the explanatory models as theories of perceptual capacities. Rather, my criticisms concern the ways that those models lead to distortions, and in particular, oversimplifications of our concepts of those capacities.
8. *Cf.* Wittgenstein (1998), 138: 'we *understand* the meaning of a word when we hear or say it; we grasp it in a flash, and what we grasp in this way is surely something different from the "use" which is extended in time!' (original italics)
9. No attempt is made to offer a conception of visual meaning incorporating these two senses. To the contrary, the assumption that these senses of meaning must rest on some deeper sense will be identified as a primary source of confusion about how conceptual meaning is to be explained.

10. For example, Fodor, in 'Could there be a theory of perception?', *Journal of Philosophy*, 63 (1966), interprets both Ryle and Wittgenstein as arguing that questions of the form 'How do we see *p*?' are appropriately understood as questions about logical grammar. As we shall argue with respect to Wittgenstein, this interpretation goes astray in conflating the claim that no genuinely philosophical questions about seeing are theoretical in nature (i.e. call for rational reconstruction) with the claim that some genuine philosophical questions about seeing are *not* theoretical in nature (i.e. must be answered by an appeal to use). Only the latter claim is made by Wittgenstein.

11. The question as to whether these implications are ones that Wittgenstein did accept, or would have accepted, as consistent with his thinking, is of secondary importance to my more general interest in visual perception. In the preface to the *Investigations*, Wittgenstein writes that, 'I should not like my writing to spare other people the trouble of thinking. But, if possible, to stimulate someone to thoughts of his own.' Since I interpret him as offering us less a theory than a technique, I am obliged to heed Wittgenstein's wish by using his technique in new theoretical contexts that he did not himself address.

12. S. Cavell, *This New Yet Unapproachable America* (Albuquerque: Living Batch Press, 1989), p. 32, draws this distinction in speaking of different ways that Wittgenstein's appeal to ordinary use can be heard.

13. Wittgenstein (1998), 291.

14. Wittgenstein (1998), 109.

1   The concept of seeing

1. Ludwig Wittgenstein, *Philosophical Investigations*, 2nd edn, G. E. M. Anscombe, trans. (Oxford: Blackwell, 1998) p. 200.

2. S. Cavell, *The Claim of Reason* (Oxford: Oxford University Press, 1982), p. 354.

3. Jaakko Hintikka and Merrill B. Hintikka, *Ludwig Wittgenstein: Half-Truths and One-and-a-Half-Truths* (Boston: Kluwer Academic, 1996), p. 41. As I shall argue below, this interpretation presupposes a simple categorial distinction between descriptions of physical and phenomenological objects, which Wittgenstein's investigations aim to undercut.

4. S. Mulhall, *On Being in the World: Wittgenstein and Heidegger on Seeing Aspects* (New York: Routledge, 1990). On Mulhall's interpretation, the point of Wittgenstein's discussion of seeing aspects, that all seeing is continuous seeing-as, is actually meant to undercut interpretive models of perception. But this reading still negatively emphasizes the concept of interpretation.

5. A. Danto, 'Description and the phenomenology of perception', in N. Bryson, M. Holly and K. Moxey, eds, *Visual Theory* (Oxford: Polity Press, 1991).

6. Ludwig Wittgenstein, *Last Writings on the Philosophy of Psychology, Vol. 1*, C. G. Luckhardt and M. E. Aue, trans, G. H. von Wright and H. Nyman, eds (Chicago: University of Chicago Press, 1982), section 172.

7. Malcolm Budd's interpretation, in 'Wittgenstein on seeing aspects', *Mind*, 96 (1987), is the only one I know of that explicitly mentions this aspect of the discussion. As he puts it, the importance of seeing aspects is that 'its irreducibility either to a purely sensory or to a purely intellectual paradigm makes it especially suitable to promote the recognition of the polymorphous character of the concept of seeing'.

8. *Cf.* Cavell (1982), p. 14. As is perhaps now apparent, I shall, to an extent, be presupposing Cavell's interpretation of Wittgenstein's notion of a criterion.

9. Wittgenstein (1998), section 373.

10. Wittgenstein (1982), p. 13.

11. S. Cavell, *This New Yet Unapproachable America* (Albuquerque: Living Batch Press, 1989), p. 51.

12. Russell offers a compelling expression of this thought.

> ... a photograph which is so smudged that it might equally represent Brown or Jones or Robinson is vague. A small-scale map is usually vaguer than a large-scale map, because it does not show all the turns and twists of the roads, rivers, etc. so that various slightly different courses are compatible with the representation that it gives. Vagueness, clearly, is a matter of degree, depending upon the extent of the possible differences between different systems represented by the same representation. Accuracy, on the contrary, is an ideal limit.

Rosanna Keefe and Peter Smith, eds, *Vagueness: A Reader* (Cambridge: MIT Press, 1999), p. 66.

13. Hintikka and Hintikka (1996) argue that Wittgenstein's interest in aspect seeing in his later work is inversely related to his earlier interest in the following sense. While in the *Tractatus* he used the Necker cube to argue the theoretical need for a phenomenological language (i.e. a language referring only to 'phenomenological objects' or inner experiences) as his 'basic language', in *Philosophical Investigations* the very same Necker cube serves as a counter-example to his thesis that physicalistic language (i.e. a language referring to public, physical objects) is basic; where 'basic' means presumably that it is the language into which all knowledge claims are to be analysed (p. 50). But while this interpretation sheds light on the relationship between Wittgenstein's earlier and later work, it arguably oversimplifies the aim of the discussion by taking Wittgenstein to be denying that we can directly refer to our experiences. For instance, the Hintikkas argue that 'When the "aspect" changes without anything's changing in the physical situation, we have something that looks quite hard to translate into a physicalistic language' (p. 42). But reading Wittgenstein as arguing that we *can* describe our visual experiences (our 'phenomenological objects') in physicalistic language (and therefore do not need to deny our experiences or to posit a phenomenological language) upholds one side of a dichotomy that Wittgenstein seems to be attacking. As Wittgenstein puts it, his aim is not to offer a classification of psychological concepts, but only to offer examples 'to enable the reader to shift for himself when he encounters conceptual difficulties'. Wittgenstein (1998), 206a.

14. Wittgenstein (1998), 193c.

15. The terms 'infer' and 'construct' can be understood to carry importantly different epistemological implications; for example, Russell's attempt to treat our knowledge of the external world as a logical construction out of, rather than an inference from, sense-data. *Cf.* Bertrand Russell, *Our Knowledge of the External World* (New York: Routledge, 1993). On the other hand, cognitive psychologist Donald Hoffman argues that for psychological purposes, 'construction' is more apt than von Helmholtz's 'unconscious inference' [*unbewusster Schluss*], since 'inference' carries with it the misleading connotation to conscious activity. Donald Hoffman, *Visual Intelligence: How We Create What We See* (New York: W. W. Norton, 2000), p. 11. For present purposes, the terms bear no important differences.

16. Unless the drawing is not of a face in an obvious sense, for example, if the drawing is of a cloud formation that can be seen as a face. But in that case, we are no longer talking about the first use of 'see'.

17. Wittgenstein (1998), 193b.

18. Ludwig Wittgenstein, *Zettel*, G. E. M. Anscombe, trans., G. H. von Wright, eds (Berkeley: University of California Press, 1970), 320.

19. Wittgenstein (1998), 193f.

20. Wittgenstein (1998), 194a.

21. Wittgenstein (1998), 196b.

22. Wittgenstein (1998), 204b.

23. This formulation of the individualist position is from Tyler Burge. As Burge spells out the supervenience thesis: 'an individual's intentional states and events (types and tokens) could not be different from what they are, given the individual's physical, chemical, neural, or functional histories, where these histories are specified non-intentionally . . .' Burge (1986b: 4).

24. 'Its *causes* are of interest to psychologists.' Wittgenstein (1998), 193d.

25. 'The psychological concept hangs out of reach of this [physiological] explanation.' Wittgenstein (1998), 212c. One important implication is that psychologists pursuing the same feeling of puzzling uncertainty are misconstruing the gist of their questions, and in such a way that '. . . problem and method pass one another by'. Wittgenstein (1998), 232a.

26. *Cf.* Ludwig Wittgenstein, *Remarks on the Philosophy of Psychology, Vol. 1*, G. E. M. Anscombe, trans. (Chicago: University of Chicago Press, 1980a), section 556: 'It is easy to imagine someone knowing his way about a city quite accurately, i.e. he finds the shortest way from one part of the city to another quite surely – and yet that he should be perfectly incapable of drawing a map of the city. That, as soon as he tries, he only produces something completely wrong . . .'

27. Wittgenstein (1998), 193f.

28. *Ibid.*

29. Wittgenstein (1998), 197h.

30. Wittgenstein (1998), 195c.

31. Wittgenstein (1998), 202b. This is my translation. Anscombe's translation here has an ambiguity which the German does not have. The statement 'I describe what I am seeing differently' could mean either that I am describing the same

image differently, or that I am seeing something different which I am describing. The German is clearer: '*Ich* beschreibe, *was ich sehe, anders*'.

32. Thinking that Wittgenstein is arguing as much motivates the idea that he is a linguistic-idealist who is denying that there is nothing we can see that we cannot speak. I shall take up this issue in the next chapter when I discuss ineffability and the private language arguments. There, I shall argue that first-person perceptual avowals are not typically proffered on the basis of criteria.

33. In other cases, it is the *absence* of a verbal report that can serve as a criterion for someone's not seeing the same thing (or having the same visual image). For example, 'I see two pictures, with the duck-rabbit surrounded by rabbits in one, by ducks in the other. I do not notice that they are the same. Does it *follow* from this that I *see* something different in the two cases? – It gives us a reason for using this expression here.' Wittgenstein (1998), 195c. Here, reporting that the same figure (i.e. the duck-rabbit) had been seen in each case would be a criterion for having seeing the same thing in each case. Likewise, not reporting is a criterion of not having seen the same thing.

34. Wittgenstein (1998), 204b.

35. Wittgenstein (1998), 194c.

36. *Cf.* Wittgenstein (1998), 209b.

37. 'For when should I call it a mere case of knowing, not seeing? – Perhaps when someone treats the picture as a working drawing, *reads* it like a blueprint.' Wittgenstein (1998), 204a.

38. Gilbert Ryle speaks of 'see' as an 'achievement verb' (as opposed to a task or process verb) in order to explain (away) epistemological problems connected with our inability to say anything in ordinary discourse about what it is that we do or undergo when we see something.

> If I descry a hawk, I find the hawk but I do not find my seeing of the hawk. My seeing of the hawk seems to be a queerly transparent sort of process . . . But the mystery dissolves when we realize that 'see', 'descry' and 'find' are not process words, experience words or activity words. They do not stand for perplexingly undetectable actions or reactions, any more than 'win' stands for a perplexingly undetectable bit of running, or 'unlock' for an unreported bit of key-turning.

Gilbert Ryle, *The Concept of Mind* (New York: Barnes and Noble, 1949), p. 152. Speaking of the term 'see' as having a particular sense, or even a variety of senses, however, suggests that it is the *sense* which determines how 'see' can be used, and what it can be used to say. This suggestion is confusing because it implies that the sense of 'see' determines these factors independently of details about occasions on which it would be used. *Cf.* John Austin's criticism of A. J. Ayer in *Sense and Sensibilia* (Oxford: Oxford University Press, 1962), pp. 78–93. Unlike Ryle, Wittgenstein does not infer from the fact that 'see' is used in different ways the idea that 'see' has different senses. Unlike Ryle, Wittgenstein is not trying to offer a 'logical geography of concepts', but only ways to avoid possible confusions, by offering reminders about what we would say when. The latter issues in neither a taxonomy of logical forms, nor a denial of the conceptual coherence of empirical theories of perception.

39. Quoted by Lawrence Weschler in his biography of conceptual artist Robert Irwin, *Seeing is Forgetting the Name of the Thing One Sees: A Life of Contemporary Artist Robert Irwin.* (Berkeley: University of California Press, 1982).
40. Wittgenstein (1970), section 467, original italics.
41. As Wittgenstein puts it, 'To interpret is to think, to do something; seeing is a state.' Wittgenstein (1998), 212d.
42. *Cf.* Wittgenstein (1980b), section 43: 'The essential thing about seeing is that it is a state, and such a state can suddenly change into another one.'
43. Wittgenstein (1998), 212e. The passage continues 'So there is a similarity in the use of "seeing" in the two contexts.'
44. Wittgenstein (1998), 206b.
45. Wittgenstein (1998), 204f.
46. *Cf.* Charles Travis, *The Uses of Sense* (Oxford: Clarendon Press, 1989).
47. *Cf.* Keefe and Smith (1999), p. 49.
48. See note 26 above.
49. 'It is as if one saw a screen with scattered colour-patches, and said: the way they are here, they are unintelligible; they only make sense when one completes them into a shape. − Whereas I want to say: Here *is* the whole. (If you complete it, you falsify it.)' Wittgenstein (1980a), 257.
50. Wittgenstein (1998), 193e.
51. Wittgenstein (1998), 196f.
52. Wittgenstein (1998), 196b.
53. Wittgenstein (1998), 194a.
54. Wittgenstein (1998), 206h.
55. Wittgenstein (1998), 194c.
56. Wittgenstein (1998), 201b.
57. To be more precise, it is not so much an analogy as it is an example meant to further determine the meaning of the concept *noticing an aspect*: it jumps the gun to draw a firm distinction between the kind of relation the similarity between two faces bears to the faces themselves, and the kind that a geometrical pattern of pencil lead bears to a smiley face.
58. Wittgenstein (1998), 194b. It is interesting to consider, in relation to this, that when being taught the names of animals like 'dog', 'bird', 'alligator', etc., children are often shown not only photographs of the animals (or if at the zoo, ostensive definitions of the creatures themselves), but also shown drawings, sculptures, toys, and other representations.
59. For example, Meyer Schapiro speaks of Cézanne as equating the art of painting with the underlying psychological mechanisms of visual experience, both being processes, governed by a definite set of rules of transformation, and operating on sensations which are 'sifted and correlated and the world of objects, solid and flat, is put into an ordered form'. Meyer Schapiro, *Worldview in Painting: Art and Society* (New York: George Braziller, 1999), p. 102.

60. In *Sense and Sensibilia,* John Austin offers forceful criticism of the use of the terms 'direct' and 'indirect' in classical sense-data theory. Nevertheless, and not withstanding the ways these terms ordinarily function, there is something apt about their use as an expression of the interpretation picture. They convey the idea of a direct line of sight being broken, of something which gets in the way of our seeing the object we think we are seeing.

61. Wittgenstein (1998), 200a.

62. *Cf.* Wittgenstein (1998), 127.

63. Wittgenstein (1998), 193g.

64. *Ibid.*

65. Of course, I might offer reformulations of the description, for example, by saying that *this* fruit is the same colour as *that* stop sign over there. But if these serve to communicate, they do so *not* by being more direct descriptions, but by substituting one expression of a rule for another.

66. For example, in distinguishing precision from accuracy, Russell argues that while accuracy concerns the truth of a belief, a belief is precise 'when only one fact would verify it'. Keefe and Smith (1999), p. 68.

67. Wittgenstein (1998), 199e.

68. Wittgenstein (1980a), 70.

69. *Cf.* Wittgenstein (1998), 197a. This sense of 'expression' must be contrasted with the way I have been using the term to refer generally to the various ways in which what we see, and how we see it, is manifested in our behaviour, and especially, our linguistic behaviour. In the latter, expressions of what we can see take such diverse forms as a verbal description, a vocal expression ('Look! A rabbit!'), a bodily gesture, a drawing, or a reaction to a drawing. On the present sense, an expression is distinguished from a description in the way it relates to what it is about. What a poetic phrase *expresses* and how it expresses it are not easily distinguished (and are perhaps only distinguishable in the case of bad poems). Hence, we speak not of the accuracy but the *genuineness* of an expression. We would not call someone's writhing a description of his experience of pain. But if crying out 'Ouch' or 'Help! I'm in pain' is simply a more refined, more instrumentally efficacious way of crying out in pain, then these words are also misleadingly thought of as descriptions of an experience or sensation of pain that the person in pain has.

70. Wittgenstein (1998), 194a.

71. *Ibid.*

72. *Ibid.*

73. *Cf.* Grice's criticism of Austin's attacks on sense-data statements in H. P. Grice, *Studies in the Way of Words* (Cambridge: Harvard University Press, 1989).

74. Wittgenstein (1998), 195b.

75. *Ibid.*

76. Mulhall (1990).

77. Mulhall (1990), p. 136.

78. *Ibid.*

79. Mulhall (1990), p. 137.

80. Mulhall (1990), p. 132.

81. *Ibid.*
82. Mulhall (1990), p. 144.
83. *Cf.* Wittgenstein (1980a), section 949: 'A metaphysical question is always in appearance a factual one, although the problem is a conceptual one.'
84. Mulhall (1990), p. 142.
85. Mulhall (1990), p. 143.
86. Martin Heidegger, *History of the Concept of Time*, T. Kisiel, trans. (Bloomington: Indiana University Press, 1992).
87. Mulhall (1990), p. 144.

2   Theories of visual meaning

1. L. Wittgenstein, *On Certainty* (New York: Blackwell, 1969), p. 126.
2. Noam Chomsky, *New Horizons in the Study of Language and Mind* (Cambridge: Cambridge University Press, 2000), p. 20.
3. P. M. S. Hacker, *Wittgenstein: Mind and Will* (Oxford: Blackwell, 2000), p. 113.
4. For example, B. Goldberg, 'The correspondence hypothesis', *The Philosophical Review*, 77 (1968) and J. Heil, 'Does Cognitive Psychology rest on a mistake?', *Mind*, 90 (1981). Both arguments are inspired by Wittgenstein's discussion of rule-following, in particular his criticism of the idea that understanding could take the form of grasping a pictorial or other representation.
5. Z. W. Pylyshyn, *Seeing and Visualizing: It's Not What You Think* (Cambridge: MIT Press, 2003), p. 51.
6. *Ibid.*, p. 43.
7. *Ibid.*, p. 39.
8. *Ibid.*, p. 64.
9. *Ibid.*, p. 66.
10. Donald Hoffman, *Visual Intelligence: How We Create What We See* (New York: W. W. Norton & Co., 2000).
11. *Ibid.*, p. 13.
12. As the diagram suggests, any given two-dimensional figure can be interpreted as representing an infinite set of objects of different shape and size. Two objects at different relative distances from the perceiver can project a retinal image of identical size, and the same applies to shape.
13. Ludwig Wittgenstein, *Zettel*, G. E. M. Anscombe, trans., G. E. M. Anscombe and G. H. von Wright, eds (Berkeley: University of California Press, 1970), section 438.
14. Chomsky makes this point in connection with anti-individualistic arguments when he says that it is 'immaterial whether people might accept the nonveridical cases as "seeing a cube" (taking "seeing" to be having an experience, whether "as if" or veridical)'. Chomsky (2000), p. 23.
15. Hoffman (2000), p. 189.
16. *Ibid.*, p. 2.
17. *Ibid.*

18. *Cf.* H. H. Price's argument for sense-data in *Perception* (London: Methuen, 1950), p. 26.

19. Hoffman (2000), p. 11.

20. *Ibid.*, p. 10.

21. In speaking of visual meaning here, I mean to refer to what is correlated to a state of visual understanding.

22. Hoffman (2000), p. 3.

23. T. Burge, 'Individualism and psychology', *The Philosophical Review*, 95 (1986), pp. 118–19.

24. Ludwig Wittgenstein, *Philosophical Investigations*, 2nd edn, G. E. M. Anscombe, trans (Oxford: Blackwell, 1998), section 355. It could be added here that the strength of Hoffman's characterization of our impression of the square as a serious error, and so an elaborate fabrication, rests on his assumption that the measurement of the photometer is not in error, and so not a construction. But if our impression is a construction, then so is the photometric result, since our taking it as a measure of visible light rests on our ordinary concepts of relative brightness. If Hoffman means to redefine 'measurement' as 'construction', then the meaning of his assertion collapses into nonsense.

25. Ludwig Wittgenstein, *Tractatus Logico-Philosophicus*, C. K. Ogden, trans. (New York: Routledge, 1999).

26. Chomsky (2000), p. 26.

27. *Ibid.*

28. *Ibid.*, p. 53.

29. *Ibid.*

30. Hoffman (2000), p. 7.

31. *Ibid.*, p. 10.

32. *Ibid.*, p. 198.

33. *Ibid.*, p. 199: 'To say that experiences provide a systematic but arbitrary guide to the relational realm is not to deny that experiences are real and must be take seriously. Snake experiences are real experiences and must be taken seriously. But they don't entail that anything in the relational realm resembles a snake, just as a trash can icon doesn't entail that circuits and software resemble a trash can.'

34. *Ibid.*, p. 22.

35. *Ibid.*, p. 25.

36. Wittgenstein (1998), 139.

37. *Ibid.*, 150.

38. *Cf.* Wittgenstein (1998), 526: 'A picture is perhaps a still-life; but I don't understand one part of it: I cannot see solid objects there, but only patches of color on the canvas. – Or I see everything as solid but there are objects that I am not acquainted with (they look like implements, but I don't know their use). – Perhaps, however, I am acquainted with the objects, but in another sense do not understand the way they are arranged.'

39. *Cf.* Wittgenstein (1998), 196: 'If you put the "organization" of a visual impression on a level with colours and shapes, you are proceeding from the idea of the visual impression as an inner object. Of course this makes this object into a chimera;

a queerly shifting construction. For the similarity to a picture is now impaired ... this by itself wrecks the comparison of "organization" with colour and shape in visual impressions.'

40. *Ibid.*
41. *Ibid.*, 197a.
42. John Searle makes this very point in his critical review of *New Horizons*: 'When Chomsky suggests that the concepts expressed by words like "carburetor" and "bureaucrat" must be innately known by every child, and that learning the meanings of words is just a matter of applying labels to concepts the child already has, you know that something has gone radically wrong.' John Searle, 'End of the Revolution', *The New York Review of Books*, 28 (2002), p. 7.
43. John Searle, *Minds, Brains and Science* (Cambridge: Harvard University Press, 1984).
44. For example, B. Goldberg, 'Mechanism and meaning', in J. Hyman, ed., *Investigating Psychology* (New York: Routledge, 1991) and Heil (1981). Both arguments are inspired by Wittgenstein's discussion of rule-following, in particular his criticism of the idea that understanding could take the form of grasping a pictorial or other representation.
45. Hoffman (2000), p. 24.
46. Wittgenstein (1998), 33: 'a move in chess doesn't consist simply in moving a piece in such-and-such a way on the board ...'
47. *Ibid.*, 200: 'imagine a game of chess translated according to certain rules into a series of actions which we do not ordinarily associate with a *game* − say into yells and stamping of feet. And now suppose those two people to yell and stamp instead of playing the form of chess that we are used to; and this in such a way that their procedure is translatable by suitable rules into a game of chess. Should we still be inclined to say they were playing a game?'

3   The experience and expression of sight

1. Ludwig Wittgenstein, *Zettel*, G. E. M. Anscombe, trans., G. E. M. Anscombe and G. H. von Wright, eds (Berkeley: University of California Press, 1970), section 341.
2. To an extent this is true, and I shall register agreement with Dennett on various points, in particular his attacks on the traditional property of incorrigibility that awareness of qualia is taken to have.
3. My interpretation will not presuppose that the philosophical puzzles surrounding qualia are fundamentally questions about language. Whether Wittgenstein is to be interpreted as believing this I think is an open question, but one not directly relevant to my interpretation.
4. Ludwig Wittgenstein, *Philosophical Investigations* 2nd edn, G. E. M. Anscombe, trans. (Oxford: Blackwell, 1998), section 304: ' "But you will surely admit that there is a difference between pain-behavior accompanied by pain and

pain-behavior without any pain?" – Admit it? What greater difference could there be? – "And yet you again and again reach the conclusion that the sensation is *nothing*." – Not at all. It is not a *something*, but not a *nothing* either! The conclusion was only that a nothing would serve just as well as a something about which nothing could be said . . .'

5. My speaking of private language *arguments* is deliberate. While speaking of a single argument against private language is not per se wrong, it does suggest misleadingly that there is some definitive argument against some clearly specifiable feature of the concept of private language. To the contrary, I shall argue that the problems with the concept of private language have to do with its lacking full intelligibility. It is this very lack of intelligibility, thus making it an indeterminate target, that leaves no space for definitive arguments. In a sense, there is nothing there to argue against, except the intuitions of the private language advocate who thinks there is.

6. From this perspective, the problem is that natural language is constrained by the pragmatic requirements for effective communication. As such it is too coarse to articulate the richness of what is immediately given. This inability, this failure of (public) language which is supposed to illustrate the sense in which the Given falls through the cracks of language, is given sense through the possibility of a phenomenologically perspicuous language. The private language is one which is not shaped by the needs of communication, and so is freed to capture in finer-grain the logical multiplicity of visual reality.

7. This way of characterizing the critical force of Wittgenstein's criterial investigations reflects my attempt to avoid presupposing that philosophical questions have a particular form or subject matter that distinguishes them from other non-philosophical kinds of questions. Hence, I shall not argue that Dennett's analysis is wrong as a philosophical analysis, or that Wittgenstein's approach is the only sensible way of construing the issue.

8. *Cf.* Jaegwon Kim's discussion of qualia as intrinsic properties in *Philosophy of Mind* (Boulder: Westview Press, 1998), p. 177.

9. S. Shoemaker, 'Qualia and Consciousness', *Mind*, 3 (1991).

10. The intuition is sharpened by considering ways of logically-detaching that *way it is like* from the background setting within which we usually talk about how things look. The case of red–green colour blindness is one example, where we can imagine not being aware that someone else cannot see a difference that we can see. A similar kind of sharpening can be effected by considerations involving the idea of machine vision. Consider a face-recognition computer used to identify ('recognize') the faces of suspected terrorists as they attempt to board an airplane. Can we speak of that computer as having the same, or analogous, visual experience that we have when we look at their face? Or imagine a much more sophisticated machine that could read facial expressions and respond to them in indefinitely many ways, depending on how its output is programmed. There could be complicated algorithms correlating particular muscular configurations, motions, even reactions to various stimuli, to various concepts. Such a machine might conceivably be able to scan a face and tell us whether that person was angry, or resentful,

or melancholic; provided that these concepts could be specified in those terms. Even so, one might argue that the machine would not be able to *see* the look of the face. The machine would not have the qualitative experience that we have.

11. Against the charge that the Cartesian flavour of this picture marks it as a target for eliminative materialism, Shoemaker feels compelled to offer a Darwinian defence of ordinary psychological concepts as an innate theory of mind qua behaviour. Shoemaker (1991), p. 7.

12. For example, M. Tye, 'Qualia, content, and the inverted spectrum', *Nous*, 28 (1994).

13. Shoemaker (1991), p. 518. As he makes the point in discussing experiences of two red objects which are indistinguishable:

> One would say that they look alike, and this might be construed as meaning that the experiences of them share the same intentional properties. They are both 'of red' ... It is also true that they are phenomenally exactly alike. But here it seems that they both represent the same shade of colour *because* they are phenomenally alike in a way that could not be true if their being phenomenally alike just meant that they represent the same shade of colour.

14. For example, Thomas Nagel, 'What is it like to be a bat?', *Philosophical Review*, 83 (1974) and Frank Jackson, 'Epiphenomenal qualia', *Philosophical Quarterly*, 32 (1982).

15. Shoemaker (1991), p. 510. On the other side, he argues that Inverted Spectrum arguments show that qualia tokens cannot be functionalized. This does not conflict with physicalism, on Shoemaker's take, since a functionalist account can be given of what it is for a property to be a qualia.

16. Daniel Dennett, 'Quining Qualia', in W. Lacan, ed., *Mind and Cognition* (Oxford: Blackwell, 1990). Dennett defines 'to quine' ironically as: 'To deny resolutely the existence or importance of something real or significant.' The other main attack cited in the debate is given in G. Harman, 'The intrinsic qualities of experience', *Philosophical Perspectives*, 4 (1990). Harman argues that the hypothesis of visual qualia is not supported by ordinary visual experience.

17. For example, despite his 'intentionalist' stance on the question of the kind of similarity that we are aware of when we introspect our qualia, Michael Tye maintains that 'there is a *general* kind of consciousness – so-called "phenomenal consciousness", which is essential to all perceptual experiences and bodily sensations', and that 'qualia are simply those features, whatever they may be, which comprise the phenomenal or subjective aspects of bodily sensations and perceptual experiences'. Tye (1994), pp. 159–60.

18. As Dennett characterizes his aim: 'I want to shift the burden of proof, so that anyone who wants to appeal to private, subjective properties has to prove first that in so doing they are *not* making a mistake.' Dennett (1990), p. 1.

19. This term is not entirely felicitous, since it seems to suggest a kind of contradiction in terms. After all, logic is the last thing one would want to call 'private'. The connotation I have in mind, however, is simply that this kind of privacy is *ex hypothesi* unbridgeable.

20. John Locke, *An Essay Concerning Human Understanding* (New York: New American Library, 1964), p. 15.

21. Thus, ordinary colour blindness does not count as a case of logical privacy in this sense just because it *can* be detected.

22. Saying that the idea of logical privacy involves the possibility of specifying the character of visual experiences independently of the objects causing them, and behavioural responses to them, does not simply mean, of course, that we must be able to distinguish our experience from what we see or how we describe what we see. Nothing could be easier (I just did it), and only the most extreme solipsist would want to deny the distinction between percept and object. Rather, the possibility of logical privacy requires that the inherent properties of the visual impression constituting its (incommunicable) look be independently specifiable, in a way analogous to the way that the word 'red' can be specified independently of referring to its meaning as the name of a colour. Only then can it make sense to speak of something that we can see but that our words, or for that matter, our gestures, paint or pixels, incompetences, cannot in principle reach, for purposes of communication.

23. Dennett (1990), p. 4.

24. *Ibid.*

25. *Ibid.*

26. The idea of an 'intuition pump' reflects Dennett's dialectical approach to the problem and is reflected in his stated aim of showing that the pre-theoretical intuition, routinely appealed to in arguments for qualia, is so thoroughly confused that any rational reconstruction would have to jettison all of those intuitive features.

27. Dennett (1990), p. 5.

28. Chase may be right in claiming that while the taste of the coffee itself has not changed, his reactive attitudes towards that taste have changed. But it may also be the case that he is wrong about the constancy of his qualia, and, so, wrong about his standards changing over the years. Or it may be a combination of changes in both qualia and his attitudes towards them. The same possibilities naturally apply to Sanborn.

29. Dennett (1990), p. 6.

30. *Ibid.*

31. Dennett (1990), p. 7.

32. Wittgenstein (1998), 109.

33. This might explain why third-party linguists cannot catch on to its meaning; like a child who cannot learn what a word means because the parent keeps giving conflicting definitions of it.

34. Unlike Dennett, Wittgenstein is not offering a theory of experience or of sensation language.

35. Wittgenstein (1998), 164.

36. This view stems largely from the fact that discussions of private language are typically focused on the issue of rule-following. My interest in the question as to what it means to follow a rule is secondary to the issue of ineffability and qualia.

37. While not assuming that there is a single argument, I shall nevertheless focus on section 207, which is concerned with the interpretation of an unknown language, as well as sections 243ff., which are generally read as being concerned with private sensations and private experience.

38. J. McDowell, 'Wittgenstein and the inner world' [abstract], *Journal of Philosophy*, 86 (1989), pp. 643–4.

39. Saul Kripke, *Wittgenstein: On Rules and Private Language* (Cambridge: Harvard University Press, 1982).

40. A third sense of privacy, which I shall spend less time on, could be identified in the interpretation offered by Hintikka and Hintikka in *Investigating Wittgenstein* (New York: Blackwell, 1986). They take the relevant sense of privacy to concern the fact that no one else can directly inspect my experiences, and use this conception, in part, to argue against interpretations which take Wittgenstein to be denying the reality of subjective experiences full stop. But this argument, which criticizes Wittgenstein for arguing that language cannot communicate anything private (in that sense of privacy), misconstrues the more radical character of the privacy Wittgenstein has in mind. As such Hintikka's criticism is actually an agreement with Wittgenstein's position, while at the same time failing to address the deeper issues about criteria raised by privacy construed as necessary unintelligibility to others. Though spending less time arguing against this view, I shall allude to problems with it in the course of developing my own interpretation.

41. Only the first way of construing privacy supports the idea of a social theory of meaning, or suggests that a metaphysical insight into the non-individualistic nature of meaning can be gleaned from the arguments.

42. In terms of the example mentioned above, this approach concerns how it is to be decided whether the private linguist is using his private symbol 'S' in accordance with its meaning *S*, or whether he only thinks he is. How does he know whether his current use accords with what he previously meant by it?

43. That is, from any rule avowed by a speaker as the rule he has followed in the past, a bent-rule can be formulated which picks out all prior uses of a term as falling under it, while specifying *prima facie* a different kind of use after that.

44. As various commentators have argued for different reasons, Kripke's dismissal of a dispositional account does not consider more sophisticated physicalist or naturalist theories which might account for mistakes in application. As Goldfarb argues, Krikpe's position seems to suppose from the outset that physicalist accounts of the normativity of rules are precluded by conceptual connections between knowing what we mean by a word and being able to offer a justification of that meaning without applying to a hypothetical physical state which causally determines that meaning. Appealing to such conceptual connections is not in itself problematic, but as Goldfarb notes, it places Kripke's position under a conceptual strain, having to defend certain features of our ordinary linguistic practices, while denying that those practices are justified. *Cf*. W. Goldfarb, 'Kripke on Wittgenstein on rules', *Journal of Philosophy*, 82 (1985), p. 479. This conceptual strain will become more apparent in what follows.

45. Wittgenstein (1998), 213.
46. Kripke (1982), pp. 51ff.
47. This interpretation thus downplays the later discussion of sensation language at 243ff and especially 377–81 as not essential to the argument, but merely taken up by Wittgenstein as a possible counterexample to earlier analysis. As I shall argue below, this interpretation exaggerates the importance of the paradox.
48. Wittgenstein (1998), 201.
49. Colin McGinn, 'Wittgenstein, Kripke and non-reductionism about meaning', in A. Miller and C. Wright, eds, *Rule-Following and Meaning* (Ithaca: McGill Queen's University Press, 2002), pp. 81–92. It has been pointed out by Colin McGinn that Kripke's interpretation rests on a suppressed premise which is both crucial and dubious; namely, that the factuality of semantic ascriptions can only by justified by reference to non-semantic facts, and that the non-reducible character of semantic facts implies the nonfactuality of semantic discourse, rather than its being irreducible to non-semantic or physical facts. While I do not disagree with this diagnosis, McGinn's non-reductionist reading misconstrues the force of the appeal to ordinary criteria in assuming that the refutation of semantic scepticism underwrites a non-reductionist *theory* of meaning.
50. The conceptual nihilism – the view that there are no concepts because there is no meaning – follows from the denial that there are facts about what someone means, which implies that no one ever means anything.
51. Kripke (1982), p. 72. Agreement with communal use does not determine the correctness of an application, but does offer conventional justification for asserting that someone meant *S* by 'S', against sceptical questioning. Strictly speaking, however, and ordinary appearances to the contrary, there is no fact about me qua individual that makes it true that I meant *S*, rather than T by 'S' in the past. Thus, these assertion-conditions, which replace traditional truth-conditions for meaning, are not subject to the sceptical attacks since they merely describe the conventional circumstances under which a meaning ascription is taken to be appropriate, and do not purport to explain normativity by referring to facts which constitute what a given rule requires.
52. Such an individual suffers conceptual nihilism in not being able to mean anything, and having no grasp of objectivity, and so must be judged to succumb to an extreme form of solipsism where, *pace* Descartes, he cannot even be said to know the contents of his own mind.
53. Kripke (1982), p. 110.
54. *Ibid.*
55. G. Baker and P. M. S. Hacker, *Scepticism, Rules and Language* (Oxford: Blackwell, 1984), p. 40.
56. Goldfarb (1985), p. 480.
57. Wittgenstein (1998), 207.
58. *Ibid.* This is not simply a situation where no rules are being followed; it is a grey area where we have reasons for and against ascribing meaning intentions to the members of the tribe.
59. Wittgenstein (1998), 242.

60. This does not mean that 'red' means what we all agree counts as red, but that if we did not agree in our responses to chromatic facts, we could not employ the term 'red' in the ways we do.

61. As Baker and Hacker (1984, p. 25) point out, Kripke's interpretation of the private language argument does not really address this possibility: 'Kripke's objection to private ostensive definitions must be that the attempt to apply any such rule must leave the agent stranded, as it were *ex officio*, on his own desert island. But this leaves open the possibility that all agents are stranded on the *same* island (that public language is a congruence of private languages built separately on private ostensive definitions).'

62. 'What am I to say about the word "red"? – that it means something "confronting us all" and that everyone should really have another word, besides this one, to mean his *own* sensation of red? Or is it like this: the word "red" means something known to everyone; and in addition, for each person, it means something known only to him? (Or perhaps rather: it *refers* to something known only to him.)' Wittgenstein (1998), 273.

63. *Cf.* Wittgenstein (1998), 243.

64. Unless there is something out of the ordinary about the situation.

65. For example, I might take him to be ostensively explaining not the general concept of red, but *this* particular shade or hue of red, or the concept of colour in general. No matter how specifically he characterizes the meaning of the sample, there are possibilities for understanding how the sample is meant to be taken in different ways.

66. 'If the mental image of the timetable could not itself be *tested* for correctness, how could it confirm the correctness of the first memory? (As if someone were to buy several copies of the morning paper to assure himself that what it said was true.)' Wittgenstein (1998), 265.

67. Wittgenstein (1998), 257.

68. Wittgenstein (1998), 258.

69. *Cf.* 'The language of sense data and private experience', in Ludwig Wittgenstein, *Philosophical Occasions*, J. Klagge and A. Nordmann, eds (Cambridge: Hackett, 1993).

70. As an extreme case, Wittgenstein considers the possibility of someone defining 'red' by pointing to something that is not red, and says 'That it is ambiguous is no argument against such a method of definition. Any definition can be misunderstood.' Wittgenstein (1998), 30.

71. Wittgenstein (1998), 31: 'When one shows someone the king in chess and says: "This is the king", this does not tell him the use of this piece – unless he already knows the rules of the game up to this last point: the shape of the king.'

72. Wittgenstein (1998), 261.

73. Wittgenstein (1998), 138.

74. It is this idea, that only I can know for sure what I am experiencing, that motivates in part the possibility of private language as a language purified of the *prima facie* epistemological infelicities with natural language. *Cf.* Wittgenstein (1998), 246.

75. This possibility is precisely what the inverted spectrum illustrates.

76. *Cf.* Wittgenstein (1998), 288.

77. If, after judging them to have normal competence with colour terms, one of them suddenly calls a red apple 'blue', or does so from time to time, we would not say that she is misidentifying her visual qualia, but that she does not yet understand what 'red' means.

78. As I shall argue below, the case of private language is different, and it is important to distinguish between what the various interlocutors in the *Investigations* have to say about private language and with what is meant as an account of the semantics of ordinary sensation terms. The distinction does break down, but only at points, for example, when it is suggested that natural language may have both a public and private semantics (*Cf.* Wittgenstein (1998), 273–4).

79. *Cf.* Wittgenstein (1998), 289–90.

80. *Cf.* Wittgenstein (1998), 377–80.

81. This is due to the fact that if a criterion is employed in using a term, it must be possible for a judgement to fit, or fail to fit, the criterion. *Cf.* Wittgenstein (1998), 288.

82. That is, the problem with private sensation language on this point is not that a private criterion could not serve to establish an is right/seems right distinction, but that that distinction makes no sense in the case of sensations. Thus, for example, attempts to defend the possibility of private language by offering an account of how a private linguist could establish, for example, conditions of acceptability for self-evaluation of judgements, seem to be beside the point.

83. There is nothing problematic about making a vocal noise whenever one feels like it, and some words can be said to function like meaningless grunts or sighs that carry no meaning or too many meanings to have any determinate significance. But such uses of a word do not count as being used to mean one particular thing, and consequently, cannot be taken as bearing a logically-private meaning.

84. The passage (section 293) quoted by Dennett is suggestive: 'Now someone tells me that *he* knows what pain is only from his own case! – Suppose everyone had a box with something in it: we call it a "beetle". No one can look into anyone else's box, and everyone says he knows what a beetle is only by look- ing at *his* beetle. – Here it would be quite possible for everyone to have some- thing different in his box.' Since no one can *say* what their beetle in the box looks like, we have no good reasons for believing that there is anything in the box. And since the existence and characteristics of the 'beetles' cannot be confirmed, they cannot be disconfirmed either. Hence, according to Dennett, Wittgenstein must 'hedge his bets by saying "It is not a *something*, but not a *nothing* either!"' Dennett (1990), p. 3.

85. This possibility could be taken to suggest a meaningful sense of the term 'private language' as referring to the speech of the genius prior to its being accepted as a genuine discovery. Doing so would in turn shed light on one of the motivations for construing experience as logically-private. After all, who doesn't like to think of himself as an undiscovered genius, with a point of view so unique that it cannot be captured in the semantic net of conventional language? The point of the private

language argument would then be to show that this possibility is, if not nonsensical, then at least unlikely.

86. For example, there are various ways we have of deciding when two colours are the same colour, and more importantly, different understandings of what it means for them to be 'similar'. In some contexts, the red of a stop sign and the red of a fire truck count as being the same colour. In other contexts, they would count as being different.

87. Wittgenstein (1998), 216.

88. For example, I go to visit a friend in the hospital. On returning, someone asks me, 'So, how did she look?' I might reply, 'She's looking better. She has got her colour back, and the swelling in her arm has gone down.' Was this an accurate and complete description of what I saw? Perhaps the swelling is actually much worse than I have described it. My friend goes to the hospital afterwards and is surprised that it is so. She returns and tells me, 'Your description was totally misleading. The swelling is much worse!' Here, we can specify, more or less, what it means to give an accurate or inaccurate description of what is seen. An ideal description would not be shaped by these criteria.

89. 'The ideal clock would always point to the time "now". This also connects up with the language which describes only my impressions of the present moment. Akin is the primal utterance that is only an inarticulate sound ... The ideal name, which the word "this" is.' Ludwig Wittgenstein, *Remarks on the Philosophy of Psychology, Vol. 1*, G. E. M. Anscombe, trans., G. E. M. Anscombe and G. H. von Wright, eds (Chicago: University of Chicago Press, 1980a), section 721.

90. Dennett (1990), p. 11.

91. *Ibid.*

92. Of course, as a purported criticism of Wittgenstein's private language arguments it cannot be said to even engage the issue, since it begins by considering an experience with public criteria. Had he considered a case of a birdwatcher who claims to hear a bird-cry that no one else can hear, that would be another matter.

93. Dennett (1990), p. 3.

4 Causality and visual form

1. Ludwig Wittgenstein, *Zettel*, G. E. M. Anscombe, trans., G. E. M. Anscombe and G. H. von Wright, eds (Berkeley: Univesity of California Press, 1970), section 223.

2. *Cf.* Bertrand Russell's criticism of Cartesian interactionism as violating the law of Conservation of Momentum by positing non-physical causes (mental states) of physical events, e.g. bodily movements. Bertrand Russell, *A History of Western Philosophy* (New York: Simon and Schuster, 1945), p. 568.

3. R. Rorty, *Essays on Heidegger and Others* (New York: Cambridge University Press, 1991), p. 51.

4. *Cf.* Gary Hatfield's discussion of this distinction in his *The Natural and the Normative* (Cambridge: MIT Press, 1990).

5. Ludwig Wittgenstein, *Philosophical Investigations* 2nd edn, G. E. M. Anscombe, trans. (Oxford: Blackwell, 1998), section 193d.

6. This is what I take to be the point of Rorty's comparison between Wittgenstein and Davidson in Rorty (1991, p. 58) in which he says that

> ... Davidson's holism is more explicit and thoroughgoing than Wittgenstein's, and so its antiphilosophical consequences are more apparent. Whereas in the *Philosophical Investigations* Wittgenstein still toys with the idea of a distinction between the empirical and the grammatical, between nonphilosophical and philosophical inquiry, Davidson generalizes and extends Quine's refusal to countenance either a distinction between necessary and contingent truth or a distinction between philosophy and science.

7. Thus, for example, the possibility of Newtonian physics presupposes, for Kant, the general lawfulness of nature as an *a priori* principle.

8. Immanuel Kant, *Critique of Pure Reason*, N. K. Smith, trans. (New York: St Martin's Press, 1929), B, vii–xxi.

9. Wittgenstein (1998), 212c.

10. Rudolf Arnheim, *Visual Thinking* (Berkeley: University of California Press, 1969), p. 19.

11. Wittgenstein (1998), 297.

12. The logical connection between cause and effect made the causal theory useful for those who wanted to use what they took to be their subjective sense impressions as a basis for inferring the existence of an external world as cause. At the same time, the logical independence of any particular subjective experience qua effect from any particular object qua cause opens up a logical gap between how the world appears to the eyes and how it might otherwise be.

13. H. P. Grice, *Studies in the Way of Words* (Cambridge: Harvard University Press, 1989).

14. *Cf.* Charles Travis' criticism of the first part of Grice's argument – his linguistic argument for the existence of sense-data – in 'The annals of analysis', *Mind*, 100 (1991). My own approach is informed by his work on Grice and elsewhere.

15. Grice (1989), p. 238.

16. *Cf.* Georges Dicker's discussion of Descartes in *Descartes: An Analytical and Historical Introduction* (New York: Oxford University Press, 1993), p. 31, where he takes it to be obvious that the statement, 'I see a pen, but it is not the case that a pen is one of the causes of my present visual experience', is a contradiction.

17. Grice (1989), p. 238.

18. This conception of behaviour as 'motions and noises' has of course fallen into disrepute, partly as a result of insuperable problems with translating statements about psychological states into statements about behavioural dispositions. Nevertheless, it is clear that contemporary functionalist thinkers employ a conception of behaviour that is in some respects more restrictive than that the older behaviourists used. *Cf.* Jennifer Hornsby's discussion of David Lewis and Brian Loar in

'Physicalist thinking and conceptions of behaviour', in P. Pettit and J. McDowell, eds, *Subject, Thought and Context* (Oxford: Oxford University Press, 1986).

19. Wittgenstein (1998), 3.
20. It is important here to distinguish between *logical behaviourism*, as a thesis about the meanings of psychological expressions, and *ontological behaviourism* which denies that there are any psychological facts over and above facts about behaviour. Nevertheless, while logical behaviourism does not deny the existence of extra-behavioural facts, it does attempt to restrict the ways in which psychological ascriptions can be understood to refer. As such, it restricts the concept of what is observable in terms of someone's behaviour.
21. Wittgenstein (1998), 178.
22. Wittgenstein (1970), 611.
23. Jaegwon Kim, *Mind in a Physical World* (Cambridge: MIT Press, 2000), p. 56. It is worth remarking here that this option, which amounts to *epiphenomenalism*, is not only offensive to physicalist sensibilities but deeply counter-intuitive to common-sense intuitions about perception, insofar as it means that our experiences cannot be said to cause us to react to them.
24. Putnam's multiple realizability argument in *Mind, Language and Reality* (1997) undermined the reductionist premise of identity theories that mental states are identical to physical states, by arguing that different physical mechanisms could realize the same mental properties, thus giving rise to functionalism. On the other hand, Davidson's argument that the principles governing the rationality of thought preclude the possibility psychophysical laws undermined the possibility of establishing laws between mental and physical types, thus establishing anoma-lous monism (or token physicalism).
25. Kim (2000), p. 9.
26. Kim (2000), p. 189.
27. Kim (2000), p. 36.
28. Or, as the idea is often characterized, that a singular causal statement implies a general statement of the form, 'whenever a, then b'.
29. G. E. M. Anscombe, 'Causality and determination', in E. Sosa, ed., *Causation and Conditionals* (Oxford: Oxford University Press, 1975), p. 65.
30. Anscombe (1975), p. 67.
31. Ludwig Wittgenstein, *Philosophical Occasions*, J. Klagge and A. Nordmann, eds (Cambridge: Hackett, 1993), p. 373.
32. *Cf.* Kim (2000), p. 126.
33. D. M. Armstrong and N. Malcolm, *Consciousness and Causality* (Oxford: Blackwell, 1984), p. 70.
34. Armstrong and Malcolm (1984), p. 71.
35. *Ibid.*
36. Donald Davidson, *Subjective, Intersubjective, Objective* (Oxford: Clarendon Press, 2001), p. 69.
37. M. Dikovitskaya, *Visual Culture: The Study of the Visual after the Cultural Turn* (Cambridge: MIT Press, 2005), pp. 48–9.

38. Anthony Woodiwiss, *The Visual in Social Theory* (New York: Athlone Press, 2001), p. 3.

39. Hal Foster, 'Preface', in H. Foster, ed., *Vision and Visuality* (Seattle: Bay Press, 1988), p. ix.

40. *Ibid.*

41. J. Crary, 'Modernizing vision', in Foster (1988), p. 31.

42. M. Jay, 'Scopic regimes of modernity', in Foster (1988), p. 20.

43. Woodiwiss (2001), p. 140.

44. This is the whole point of writing dialogues in which context and perspective are given a nuanced epistemological acknowledgement.

45. P. Feyerabend, *Conquest of Abundance* (Chicago: University of Chicago Press, 2001), p. 143.

46. H. Putnam, *Words and Life* (Cambridge: Harvard University Press, 1995), p. 299.

47. C. Alexander, *The Phenomenon of Life: The Nature of Order, Book 1* (Berkeley: The Center for Environmental Structure, 2003), p. 16.

48. *Ibid.*

5   Aesthetic experience

1. Ludwig Wittgenstein, *Culture and Value*, P. Winch, trans. (Chicago: University of Chicago Press, 1980c), p. 5.

2. A. Danto, *The Abuse of Beauty: Aesthetics and the Concept of Art* (Chicago: Open Court Books, 2003), p. 83.

3. Marshall McLuhan, *Understanding Media: The Extensions of Man* (New York: Signet Books, 1964), p. 170.

4. Daniel Dennett, *Kinds of Minds: Towards an Understanding of Consciousness* (New York: Basic Books, 1996), p. 143. This view relates to his naturalistic interpretation of the private language arguments that I critiqued in Chapter Three. On this view, the greater realism of photography is due to its lack of syntactically-mediated structure. A painter may be able to paint a particular quality *S* of her visual experience, but according to Dennett, she should be able to photograph it.

5. http://www.stanfordalumni.org/news/magazine/2001/mayjun/features/muybridge.html

6. *Cf.* E. H. Gombrich, *Art and Illusion: A Study in the Psychology of Pictorial Representation* (Hong Kong: Princeton University Press, 2000), p. 36.

7. Ludwig Wittgenstein, *Remarks on the Philosophy of Psychology, Vol. 1*, G. E. M. Anscombe, trans., G. E. M. Anscombe and G. H. von Wright, eds (Chicago: University of Chicago Press, 1980a), section 443.

8. James Elkins, *The Object Stares Back* (New York: Harvest Books, 1997), p. 28.

9. Gombrich (2000), p. 90.

10. *Ibid.*

11. Robert Hughes, *Nothing if Not Critical* (New York: Alfred Knopf, 1990), p. 144.

12. It is interesting to note here that some of van Gogh's most vivid drawings are actually copies he made of his own paintings.

13. Some will object here that Valery's statement cannot be taken as a definition because it does not offer anything in the way of necessary and sufficient conditions for applying the concept of seeing. As may be apparent by now, I am using the concept of definition, in one of its perfectly justifiable senses, as a statement that explains what a word means by indicating how the word is to be used. In this sense, the success of the definition does not turn on its form, but on whether it serves to indicate the use.

14. Hughes (1990), p. 146.

15. Wittgenstein (1980c), p. 36, original italics.

16. There is, naturally, a problem with generalizing about the interest that *all* artists have with perception. No doubt there are also a great deal of overlapping interests between artists and scientists. It may be more useful to talk about what it means to have an aesthetic interest in what is seen, as something that could be pursued or avoided by either profession.

17. Semir Zeki, *Inner Vision: An Exploration of Art and the Brain* (Oxford: Oxford University Press, 1999), p. 2.

18. Zeki (1999), p. 1.

19. Zeki (1999), p. 4.

20. A. Danto, *The Transfiguration of the Commonplace* (Cambridge: Harvard University Press, 1989), p. 8.

21. Zeki (1999), p. 40.

22. Zeki (1999), p. 3.

23. Zeki (1999), p. 113.

24. Plato, *Symposium* (Oxford: Oxford University Press, 1998).

25. This formulation of the connection is from the brilliant feminist philosopher Jen L. Taylor. It's an intriguing way to understand the connection between ethics and aesthetics because it does not begin by distinguishing perception from the will. Like love, the perception of beauty turns out to be something we can be said to have a responsibility to see (private discussion).

26. As Alexander puts it: 'What I call wholeness is, to a very rough degree, a mathematical representation of the overall gestalt which we perceive, or which we are aware, which gives the character to the configuration, and which forms, what an artist might call, his most intuitive apperception of the whole.' Christopher Alexander, *The Process of Creating Life: The Nature of Order, Book 2* (Berkeley: The Center for Environmental Structure, 2002), p. 20.

27. Ludwig Wittgenstein, *Philosophical Investigations* 2nd edn, G. E. M. Anscombe, trans. (Oxford: Blackwell, 1998), section 66.

28. S. Hagen, *Buddhism is Not What You Think* (San Francisco: HarperSanFrancisco, 2003), p. 61.

29. Zeki (1999), p. 13.

30. Zeki (1999), p. 73.

31. Rudolf Arnheim, *Visual Thinking* (Berkeley: University of California Press, 1969), Chap. 1.

32. Friedrich Nietzsche, *The Gay Science* (New York: Vintage Books, 1974), p. 328.
33. Nietzsche (1974), p. 329.
34. Nietzsche (1974), p. 324, original italics.

Epilogue: Wittgenstein as an ecologist of meaning

1. Ludwig Wittgenstein, *Culture and Value*, P. Winch, trans. (Chicago: University of Chicago Press, 1980c), p. 7.
2. Ludwig Wittgenstein, *Philosophical Investigations* 2nd edn, G. E. M. Anscombe, trans. (Oxford: Blackwell, 1998), section 124.
3. Wittgenstein (1998), 200.
4. E. Gellner, *Language and Solitude: Wittgenstein, Malinowski and the Habsburg Dilemma* (Cambridge: Cambridge University Press, 1999), pp. 72–73.
5. Of course, having ordinary linguistic competence does not rule out logically the possibility, and desirability, of learning one's language better; knowing, not simply when to call *this* 'red', but when to call *this* a 'spade'.
6. Wittgenstein (1998), section 109.
7. This is not to say that truth is a matter of decision, but only that meaning is. *Cf.* Wittgenstein (1998), 241: ' "So you are saying that human agreement decides what is true and what is false?" – It is what human beings *say* that is true and false; and they agree in the *language* they use.'
8. A. Danto, 'Description and the phenomenology of perception', in N. Bryson, M. Holly and K. Moxey, eds, *Visual Theory* (Oxford: Polity Press, 1991), p. 204.
9. '. . . it may need a good deal of historical imagination to recapture the thrill and the shock which the first illusionist images must have caused when shown on the stage or on the walls of Greek houses . . . How did they achieve . . . what had been denied the Egyptians, the Mesopotamians, and even the Minoans?' E. H. Gombrich, *Art and Illusion: A Study in the Psychology of Pictorial Representation* (Hong Kong: Princeton University Press, 2000), p. 127.
10. Gombrich (2000), p. 128.

Bibliography

Alexander, C., *The Phenomenon of Life: The Nature of Order, Book 1* (Berkeley: The Center for Environmental Structure, 2003).

— *The Process of Creating Life: The Nature of Order, Book 2* (Berkeley: The Center for Environmental Structure, 2002).

Anscombe, G. E. M., 'Causality and determination', in E. Sosa, ed., *Causation and Conditionals* (Oxford: Oxford University Press, 1975).

Armstrong, D. M., *A Materialist Theory of Mind* (London: Routledge & Kegan Paul, 1968).

Armstrong, D. M. and Malcolm, N., *Consciousness and Causality* (Oxford: Blackwell, 1984).

Arnheim, R., *Visual Thinking* (Berkeley: University of California Press, 1969).

Austin, J. L., *Sense and Sensibilia* (Oxford: Oxford University Press, 1962).

Baker, G., 'Criteria: a new foundation for semantics', *Ratio*, 16 (1974).

Baker, G. and Hacker, P. M. S., *Scepticism, Rules and Language* (Oxford: Blackwell, 1984).

Boghossian, P., 'The rule-following considerations', *Mind*, 98 (1989).

Bois, Y. and Krauss, R., *Formless: A User's Guide* (New York: Zone Books, 1997).

Budd, M., 'Wittgenstein on seeing aspects', *Mind*, 96 (1987).

— 'Wittgenstein on sensuous experiences', *The Philosophical Quarterly*, 36 (1986).

Burge, T., 'Cartesian error and the objectivity of perception', in P. Pettit and J. McDowell, eds, *Subject, Thought and Context* (Oxford: Clarendon Press, 1986a).

— 'Individualism and psychology', *The Philosophical Review*, 95 (1986b).

Cavell, S., *The Claim of Reason* (Oxford: Oxford University Press, 1982).

— *This New Yet Unapproachable America* (Albuquerque: Living Batch Press, 1989).

Chihara, C. S. and Fodor, J. A., 'Operationalism and ordinary language: a critique of Wittgenstein', *American Philosophical Quarterly*, 2 (1965).

Chomsky, N., *New Horizons in the Study of Language and Mind* (Cambridge: Cambridge University Press, 2000).

Crary, J., 'Modernizing vision', in H. Foster, ed., *Vision and Visuality* (Seattle: Bay Press, 1988).

Danto, A., *The Abuse of Beauty: Aesthetics and the Concept of Art* (Chicago: Open Court Books, 2003).

— 'Description and the phenomenology of perception', in N. Bryson, M. Holly and K. Moxey, eds, *Visual Theory* (Oxford: Polity Press, 1991).

— *The Transfiguration of the Commonplace* (Cambridge: Harvard University Press, 1989).

Davidson, D., *Subjective, Intersubjective, Objective* (Oxford: Clarendon Press, 2001).

Davies, M., 'Individualism and perceptual content', *Mind*, 100 (1991).

Dennett, D., *Brainstorms* (Cambridge: MIT Press, 1986).

— *Kinds of Minds: Towards an Understanding of Consciousness* (New York: Basic Books, 1996).

— 'Quining Qualia', in W. Lycan, ed., *Mind and Cognition* (Oxford: Blackwell, 1990).

Diamond, C., *The Realistic Spirit* (Cambridge: MIT Press, 1995).

Dicker, G., *Descartes: An Analytical and Historical Introduction* (New York: Oxford University Press, 1993).

Dikovitskaya, M., *Visual Culture: The Study of the Visual after the Cultural Turn* (Cambridge: MIT Press, 2005).

Donagan, A., 'Wittgenstein on sensation', in G. Pitcher, ed., *Wittgenstein: The Philosophical Investigations* (South Bend: University of Notre Dame Press, 1968).

Elkins, J., *The Object Stares Back: On the Nature of Seeing* (New York: Harvest Books, 1997).

Feyerabend, P., *Conquest of Abundance: A Tale of Abstraction versus the Richness of Being* (Chicago: University of Chicago Press, 2001).

Fodor, J., 'A Science of Tuesdays', review of *The Threefold Chord: Mind, Body and World* by Hilary Putnam, *London Review of Books*, 22 (2000).

— 'Could there be a theory of perception?', *Journal of Philosophy*, 63 (1966).

Foster, H., 'Preface', in H. Foster (ed.), *Vision and Visuality* (Seattle: Bay Press, 1988).

Gellner, E., *Language and Solitude: Wittgenstein, Malinowski and the Habsburg Dilemma* (Cambridge: Cambridge University Press, 1999).

Gibson, J. J., *The Perception of the Visual World* (Cambridge: Riverside Press, 1950).

Goldberg, B., 'The correspondence hypothesis', *The Philosophical Review*, 77 (1968).

— 'Mechanism and meaning', in J. Hyman, ed., *Investigating Psychology: Sciences of the Mind after Wittgenstein* (New York: Routledge, 1991).

Goldfarb, W., 'Kripke on Wittgenstein on rules', *Journal of Philosophy*, 82 (1985).

— 'Wittgenstein on understanding', *Midwest Studies in Philosophy*, 16 (1992).

Gombrich, E. H., *Art and Illusion: A Study in the Psychology of Pictorial Representation* (Hong Kong: Princeton University Press, 2000).

Grice, H. P., *Studies in the Way of Words* (Cambridge: Harvard University Press, 1989).

Hacker, P. M. S., *Insight and Illusion: Themes in the Philosophy of Wittgenstein* (Bristol: Thoemmes Press, 1997).

— 'Seeing, representing and describing: an examination of David Marr's computational theory of vision', in J. Hyman, ed., *Investigating Psychology: Sciences of the Mind after Wittgenstein* (New York: Routledge, 1991).

— *Wittgenstein: Mind and Will* (Malden: Blackwell, 2000).

— *Wittgenstein's Place in Twentieth-Century Analytic Philosophy* (Malden: Blackwell, 1996).

Hagen, S., *Buddhism is Not What You Think* (San Francisco: HarperSanFrancisco, 2003).

Harman, G., 'The intrinsic qualities of experience', *Philosophical Perspectives*, 4 (1990).

Hatfield, G., *The Natural and the Normative: Theories of Spatial Perception from Kant to Helmholtz* (Cambridge: MIT Press, 1990).

Heidegger, M., *History of the Concept of Time*, T. Kisiel, trans. (Bloomington: Indiana University Press, 1992).

Heil, J., 'Does Cognitive Psychology rest on a mistake?', *Mind*, 90 (1981).

Hintikka, J. and Hintikka, M. B., *Investigating Wittgenstein* (New York: Blackwell, 1986).

— *Ludwig Wittgenstein: Half-Truths and One-and-a-Half-Truths* (Boston: Kluwer Academic, 1996).

Hoffman, D., *Observer Mechanics: A Formal Theory of Perception* (New York: Harcourt Brace Jovanovich, 1989).

— *Visual Intelligence: How We Create What We See* (New York: W.W. Norton & Co., 2000).

Hornsby, J., 'Physicalist thinking and conceptions of behaviour', in P. Pettit and J. McDowell, eds, *Subject, Thought and Context* (Oxford: Oxford University Press, 1986).

Hughes, R., *Nothing If Not Critical: Selected Essays on Art and Artists* (New York: Alfred Knopf, 1990).

Hume, D., *A Treatise of Human Nature*, 2nd edn, P. H. Nidditch, ed. (Oxford: Clarendon Press, 1978).

Hyman, J., 'The causal theory of perception', *The Philosophical Quarterly*, 42 (1992).

Jackson, F., 'Epiphenomenal qualia', *Philosophical Quarterly*, 32 (1982).

Jackson, F. and Pettit, P., 'Functionalism and broad content', *Mind*, 47 (1988).

Jay, M., 'Scopic regimes of modernity', in H. Foster, ed., *Vision and Visuality* (Seattle: Bay Press, 1988).

Kant, I., *Critique of Pure Reason*, N. K. Smith, trans. (New York: St. Martin's Press, 1929).

Keefe, R. and Smith, P., eds, *Vagueness: A Reader* (Cambridge: MIT Press, 1999).

Kim, J., *Mind in a Physical World* (Cambridge: MIT Press, 2000).

— 'Perception and reference without causality', *Journal of Philosophy*, 74 (1977).

— *Philosophy of Mind* (Boulder: Westview Press, 1998).

— *Supervenience and Mind* (Cambridge: Cambridge University Press, 1993).

Köhler, W., *Gestalt Psychology* (New York: New American Library, 1947).

Kripke, S., *Wittgenstein: On Rules and Private Language* (Cambridge: Harvard University Press, 1982).

Locke, J., *An Essay Concerning Human Understanding* (New York: New American Library, 1964).

Lycan, W., *Philosophy of Language: A Contemporary Introduction* (New York: Routledge, 2000).

Malcolm, N., 'Wittgenstein: the relation of language to instinctive behavior', *Philosophical Investigations*, 5 (1982).

Marr, D., *Vision: A Computational Investigation into the Human Representation and Processing of Visual Information* (New York: W. H. Freeman and Co., 1982).

McDowell, J., 'Meaning and intentionality in Wittgenstein's later philosophy', *Midwest Studies in Philosophy*, 17 (1992).

— 'Wittgenstein and the inner world' [abstract], *Journal of Philosophy*, 86 (1989).

McGinn, C., 'Wittgenstein, Kripke and non-reductionism about meaning', in A. Miller and C. Wright, eds, *Rule-Following and Meaning* (Ithaca: McGill-Queen's University Press, 2002).

McLuhan, M., *Understanding Media: The Extensions of Man* (New York: Signet Books, 1964).

Mulhall, S., *On Being in the World: Wittgenstein and Heidegger on Seeing Aspects* (New York: Routledge, 1990).

Nagel, T., 'What is it like to be a bat', *Philosophical Review*, 83 (1974).

Nietzsche, F., *The Gay Science* (New York: Vintage Books, 1974).

Peacocke, C., 'Rule-following: the nature of Wittgenstein's arguments', in S. Holtzman and C. Leich, eds, *Wittgenstein: To Follow a Rule* (Boston: Routledge & Kegan Paul, 1981).

Pears, D., *The False Prison: A Study of the Development of Wittgenstein's Philosophy, Vol. 2* (Oxford: Clarendon Press, 1990).

Pinker, S., *How the Mind Works* (New York: W. W. Norton & Co, 1997).

Plato, *Symposium* (Oxford: Oxford University Press, 1998).

Price, H. H., *Perception* (London: Methuen, 1950).

Putnam, H., *Mind, Language and Reality: Philosophical Papers, Vol. 2* (New York: Cambridge University Press, 1997).

— *The Threefold Cord: Mind, Body, and World* (New York: Columbia University Press, 1999).

— *Words and Life* (Cambridge: Harvard University Press, 1995).

Pylyshyn, Z. W., *Seeing and Visualizing: It's Not What You Think* (Cambridge: MIT Press, 2003).

Quine, W. V. O., *Word and Object* (Cambridge: MIT Press, 1960).

Rhees, R., *Discussions of Wittgenstein* (London: Routledge & Kegan Paul, 1970).

Robinson, H., *Perception* (New York: Routledge, 1994).

Rorty, R., *Essays on Heidegger and Others* (New York: Cambridge University Press, 1991).

— *Philosophy and the Mirror of Nature* (Princeton: Princeton University Press, 1982).

Russell, B., *A History of Western Philosophy* (New York: Simon and Schuster, 1945).

— *Our Knowledge of the External World* (New York: Routledge, 1993).

— 'Vagueness', in R. Keefe and P. Smith, eds, *Vagueness: A Reader* (Cambridge: MIT Press, 1999).

Ryle, G., *The Concept of Mind* (New York: Barnes and Noble, 1949).

Schapiro, M., *Worldview in Painting: Art and Society* (New York: George Braziller, 1999).

Schulte, J., *Experience and Expression: Wittgenstein's Philosophy of Psychology* (New York: Oxford University Press, 1995).

Searle, J., 'End of the Revolution', review of *New Horizons in the Study of Language and Mind* by Noam Chomsky, *The New York Review of Books*, 28 (2002).

— *Minds, Brains and Science* (Cambridge: Harvard University Press, 1984).

Shoemaker, S., 'Qualia and consciousness', *Mind*, 3 (1991).

Travis, C., 'The annals of analysis', *Mind*, 100 (1991).

— *Unshadowed Thought* (Cambridge: Harvard University Press, 2000).

— *The Uses of Sense* (Oxford: Clarendon Press, 1989).

— 'Vagueness, observation, and sorites', *Mind*, 94 (1985).

Tye, M., 'Qualia, content, and the inverted spectrum', *Nous*, 28 (1994).

Weschler, R., *Seeing is Forgetting the Name of the Thing One Sees: A Life of Contemporary Artist Robert Irwin* (Berkeley: University of California Press, 1982).

Wittgenstein, L., *The Blue and Brown Books* (New York: Harper Torchbooks, 1960).

— *Culture and Value*, P. Winch, trans. (Chicago: University of Chicago Press, 1980c).

— *Last Writings on the Philosophy of Psychology, Vol. 1*, C. G. Luckhardt and M. E. Aue, trans, G. H. von Wright and H. Nyman, eds (Chicago: University of Chicago Press, 1982).

— On Certainty (New York: Blackwell, 1969).

— *Philosophical Investigations*, 2nd edn, G. E. M. Anscombe, trans (Oxford: Blackwell, 1998).

— *Philosophical Occasions*, J. Klagge and A. Nordmann, eds (Cambridge: Hackett, 1993).

— *Remarks on Colour*, L. McAlister and M. Schättle, trans, G. E. M. Anscombe, eds (Berkeley: University of California Press, 1977).

— *Remarks on the Philosophy of Psychology, Vol. 1*, G. E. M. Anscombe, trans, G. E. M. Anscombe and G. H. von Wright, eds (Chicago: University of Chicago Press, 1980a).

— *Remarks on the Philosophy of Psychology, Vol. 2*, C. G. Luckhardt and M. A. E. Aue, trans, G. H. von Wright and H. Nyman, eds (Chicago: University of Chicago Press, 1980b).

— *Tractatus Logico-Philosophicus*, C. K. Ogden, trans. (New York: Routledge, 1999).

— *Zettel*, G. E. M. Anscombe, trans., G. E. M. Anscombe and G. H. von Wright, eds (Berkeley: University of California Press, 1970).

Woodiwiss, A., *The Visual in Social Theory* (New York: Athlone Press, 2001).

Wright, C., 'Does *Philosophical Investigations I*, §§258–60 suggest a cogent argument against private language?', in P. Pettit and J. McDowell, eds, *Subject, Thought and Context* (New York: Oxford University Press, 1986).

— 'Wittgenstein's later philosophy of mind: sensation, privacy and intention', *Journal of Philosophy*, 7 (1989).

Zeki, S., *Inner Vision: An Exploration of Art and the Brain* (Oxford: Oxford University Press, 1999).

Index

Lightning Source UK Ltd.
Milton Keynes UK
UKOW02n1139120214

226314UK00009B/110/P